JAZZ
IN BLACK
AND WHITE

JAZZ IN BLACK AND WHITE

Race, Culture, and Identity in the Jazz Community

Charley Gerard

 PRAEGER

Westport, Connecticut
London

Library of Congress Cataloging-in-Publication Data

Gerard, Charles D.
    Jazz in black and white : race, culture, and identity in the jazz
community / Charley Gerard.
      p. cm.
    Includes bibliographical references and index.
    ISBN 0–275–96198–2 (alk. paper)
    1. Jazz—History and criticism. 2. Music and race. 3. Afro-
Americans—Race identity. 4. United States—Race relations.
I. Title. II. Series.
ML3508.G47 1998
781.65′0973—DC21   97–33018

British Library Cataloguing in Publication Data is available.

Library of Congress Catalog Card Number: 97–33018
ISBN: 0–275–96198–2

First published in 1998

Praeger Publishers, 88 Post Road West, Westport, CT 06881
An imprint of Greenwood Publishing Group, Inc.

Printed in the United States of America

The paper used in this book complies with the
Permanent Paper Standard issued by the National
Information Standards Organization (Z39.48–1984).

10 9 8 7 6 5 4 3

Contents

Acknowledgments

With my grateful thanks to:

Paul Berman, Phillip Gerard, Donald Gerard, Irene Gunther, Mark Schone, Evan Sarzin, Don Schott, Phillip Schuyler, and Thomas Owens for reading the manuscript. I couldn't have written this book without your invaluable suggestions and comments.

Judith Weinstock, my wife and partner, with whom I have exchanged thoughts about the color of jazz for twenty-five years. Your brilliant mind, abetted by a profound love and knowledge of music, contributed to the genesis of most of the ideas in this book.

Cynthia Harris, Norine Mudrick and my other editors at Greenwood Publishing Group for taking an interest in my manuscript.

Alva Nelson, John Loehrke and Ron Welburn for your whole-hearted cooperation.

Introduction

Bettina studied music, she even wrote a few compositions, and so had some basis for understanding what was new and beautiful about Beethoven's music. Nevertheless, I ask this question: was it Beethoven's music that captivated her, its notes, or was it rather what the music *represented,* in other words, its vague affinity to the ideas and attitudes that Bettina shared with her generation? Does love for art really exist and has it ever existed? Is it not a delusion? When Lenin proclaimed that he loved Beethoven's *Appassionata* above all else, what was it he really loved? What did he hear? Music? Or a majestic noise that reminded him of the solemn stirrings in his soul, a longing for blood, brotherhood, executions, justice, and the absolute? Did he derive joy from the tones, or from the musings stimulated by those tones, which had nothing to do with art or with beauty?

—Milan Kundera, *Immortality*

I fell in love with jazz when I was still in my teens. While my classmates were listening to the Beatles, I was discovering Ornette Coleman. I also was making contact with like-minded musicians. Although it seemed unlikely that in the distant suburbs I would come upon anyone serious about a genre inextricably linked to city life, I did find such people and without any difficulty. In the private school I attended, there were two drummers, one a student of Stanley Spector, a famous jazz drum teacher, the other a student of the late Charles Moffett, Ornette Coleman's drummer in the late 1960s. In the general neighborhood I also met a trumpeter who had played in a rehearsal band led by Paul Jeffries, and a pianist who recorded in the 1970s with Pat Martino and Eric Kloss. In my senior year of high school I began studying with Jimmy Giuffre in his Manhattan studio on 15th Street. By then, I had made the switch from reluctant classical clarinet player to devoted avant-garde jazz saxophonist.

In the process of discovering the music, I also explored the literature of jazz. Two books had an especially profound effect: A. B. Spellman's *Four Lives in the Bebop Business* and Amiri Baraka's *Blues People: The Negro Experience in White America and the Music That Developed From It.* (Baraka was known as LeRoi Jones at the time of *Blues People's* publication.) Spellman's book is a portrait of four musicians: Ornette Coleman, Cecil Taylor, Jackie McLean, and Herbie Nichols. Each chapter offers lessons—"warnings" might be a better word—to someone interested in a jazz career. The chapter on Herbie Nichols made it clear that early death from sickness, poverty, and neglect was possible, even likely. The chapter on McLean showed how drugs ruined the lives of a lot of jazz musicians. The chapters devoted to Coleman and Taylor were studies in racial ambivalence, with Coleman finding it necessary to apologize for his reliance on white bassists and Taylor apologizing for his conservatory education and familiarity with white composers.

Amiri Baraka's book deals with musical genres like the blues as African-American expression, "the result of certain attitudes, certain specific ways of thinking about the world (and only ultimately about the *ways* in which music can be made)."[1] Baraka seems to hear an underlying racial message in practically any sound, from the swing generated by a rhythm section to a horn solo. Like Czech writer Milan Kundera when he is discussing his character Bettina's musical interests, I occasionally wonder if it is the music that captivates Baraka or simply "its vague affinity" to his political ideas and attitudes. But at least he recognizes the importance of race and culture in the music. Those who prefer to dismiss entirely its social implications reveal an almost complete lack of political insight. Consider the response of the white British blues player John Mayall to the idea that the musical form derives from the African-American experience: "What is *black* music? Music isn't black or white. There's no such thing as *black* music."[2]

Spellman's and Baraka's books brought home to me how my background as a private-school student from a financially secure family with a European heritage almost automatically destined me to a marginal place within the music I was most drawn to. Jazz musicians lived in a world of drug addicts, alcoholics, and crazy eccentrics that I knew nothing about. But apart from our differing lifestyles, there was an even more insurmountable barrier between me and the artists I admired: For them the music called jazz was more than a deeply satisfying aesthetic experience; it was an integral part of the African-American identity. No matter how many lifetimes I spent in the jazz community, that music would never define me as it did them. Although from their perspective my devotion to jazz was wrong-headed, I strongly believed that the music had chosen me as much as I had chosen it.

Race was an important issue for a musician entering the jazz world in the late 1960s. These were years when the Black Power movement was reaching its peak. As a protégé of a white pianist who had befriended the members of the house rhythm section, I participated in several open jazz sessions at a bar in Germantown, a black Philadelphia suburb. I never knew if it was my age, race, or lack of musical credentials that made it so difficult for me to get a chance to play until shortly before closing time—if at all. I sensed that the non-musicians did not like having their bar encroached on by whites, and the black band leader was surely trying to limit access to the few well-established white musicians in attendance. I was there partly to find a job with a black band in order to get established in the jazz community. For a white, being hired by a black band was a sure way to make one's reputation. After I had sat in with the band several times, the band leader praised my playing but advised me to look for work among white musicians.

In jam sessions at New York City clubs I received more of the cold shoulder from black musicians, if not downright hostility. At one East Village club, Anthony Braxton, who was just starting to get international attention as an important jazz figure, interceded on my behalf. But the session leader never gave me permission to play, although I stayed until 2 A.M.[3]

As I became more aware of the intense competition for the few available opportunites in jazz, I reconciled myself to the fact that being excluded for racial reasons was not necessarily a result of anti-white racism. There was a good reason why whites weren't being hired. If given a choice between an inexperienced black musician and a comparable white musician, most black professional musicians preferred to help out the black musician.

Being shut out of the black jazz scene was a confusing experience for someone who thought that black rejection came only to the untalented. It seems to me now that I was naïvely expecting black jazz musicians to greet me with a brotherly spirit based on our shared musical interests. Apparently, large chunks of the jazz community were untouched by the counter-cultural ethos then in vogue, in which racial differences were downplayed. It was a time when Jimi Hendrix, Miles Davis, Sly Stone, and other influential musicians were wearing hippy clothes and fronting bands in which white musicians were well represented, when it seemed that anyone with talent could be a "brother."

Twenty years later, racial identity is every bit as perplexing as it was then. After writing this book I am still unable to decide once and for all whether jazz belongs to anyone who has the talent to play it, or if it belongs to African Americans who perceive it as "a kind of symbolic commentary through which [they] observe and understand the perspective of black people."[4]

One thing remains clear. Many jazz musicians, both white and African-American, have a nagging suspicion that there is a strong correlation between artistic success in jazz and being African-American. In the history books, blacks clearly dominate—as they do in basketball. For every Larry Bird in jazz, there are five or more Wilt Chamberlains. The history of jazz is portrayed as a series of major African-American artists whose original styles caught the interest of their respective musical generation. Opinions vary among members of the jazz community, but the African Americans who developed their reputations playing bebop are on everybody's list, along with swing-era musicians like Louis Armstrong, Fletcher Henderson, Count Basie, Sidney Bechet, Duke Ellington, and the notable members of their respective bands. Jazz fans and musicians are unified by their almost religious devotion to these artists. They are referred to as the "master musicians," and members of the jazz community are intimately familiar with their lives both from an oral tradition and from reading about them in magazines and books. Their views on music and life are closely studied and revered. Jazz musicians and devoted fans have developed an intimate familiarity with these masters and refer to them confidently with the correct appellation. Dizzy Gillespie and Miles Davis are known by their first names, John Coltrane is called " 'Trane," and Charlie Parker is "Bird." A musician seeking to rise above the lowest levels of the jazz community must receive the approval of musicians who have played with the masters, and in order to reach the topmost level, he or she must become a longtime associate of one of the masters themselves.

Few members of the jazz community have more than a few whites on their private lists of jazz masters, if they have any at all. White musicians are regarded as either epigones or as outsiders to the tradition. Indeed, there is some validity to the downplaying of white accomplishments in the jazz history books. Many important white artists such as George Gershwin and Raymond Scott were strongly influenced by jazz but were not exactly jazz musicians. Even white musicians such as Paul Desmond who perform more or less within the jazz tradition and stick to the established jazz literature tend to be artistic loners whose interests turn them away from the stylistic developments of their generation.

The obsession with race is disturbing to those who wish to direct attention away from differences that, after all, are grounded in theories that were originally used to keep African Americans from participating freely in American society. Nevertheless, it must be admitted that for stylistic reasons alone, race is an important aspect in critically assessing jazz musicians. For one thing, the racial identity of the artist tells something about his or her music. White musicians tend to develop their artistic slant from performing with white bands, black musicians with black bands. As a result, white musicians share musical styles with other whites, black musicians with other blacks.

A CHRONOLOGICAL OVERVIEW OF THE LITERATURE ON RACE AND JAZZ

Pre-World War II jazz musicians were proud of their efforts to integrate America. They kept their own racial problems out of the press. Nat Hentoff was one of the first jazz critics to break the silence. In "Race Prejudice in Jazz" for *Harper's* in 1959 and "The Murderous Modes of Jazz" for *Esquire* in 1960, he reported on the resentments of black musicians who felt that whites had received an unfair share of acclaim and financial success, and the suspicions of white musicians who believed that blacks did not respect their talents as jazz musicians. Hentoff made clear that opinions about the relative merits of white and black musicians were not contained within racial borders. He cites blacks who praise white musicians and whites who believe that a band needs black musicians to make the music swing.

Amiri Baraka's *Blues People* (1963) was the first book to argue that jazz is essentially the music of African Americans. With subsequent books, Baraka emphasized the relationship to African religious beliefs of the music he saw fit to call "black music." Baraka's views were enthusiastically taken up by black nationalists who found African precedents for many facets of African-American culture, particularly, it seemed, for those they saw fit to praise. Essays by several articulate although tendentious jazz critics writing from this perspective (subsequently labeled Afrocentrism) are contained in *The Black Aesthetic*, edited by Addison Gayle, Jr.

Beginning in the 1940s scholars familiar with African art and music have provided academic credentials to the politically volatile notion that African-American culture is continuously being replenished by African culture. In anthropology there was Melville Herskovits, whose *Myth of the Negro Past* (1941) had a profound influence on Amiri Baraka. In the 1950s ethnomusicologist Richard Alan Waterman, a student of Herskovits, made more detailed comparisons between jazz and African music. In the 1960s art historian Robert Farris Thompson began his life work of describing an African aesthetic that exerts a powerful impact on the latest trends in African-American culture just as it affects cultural developments throughout the African continent. *Flash of the Spirit: African & Afro-American Art & Philosophy* (1983) is one of his most notable efforts. John Miller Chernoff, an ethnomusicologist and performer of West African musical styles, continued in Thompson's footsteps. In *African Rhythm and African Sensibility: Aesthetics and Social Action in African Musical Idioms* (1971) he adhered to Thompson's "cool aesthetic" as a valid starting point for examining African and African Diasporan music and art. He wrote that the music of James Brown and the Dagomba music he learned to play while living in Ghana were kindred expressions based on this aesthetic.

Norman C. Weinstein's *A Night in Tunisia: Imaginings of Africa in Jazz* (1992) was the first book-length study of the African legacy in jazz. Rather than dealing with the actual influences of African music on jazz, Weinstein chose to act as a "chronicler detailing the way jazz composers creatively have struggled over time with the African theme." The book is a study of twelve figures: Duke Ellington, discussed through the voice of Madame Zzaj, Ellington's imagined personification of jazz; John Coltrane; George Russell; John Carter; Count Ossie, an early Rastafarian musician who led a jazz-influenced group until his death in 1976; Randy Weston; Max Roach; Pierre Dørge, a Danish avant-garde jazz guitarist who studied with kora player Foday Musa Suso; Archie Shepp; Yusef Lateef; Sunny Murray; and Ronald Shannon Jackson. In addition, there is a chapter on Dizzy Gillespie's *Night in Tunisia,* a piece that has become the vehicle par excellence for jazz musicians to metaphorically explore their African roots. Weinstein evaluates the different interpretations it has been given by the composer and by Art Blakey, Eddie Jefferson, Sarah Vaughan and Herbie Mann. Weinstein is not interested in making a literal analysis of the song; whether it is Tunisian, African, or Afro-Cuban is beyond the point. What is essential to Weinstein is the way that the song has become a vehicle for jazz musicians' imaginations.

The black nationalist jazz-as-black-music perspective dominated jazz criticism for years. In the early 1980s jazz educators like Dr. Billy Taylor promoted an alternative, race-neutral vision of jazz as an art form that had outgrown African-American culture to become "American classical music," a universal idiom. In public forums and writings such as *Jazz Piano: A Jazz History* (1982) Taylor had sown the seeds of a frontal attack on the black music perspective.

Two jazz writers, James Lincoln Collier and Gene Lees, recently took on the task of battling what they consider to be the anti-white slant of jazz musicians and critics. Collier's views on the excesses of black-music ideology are laid out in a chapter of *Jazz: The American Theme Song* (1993). Lees addresses the topic in the final chapter of *Cats of Any Color* (1994).

Collier and Lees helped stimulate a long-overdue appraisal of race and culture. It is only regrettable that their agenda appears to be not only to correct inaccuracies in the literature but to cast doubt on the premise that African Americans have a culture of their own, distinct from white American culture, and to conveniently disregard the dominance of black culture on jazz.

Lees' chapter on race inspired several magazine articles. Terry Teachout in his 1995 *Commentary* article "The Color of Jazz" agrees with Lees that white musicians are getting shafted by the black jazz establishment's reverse racism. Sandy Carter wrote a perceptive review of Lees' book for the progressive publication *Z Magazine* in which she notes that Lees' professed skin color-blindness causes him to "hear in jazz only abstract humanity."[5] Collier's criticism of Wynton Marsalis's leadership as artistic director of the jazz program at Lincoln Center inspired a series of acerbic exchanges in the *New York Times Review of Books* and a debate between Collier and Marsalis that took place in front of a Lincoln Center audience. The jazz press typically does not address social issues, so it was especially noteworthy that *Jazz Times* elected to print "Racism and Jazz: Same as It Ever Was ... Or Worse?" by the late James T. Jones IV. It served to give recognition to the fact that the jazz community, in conflict over the recently gained clout of African Americans in positions of leadership in arts organizations and recording companies, was no more a haven from racial conflicts than the rest of American society.

In January 1996, National Public Radio began a two-part series, "Jazz Musicians Discuss Racism in the Jazz World," moderated by Dean Olsher to address two issues: discriminatory hiring practices in the jazz world and jazz as black music. Instead of interviewing Wynton Marsalis and other young musicians who were described as over-represented in the media, Olsher turned toward older musicians, some of whom were very old, like ninety-year-old Doc Cheatham and eighty-seven-year-old Lionel Hampton. There was little controversy stirred up over the well-documented discriminatory practices of the past, and little said about the present. No one addressed the near absence of whites in black groups. Archie Shepp's suggestion that white big bands discriminate against blacks was rebutted by Japanese pianist and arranger Toshiko Akiyoshi, whom Olsher describes as the leader of a white big band despite her obvious lack of Caucasian characteristics and European heritage. The more complex and heated issue of whether African Americans have a right to claim jazz as their own was ridiculed by black trumpeter Doc Cheatham ("Race has got nothing to do with jazz anyhow") and dismissed as historically inacurate by white saxophonist Gerry Mulligan. White guitarist Jim Hall, who considers the jazz community to be his "family," asserted that few members of that community support the idea of jazz as black music. Hall was upset over a recent *New York Times Magazine* article on tenor saxophonist Joe Lovano that made Lovano out to be the great white hope in a field of black contenders. With just one musician, Archie Shepp, supporting the idea of jazz as black music—and someone whose political and musical ideas are often extreme—the listeners got the false impression that few jazz scholars and musicians recognize the persistent influence of African-American culture on jazz.

Jazz in Black and White is the first book-length view of racial attitudes in the jazz community. While it attacks outright errors, it discusses racial identities without assigning judgment as to their worth and validity. A firm belief that how one chooses one's identity is beyond the pale of reason has guided the writing. If someone chooses his or her identity based on a baggage of mistaken ideas, so be it. Why should she or he be any different than anyone else? As the philosopher Kwame Anthony Appiah wisely points out, cultural identity is very complex and often as not based on a misreading of history:

Every human identity is constructed, historical; every one has its share of false presuppositions, of the errors and inaccuracies that courtesy calls "myth," religion "heresy," and science "magic." Invented histories, invented biologies, invented cultural affinities come with every identity; each is a kind of role that has to be scripted, structured by conventions of narrative to which the world never quite manages to conform.[6]

Jazz in Black and White is about the formulation of identity in the face of racial difference. Jazz has been and continues to be a music whose developments are closely linked to the ways in which African Americans have adopted different strategies of achieving sociopolitical goals. Their music reflects these goals and acts as a rallying force. The promotion of lower-class black Southern culture and inner-city styles like rhythm-and-blues and rap as a means of achieving black racial solidarity has led to the development of new jazz styles as well, which I examine in Chapter 1, "Black Music, Black Identity." Identification with Africa has itself fostered a large body of music, which I write about in Chapter 2, "African Music, African Identity."

The pressures of being black in America have influenced the formulation of black jazz musicians' personal identities. I discuss their conversion to Islam and other Eastern religions in Chapter 3, "Race and Religious Identity." Black musicians have attempted to deal with the insecurities engendered by racism by joining communities that give them a firm sense of identity. In Chapter 4, "Race and Jazz Communities," I begin by discussing a community united by heroin use, an activity that has had a profoundly deleterious effect on jazz. Then I turn to the jazz collectives of the 1960s formed in response to black musicians' sense of powerlessness in the music business.

In Chapter 5, "Black Music, White Identity," I examine the close relationship of whites with black culture and the problematic situation of the white jazz musician—having to create in an art form rooted in black culture and marked by the stylistic imprints of black innovators.

Chapter 6, "Colorless Swing," is an examination of the assimilation of jazz into the wider American culture. In Chapter 7, "Racial Identity and Three Lives," I interview John Loehrke and Alva Nelson, two perceptive jazz musicians whose lives have been taken up with the issue of race, and Ron Welburn, who re-evalutes the black nationalist stance he took nearly three decades ago in his important essay, "The Black Aesthetic Imperative." In Chapter 8, "Racial Identity Embedded in Performance," I analyze two very different performances: Aretha Franklin's version of *You Are My Sunshine* and The Jimmy Giuffre Three's version of *Blue Monk*. Finally, Chapter 9, "The Right of Swing" (a punning reference to Stravinsky's *Rite of Spring*), is about establishing a pedigree in the musical world.

I have approached this study of jazz with the belief that music is a container of cultural data, and that the elements of music, although they do not have the precision of speech, still convey meanings. These meanings are not inherent in a piece of music in the same way they are, say, in a computer manual. As ethnomusicologist Ruth M. Stone points out, meaning in music is created when the participants in a performance (or the listeners of a recording) actively refer to knowledge they have about the present performance, their stock of knowledge about music in general, as well as other aspects of culture that bear on the music.[7] Just as meaning in music is multi-faceted, so too are the ways in which it can be interpreted.

Black Music, Black Identity

For a short while, many Americans, both blacks and whites, considered jazz to be a form of white dance music. The first jazz recordings were performed by white musicians, and numerous African Americans first learned about jazz from recordings of white groups like the Original Dixieland Jazz Band. By the mid-1920s, however, most Americans had learned that jazz came from African-American culture and accepted the fact with equanimity.

But they were not prepared to give it back. Jazz had been thoroughly assimilated into the American fabric. While Jews played Jewish music, Cajuns played Cajun music, Italians played Italian music, and Mexicans played Mexican music, jazz was music for the taking. Jazz became paradoxically both a music shared by all Americans yet still, somehow, intrinsically African-American. The ambiguity was not lost on the Harlem Renaissance writer Joel Augustus Rogers. In "Jazz at Home," Rogers, who gained fame as the author of several books, including *The World's Greatest Men of African Descent,* concluded that it was "difficult to say whether jazz is more characteristic of the Negro or of contemporary America."[1]

Both whites and blacks made a distinction between jazz and the blues-based music of the rural South and Northern black ghettoes that record la-

...lled "race music." Whites and middle-class blacks shared a disdain for this working-class, rural black music. Some of the leading jazz figures of the 1920s denigrated race music. Milt Hinton and Cab Calloway shared the belief that African-American Southerners "had nothing really musically uplifting to listen to. It was all this old crud." Moreover, it "kept the black mind in the South down."[2]

While race music held blacks to their roots like an ethnic glue, jazz released them into a world of opportunity in which talented, savvy musicians with the right connections could compete with whites. Radio and the recording industry opened their doors to musicians who could supply white America's endless thirst for jazz. While the music industry continued to give preference to whites, they were willing to promote the popular black bands that appealed to whites.

While African Americans were in the process of gaining a foothold in the music business, black musicians did not at first have much interest in claiming credit for creating jazz. According to saxophonist great Benny Carter, few musicians were interested in whether what they were playing was jazz or black music.

One can only guess why this was so. Perhaps because African Americans' successes were tenuous, they kept quiet their beliefs that jazz was a species of black music. Or else it took the civil rights movement to make jazz musicians and middle-class blacks proud enough of black culture that they were no longer ashamed of associating race music with jazz.

Amiri Baraka's *Blues People* (1963) was the first book to argue that jazz is essentially the music of African Americans. With subsequent books he began calling it "black music," and emphasized its relationship to African religious beliefs. Along with a few white supporters like critic Frank Kofsky, many African-American musicians and critics have since proclaimed their enthusiasm for Baraka's thesis. But the idea that jazz is an expression of African-American culture is not new. In the late 1940s, according to soprano saxophonist Bob Wilber, "some jazz critics" had spread the message that jazz was black music.[3]

Duke Ellington was probably the first musician to call his own work "Negro music." Of all the early jazz musicians, Duke Ellington was especially dedicated to creating a body of work in which African-American culture took center stage. Although Ellington told Nat Hentoff in 1965 that jazz no longer should be called Negro music since "it has become so integrated you can't tell one part from the other so far as color is concerned,"[4] Ellington was nevertheless an important influence on the development of the black music perspective.

What are the elements that constitute black music as an ideology? Its proponents believe that African Americans are an ethnic group, a term defined by sociologists Michael L. Hecht, Mary Jane Collier, and Sidney Ribeau as "a self-perceived community of people who hold a common set of traditions not shared by those with whom they are in contact."[5] The use of the term "ethnic group" as a less vitriolic replacement for race has been attributed to anthropologist Ashley Montague in a speech given for the inauguration of UNESCO in 1950.[6] African Americans have chosen to retain race as an ethnic identifier, despite their awareness that few of them descend from families without white blood. Jon Michael Spencer, a professor in African and Afro-American studies at the University of North Carolina, explains that for African Americans, "race is a useful metaphor for cultural and historic difference, because it permits a level of social cohesion among oppressed people."[7]

From the black music perspective, black music is the ethnic expression of the African-American people. Adherents to the black perspective dispute the view that jazz, blues, gospel, rap, and other idioms are disparate entities. Instead, they see all the music created by African Americans as one unified idiom rather than as a composite of different styles. This holistic vision of black music has been influenced by a sociopolitical goal: to promote the unity of African Americans.

Black music is not an idiom made up of rules that can be taught and transmitted like any other musical form. It is based on the blues, and proponents of the black music ideology believe that the blues is not just a music but a world view. The blues is not something that African Americans *do* but how they *live.* They are *blues people*—hence the title of Baraka's book. In the literature of black music ideology, the music is regarded as the story of the blues people in America.

By establishing jazz as part of an entity called black music, jazz is knocked off its pedestal as an elite style. Although the black music ideologists consider that jazz is not *better* than other black idioms, they recognize that it *is* different. They refer to jazz as "Black [or African-American] classical music." Black music ideologists are opposed to the use of the term "classical music" without a further qualifier. Such usage implies that any music other than the art-music tradition established by European composers is "popular" music. As a result they typically refer to "black classical music" and "European classical music."

ESSENTIALISM

Essentialism is defined by the brilliant cultural theorist bell hooks as "the assumption that there is a black essence shaping all African-American experience, expressed traditionally by the concept of 'soul.' "[8]

Soul means putting all you can into your efforts. The soul ideology stresses honest trying over success or failure. Ethnomusicologist Charles Keil describes this attitude as "You can make it if you try." Soul is making an effort despite societal handicaps like racism or a history of personal setbacks. This aspect of soul is glossed by the motto, "Keep on pushing." Soul is expressing oneself without constraint and giving others encouragement to express themselves freely as well. Soul is "telling it like it is"—talking in a forthright manner about sex, heartbreak, and the battle between the sexes. Soul is appropriate behavior and proper timing, being able to initiate or respond with just the right line, gesture, and intonation. It is also the ability to appreciate the responses of others. Soul is a celebration of African-American, Southern, rural culture: its food, religion and music. The soul movement especially embraced those African-American traits that had been a source of shame for upwardly mobile blacks. In a reversal of such attitudes, the adjective "funky," meaning bad-smelling, became a term of praise. Most important, soul has to do with a conviction that other African Americans are brothers and sisters. In this respect, soul is solidarity.

The soul ideology "encompasses many opposites and defines a paradox, the Negro's acceptance of life in all its bitter-sweetness, joyful-sadness and painful-pleasures."[9] It is rife with ironies in its celebration of African-American traditions such as "the dozens," the insult game that simultaneously imparts camaraderie and incites hostility.

The idiom known as soul music was based on a simple transmutation of the sacred to the secular. Yet simultaneously it possessed a complex network of nonverbal symbols referring back to the sacred even when the terminology was about making love or breaking up with a lover. What are some of these symbols that transport the listener from mere secular concerns into a spiritual realm? Keil enumerated a few: "Constant repetition coupled with small but striking deviations; similar wails and cries linked to various tumbling strains and descending figures; or simply statements and counter-statements"—all of which equal 'soul.' "[10]

The essence of soul music is more than technical devices, although these are important elements. It is an urgent and effort-laden message of sincerity. When, in her recording of *You Are My Sunshine*, Aretha Franklin keeps repeating the incomplete thought, "And I believe it, I believe it, I believe it because," the effect is that of convincing the audience that she is expressing her deepest feelings and is almost unable to verbalize them. It sounds as if she is in church, testifying her faith in front of a congregation. Music informed by these qualities inevitably refers back to the church no matter what the actual context may be. Ray Charles said that Aretha Franklin "could do *Stardust* but if she did *her* thing on it, you'd hear the church all over the place."[11]

The soul movement was full of ironies. One of its greatest was that whites participated in creating the music. Several composers of songs written for the African-American pop market were white, like Jerry Lieber and Mike Stoller, and Carole King and Gerry Goffin. Aretha Franklin's most famous albums were arranged by the Turkish-American Arif Mardin and performed by Southern white studio musicians. Two of the busiest musicians in soul music were bassist Donald "Duck" Dunn and and guitarist Steve Cropper, both white musicians in the group Booker T and the MGs. The soul jazz classic *Mercy, Mercy, Mercy* was composed by the Austrian pianist Joe Zawinul.

The soul movement had a very strong influence on jazz in the 1950s. It produced a new style called "soul jazz" or "hard bop": jazz with a tough sound and a hard-driving beat. The style, whose first major artists were Art Blakey and Horace Silver, began as a blend of the harmonic language of bebop with the sound of the blues and the propulsive beat of gospel and of rhythm and blues. It reached a high level of intensity also derived from gospel music that was especially evident in the music of Charles Mingus. In hard bop, African-American elements were proudly and at times vociferously emphasized, reflecting the growing belief on the part of black musicians that, in the words of Amiri Baraka, their roots "are a valuable possession, rather than the source of ineradicable shame."[12] Musicians took pride in their heritage by "being funky"—utilizing blues phrasing, blues-scale melodies, gospel harmonies, and a strong backbeat. They named their compositions after events and people important to African-American culture and frequently used African-American linguistic idioms in the titles.

JAZZ AS BLACK INTELLECTUAL PROPERTY

> Black music should not be allowed to become popular outside the black community, which means that the black community must support the music.
>
> —Ron Welburn, "The Black Aesthetic Imperative"[13]

Black music ideologists are offended that each style of jazz—and each variety of blues, rhythm-and-blues, and rap, for that matter—has been appropriated from the African-American community almost from the day after it was first heard there. Musical idioms created by African Americans are considered to be in the public domain, while the musical idioms of other ethnic groups tend to retain their ethnic roots. For instance, authentic Latin music (in contrast to the ersatz variety made for non-Latinos) has throughout its history remained a music made primarily by and for Latinos. It was not because of the language barrier alone. Even Latin music with English lyrics such as the bugalú of the early 1960s was created by Latinos for their own people.

White musicians occupy an unenviable role in black music ideology. They are called thieves for making money from the music and exploiters for benefiting from African-American talent. The proponents of the black music ideology believe that nearly all of the white musicians who have been involved in jazz have been imitators of black innovators. This point of view has had wide currency among African-American musicians and it predates the publication of *Blues People*. An anonymous California musician told jazz historian J. E. Berendt in the early 1950s that "there has not been a single white man, perhaps leaving aside Bix [Beiderbecke], who has had an idea. Only the colored men have ideas."[14] The accomplishments of white innovators, when they are recognized at all, are trivialized because they did not evolve out of African-American culture. Thus, cool jazz and fusion are considered to be dead-ends in jazz history because whites played important roles in these movements.

Black music ideologists believe that whites refuse to give credit to the African-American originators of the music. To Frank Kofsky's way of thinking, this is because whites refuse to recognize that African-Americans "can create anything of durable value."[15] Miles Davis believed it is because "the white man likes to win everything. White people like to see other white people win . . . and they can't win when it comes to jazz and the blues because black people created this."[16] The inability of whites to credit African-American talent is often used to explain why white practitioners have gotten far richer and more famous than the originators of the music. While there is much truth to this view, it can be carried too far. Most of the entertainers and musicians to whom America has accorded fame and fortune have added a white influence that has cushioned the African-American qualities of their work. For instance, Elvis Presley, whom Davis considers to be nothing but a third-rate copy of African-

American musicians, was a more complex mix of white and African-American elements than Davis cares to recognize. While condemning white taste, Davis forgets an important consideration: Whites have been more than partly responsible for his success.[17]

In the early 1960s black music ideologists were motivated to put a needed spotlight on the innovations of black musicians, who had not received their due credit. Since that time black music ideologists have been carried away by the spirit of reclaiming credit for blacks, making some absurd claims.

In his autobiography, Miles Davis did his best to bring cool jazz—or at least his own role in the style—back into the spectrum of African-American culture. He argues that, since its sources of inspiration were whites whose music was based on the work of black musicians of an earlier era, cool jazz therefore grew out of black roots: "*Birth of the Cool* came from black musical roots. We were trying to sound like Claude Thornhill, but he had gotten his shit from Duke Ellington and Fletcher Henderson. Gil Evans himself was a big fan of Duke's and Billy Strayhorn's, and Gil was the arranger on *Birth of the Cool*."[18]

Ben Sidran describes *Birth of the Cool* as a brief stage in the evolution of black consciousness. His analysis of the album is loaded with musical symbolism—and silly mistakes. Consider the errors in the following statement:

> A tuba replaced the more volatile string bass and achieved a fluid rhythmic motion; significantly, the drums, too, played a minor supporting role. In fact, it is possible to listen to this record and imagine that the total effect would be the same if there were no drums used at all. The lack of rhythmic propulsion indicated the guarded nature of the black community, inasmuch as rhythmic assertion had always characterized black cultural assertion.[19]

To begin with, bassists played on all three of the *Birth of the Cool* recording sessions: Al McKibbon, Joe Shulman, and Nelson Boyd. Sidran assumes his readers share his strange opinion that a tuba is less "volatile" than a bass. With regard to his complaint about the minor role of drums in the recording, this remains a matter of musical judgment. But there is another explanation. The drums on many recordings done before the advent of the LP are scarcely audible. In any case it seems silly to make "rhythmic propulsion" the end-all and be-all of African-American music. African-American artists have expressed themselves in more ways than one. Are we to conclude that the famous Ellington-Blanton bass-and-piano duets are lacking in "black cultural assertion" because the drums were absent?[20]

Neither Sidran nor Davis makes a good case that cool jazz has its roots in African-American culture. Part of Sidran's problem is that he ascribes too much importance to the coincidence that "cool" was the name of a mode of behavior coming to prominence in African-American culture around the same time that *Birth of the Cool* was recorded. This behavior, which began with the bebop musicians of the 1940s, had little, if anything, to do with cool jazz except for the shared name. In *Blues People* Amiri Baraka noted the irony that "the music seemed to represent almost exactly the opposite of what *cool* as a term of social philosophy had been given to mean."[21]

Why Davis wished to credit blacks for the inspiration of cool jazz is anyone's guess. Davis's own relations with white musicians were troublesome and complex. Although he often made disparaging comments about white musicians, he had no qualms about hiring them if it suited his purposes. He certainly never "repudiated" cool jazz, as Kofsky claims. He was to continue collaborating with Gil Evans, one of the architects of the cool style, for the rest his career.

SHUTTING WHITES OUT

With their proprietary interest in jazz, black music ideologists have tried to keep its expression confined to the African-American community. The term "Crow Jim" was coined in the 1940s by the editors of *Metronome* to describe the so-called reverse discrimination that a few black band leaders appeared to be practicing.[22] Crow Jim behavior was explained away by some African-American musicians who believed that African Americans have a responsibility to employ their own kind. Why hire whites when there are plenty of unemployed black musicians? While this attitude has had a chilling effect, it has not kept most of the famous African-American bandleaders from hiring white musicians. The practice of hiring white musicians is widespread, and representatives of nearly every style of jazz, from Louis Armstrong, Count Basie, and Duke Ellington to Miles Davis, Dizzy Gillespie, Thelonious Monk, Ornette Coleman, and Jack DeJohnette, have had whites in their bands. It is remarkable that the very musicians who have made the nastiest statements about white musicians have nevertheless hired them. Art Blakey, the same man who said that "the only way the Caucasian musician can swing is from a rope," helped start the career of a number of whites such as Geoff Keezer and Valery Ponomarev. Archie Shepp, one of the most vocal black nationalists in the jazz community, had Roswell Rudd and Cameron Brown in his bands for long periods of time. The list of outspoken African-American musicians who have hired white musicians also includes Charles Mingus.

White jazz bebop musicians like Art Pepper indicate that reverse discrimination gained momentum in the 1950s. Pepper had a band that employed African Americans in its rhythm section. One night when Pepper completed a performance, some friends pointed out that the bassist and drummer, Curtis Counce and Lawrence Marable, had been making fun of him behind his back while he was playing. Over the course of the next few nights Pepper indeed found them to be sneering at him. He confronted Lawrence Marable, who told him, "None of you white punks can play."[23] Several prominent musicians, Red Rodney and Buddy DeFranco among them, left jazz altogether as a result of such experiences. Since the 1960s the influence of Malcolm X further encouraged this line of separatism.

More recently, white complaints have shifted to the gate-keepers of the music world as African Americans have risen to power in record companies, cultural centers, and arts organizations. Among the most visible targets of these complaints is Wynton Marsalis in his role as the first artistic director of *Jazz at Lincoln Center*.

Marsalis has been attacked for never presenting a program featuring the music of a white jazz musician. His response to the charge is simple: He is the artistic director, and he has been chosen for that post to make programming decisions based on his artistic vision. But Marsalis is promoting a limited range of music. Although it spans the history of jazz from Jelly Roll Morton through John Coltrane, it does not include several important jazz styles such as cool jazz and avant-garde jazz. He dislikes the work of jazz musicians whose music is heavily indebted to classical music. Marsalis prefers the styles in which African Americans have dominated, and dislikes styles in which whites have been successful. As a result, he comes up with an aesthetic rationale for rejecting the music of the most prominent white musicians (Gil Evans and Dave Brubeck, for example). It is not a simple racist choice. Marsalis also vetoed a commission to the African-American composer George Russell, whose music, like that of Gil Evans, is influenced by contemporary classical music and fusion.

Lees and Collier believe there is an issue of parity not being addressed at Lincoln Center. In addition to the absence of programs celebrating the music of white musicians, the number of white musicians used at Lincoln Center has been small. The jazz critic Whitney Balliett has suggested that such hiring policies are racist. In the October 14, 1991, issue of *The New Yorker* he wrote, "Just six of the fifty-four performers used this week at Lincoln Center were white. Blacks invented jazz, but nobody owns it."[24]

Based on his hiring policies, it is apparent that Marsalis does not believe that there are many first-rate white musicians around and believes that African-American musicians are more deserving of his sponsorship since they are under-represented at other major cultural centers. After all, Marsalis has only to look into the rosters of the symphony orchestras that play at Lincoln Center. He knows he will find few African Americans.

How obligated is Marsalis to give a race-neutral program? Should he be required to follow standards of hiring adopted by trade unions? Should these standards be required by the sponsors of all cultural events? Should James Brown have been required to hire Korean musicians before permitting him to perform at the Apollo? Should the Juilliard String Quartet have been mandated to add an African-American cellist when their cellist retired from the group several years ago? Willard Jenkins, executive director of the National Jazz Service Organization (and no Marsalis advocate), is disturbed by the demands for parity in hiring. He asks: "Why are these questions only asked when something appears to be 'too black' for certain folks' comfort zones?" Lees responds that several figures in the jazz community asked the same questions when jazz was "too white." And, he adds, they did something to correct the situation. Benny Goodman, Artie Shaw, John Hammond, and others integrated jazz bands, and jazz critics such as Leonard Feather worked to secure deserved acclaim for African-American musicians.

At the crux of the problem is the argument of whether jazz is about the African-American experience in America or if it is a universal expression. Suppose that jazz were indeed an ethnic expression, as is Latin music. White musicians would then function in the jazz idiom much as they do in Latin music. There are several non-Latinos who have become prominent in Latin music, but most of them have occupied subsidiary roles as sidemen or arrangers. The few who have become leaders have chosen Spanish-sounding names. Consider the case of Larry Harlow, who is probably the most prominent non-Hispanic member of the Latin music community. Born Lawrence Ira Kahn, Harlow traveled to Cuba as a young man and learned Spanish. When he performs, he is in a sense masquerading as a Latino. This is his stage persona. Harlow delights in the absurdity of his situation, and used to have his vocalist refer to him as "el judío maravilloso"—the Wonderful Jew. After being on the scene so long, he has become an honorary Latino.

When Latin music is presented, Latin bandleaders and musicians are given priority. In recent years, the Japanese band Tierra del Sol has appeared at several salsa concerts, but it is considered a curiosity. Yet, there are no outcries about anti-white discrimination. No Latin music critic complains that only six out the fifty-four musicians who performed in the course of one week at some Latin jazz venue were white. The expectation is that, since Latin music is an ethnic music, Latinos should predominate. There may be other ethnic battles raging—for instance, between Puerto Ricans and Dominicans—but within the broad umbrella of Latin-American music, no one is staking a claim for non-Latinos.

ESSENTIALIST CRITICISMS OF BLACK MUSICIANS

bell hooks bemoans the influence of black nationalists who insist "that there is only 'one' legitimate black experience," and who condemn black individuals for not acting black enough.[25]

Proponents of the black music perspective blasted African-American artists who they believed had abandoned black culture and embraced European culture, defined broadly to include white America as well as the European continent. Amiri Baraka abhorred the music of Europe and white America, considering it a decadent art form antithetical to the African-American experience. Baraka warned African-American artists to steer clear of white musical influences: "To play their music is to be them and to act out their lives, as if you were them. There is, then, a whole world of most intimacy and most expression, which is yours, colored man, but which you will lose playing melancholy baby [sic] in B flat, or the *Emperor Concerto,* for that matter. Music lessons of a dying people."[26]

Exponents of the black music ideology do not all share Baraka's contempt for the music of Europe and white America. Baraka himself began to express this attitude only in writings published after *Blues People.* Reading his landmark study, one pictures the author vainly struggling not to condemn white musicians like Bix Beiderbecke just because of their "whiteness."

Wynton Marsalis, whose interviews suggest he considers jazz to be a black music, is no stranger to classical music. Indeed, he has proven himself to be in the top rank of classical trumpeters. But Marsalis is touchy about his interest in classical music. He is certainly aware that there are many African-American intellectuals who think that blacks have no business playing Haydn. In a recent interview he justified his involvement with classical music by remarking that "classical music is *not* white music" and "has nothing to do with racial situations" [emphasis in original]. Marsalis's defensiveness reached its most absurd heights when he likened Beethoven to Louis Armstrong: "His music has the same type of freedom and struggle for abolition of the class system, as Louis Armstrong's music is a celebration of that abolition. See, Beethoven's music has that struggle in it. Louis Armstrong is the resolution of that."[27]

In writing the history of postwar developments in jazz, scholars writing from the black music perspective have excoriated the influence of European music and criticized those musicians who they believe turned their backs on African-American culture when they looked to Europe for inspiration. James Lincoln Collier, a controversial figure in the jazz world because of his unflattering and idiosyncratic biographies, has expanded on the notion that bebop musicians were leaning toward European concepts alien to African-American culture.[28] But he goes a bit overboard by claiming that Gillespie's beret and Parker's British accent were indications that jazz was becoming more and more European. A full picture of bebop shows that for every European affectation there was a home-grown innovation in dress and vocabulary. Complementing Parker's Britishisms were jive words that originated in Harlem. And Gillespie's French beret was augmented by sunglasses and a zoot suit. Even if some of the elements originated in Europe, the total style was an American original.

Collier's contention that bebop exhibited a strong European bias makes more sense when he deals with purely musical phenomena. He supports his argument by citing the bebop musicians' fondness for harmonic structures and scales found in classical music and their abandonment of the fluid approach to pitch typical of blues players and early jazz musicians as evidence of this trend. Several of the bebop musicians studied with well-known composition teachers or befriended famous composers. Before he died Charlie Parker told Edgard Varèse that he was tired of the jazz world and wanted to be able to write orchestral scores.[29]

But Collier's argument is not without flaws. From his account of the music the uninformed reader could form the notion that the state of jazz harmony before bebop was primitive. Collier is just plain wrong in stating that "the old 'barbershop' harmonies of jazz were going in favor of advanced harmonies using a high degree of dissonance."[30] Interest in European forms among African Americans goes back to the nineteenth century, when a few black musicians studied with prominent European musicians. Among them was Will Marion Cook, who studied with Antonin Dvorák. There was nothing especially new about harmonic interest in the jazz community either. Much of the harmonic vocabulary of bebop can be found in Art Tatum's music. Bebop came about when horn players became as sophisticated about harmonies as pianists such as Tatum were, and then constructed melodic lines using higher chord intervals (seventh, ninth, eleventh and thirteenth scale degrees). By and large, this is how bebop came into being, not through studying classical music per se.

In a review of Miles Davis's autobiography and career, Stanley Crouch assailed the Davis-Evans cool jazz collaborations such as *Sketches of Spain* for relying on the canons of Western music and European aesthetics.[31] To Crouch's way of thinking, "European" and "Western" are terms of disapprobation as far as jazz is concerned. He suggests that good jazz is not Western music. Thus, for example, Monk's playing "is as far from European convention as bottleneck guitar work." He speaks of European music as if it were a compact entity that could be effortlessly characterized and then dismissed. He writes about Davis as if he were an unsophisticated pawn of European aesthetics. Consider the following two passages in Crouch's article: "Davis could be taken in by pastel versions of European colors" and "Davis turns out to have been overly impressed by the lessons he received at Juilliard."[32] It is difficult to reconcile these statements with the trumpeter's personality we have come to know from his autobiography and his many interviews. He is invariably pictured as a tough individual married to no point of view and uninterested in adhering to anyone's standards but his own.

The problem with Crouch's criticism is that he uses racially loaded terms. But I am certainly not crediting him for originating a rhetoric in which "European," "white," and "Western" are bad, while "black" and "African" are good; jazz writers have been doing it for decades. And, like these writers, Crouch uses these terms habitually rather than trying for more substantive criticism. On the other hand, perhaps Crouch doesn't really have anything on his mind other than racial stereotypes. At times, his writing reads like those ballet critics who, when reviewing African-American dancers, dwell on their physical differences from white dancers.

There is, of course, nothing the matter with denigrating *Sketches of Spain.* It is the manner in which Crouch sets about doing it that is wrong. There is a difference between condemning Gil Evans for writing "television music" and for writing music that is European, white, Western, and so on. While the former characterization is sociopolitically neutral (unless you happen to be a television-music composer), the latter terms transport the reader into the realm of black nationalism and its beliefs in the superiority of the "Afro-Asian world" and the "decay of Western civilization." It is strange to find Crouch in this territory, since in his nonmusical essays he unerringly condemns it. In *Notes of a Hanging Judge,* he refers to the "imbecility" of "ethnic nationalist black Americans" and to "the ersatz Africans of America who confused identity with pretentious name changing, costumes, and rituals that turned ethnicity into a hysterically nostalgic social club."33

Black music ideologists have attacked the bebop musicians for considering themselves to be disengaged outsiders for whom art was their religion, a refuge from the conventional world.34 Being an artist and trying to gain the status of "genius" was just another way of seeking white approval. According to poet-musician Jimmy Stewart, the black musicians of the 1940s and 1950s had fallen "prey for [*sic*] the aesthetic ideological traps the whites had laid for [them]."35

Perhaps in the context of the black nationalism of the 1960s, the bebop musician's devotion to art was a mistake. But back in the 1940s, claiming that one deserved to be treated as an artist was a revolutionary concept in the music business. While it is true that the image of the uncompromising artist is a purely Western invention, bebop musicians had no alternative role models with which to pursue their musical interests unfettered and be treated with respect. They saw their musical freedom as a metaphor for, and the musical equivalent of, the quest for political freedom being undertaken by Justice Thurgood Marshall and other civil rights leaders. They didn't want to be boxed in to any restrictive categories, as Gillespie makes clear in his autobiography:

> We never wished to be restricted to just an American context, for we were creators in an art form which grew from universal roots and which had proved it possessed universal appeal. Damn right! We refused to accept racism, poverty, or economic exploitation, nor would we live out uncreative humdrum lives merely for the sake of survival.36

While jazz musicians of previous generations often had one foot in jazz and the other in more popular African-American expressions such as the blues, bebop musicians wished to keep their idiom pure of popular influences. According to Gillespie, many of them looked down on the blues and were embarrassed to perform it in front of white audiences in a blues style. Gillespie was unhappy to find himself being criticized by fellow musicians for wanting to give his music more of a blues feel, more of a beat:

> People wanted to hear the beat and the blues, but the bebop musicians didn't like to play the blues. They were ashamed. The media had made it shameful. Blues artists at that time hardly ever played before white people, and we played mostly for white audiences. When I'd play a blues, guys would say, "Man, you're playing that?"
>
> I'd tell them, "Man, that's my music, that's my heritage." The bebop musicians wanted to show their virtuosity. They'd play the twelve-bar outline of the blues, but they wouldn't blues it up like the older guys they considered unsophisticated. They busied themselves making changes, a thousand changes in one bar. Why make one change in a bar if you could put a thousand more? Drummers wouldn't play back beats; they all wanted to play like Max Roach.[37]

Gillespie's disparaging comments give the reader an inaccurate idea of how his peers saw the blues. They were not turning away from the musical form considered to be at the heart of black music, merely from how it had been played in the past. The sensibilities of blues musicians were eschewed as too rural, unsophisticated. Bebop musicians wanted a new blues, fashioned for a new era. But by no means were they turning away from the blues. In fact, it is impossible to evaluate bebop properly without recognizing the centrality of the blues, especially in Charlie Parker's work. Parker performed and composed a large number of blues, and has been recognized as a major blues stylist.[38] The bebop revolution actually brought blues back to the central stage of the jazz world after years in which swing bands had marginalized it. This revival derived from Count Basie's orchestra, which provided the jazz world with a hint of how blues could be reinterpreted in a modern spirit.[39]

Although bebop musicians had not turned their backs on the blues, they had created a style of music that reflected an ambivalence toward popular blues styles. It was left to the next generation of African-

American jazz musicians, who had grown up performing and enjoying popular black music, to resolve this ambivalence. These younger musicians would verbally call attention to African-American roots and incorporate attributes of African-American popular musical idioms that were in some respects new to jazz. In the meantime, the ambivalence would grow even greater with a new style, cool jazz, in which elements of contemporary classical music sometimes predominated over African-American traits.

What forms of music meet the black music ideologists' essentialist criteria? Although hard bop had strong roots in black popular music, Amiri Baraka preferred avant-garde jazz, a music with little appeal for inner-city audiences. For him hard bop was more valuable as an affirmation of African-American culture than as a musical style. Baraka was disturbed to hear the hard bop musicians, many of whom were college-educated, urban African Americans, using the field hollers and ancient blues riffs of the rural South. Baraka believed that these musicians were pretending, "perhaps in all sincerity," to have "the same field of emotional reference as their slave ancestors."[40] He considered that because the musicians' re-evaluation of their roots was wrong-headed and possibly phony, it yielded poor musical fruits.

Baraka is appalled that much of hard bop was so easily accessible to the uninitiated, and that many of its creators wanted only to create appealing, emotionally riveting music:

> The opportunities for complete expression within its hardening structure and narrowly consistent frame of emotional reference grow more limited each time some mediocre soloist repeats a well-chewed phrase or makes of the music a static insistence rather than an opening into freer artistic achievement. It has become a kind of "sophistication" that depends more on common, then banal, musical knowledge, instead of truth or meaning suddenly revealed. What results, more often than not, is a self-conscious celebration of cliché, and an actual debilitation of the most impressive ideas to come out of bebop. One has the feeling, when listening to the most popular hard bop groups of the day, of being confronted merely by *a style,* behind which there is no serious commitment to expression or emotional profundity.[41]

When he derides the music for its static rhythms, one wonders whether he thinks gospel-influenced music can be anything other than repetitious. Baraka seems unable to accept the value of a good dance groove. Perhaps this is why he was such a champion of avant-garde jazz. I am reminded of an observation John Storm Roberts penned in the opening pages of *Black Music of Two Worlds:* "Those who use the word 'monotonous' in criticism of black music are on the wrong cultural wave length."[42]

BLACK-MUSIC EVALUATIONS OF WHITE MUSICIANS

Despite their ambivalence toward white musicians, black music ideologists have rarely, if ever, discouraged white musicians from playing black music. Several of the musicians who were the most ardent supporters of the black music ideology hired white musicians to perform in their bands. Archie Shepp brought the white trombonist Roswell Rudd to the attention of the jazz audience, and Rudd received good notices from Amiri Baraka.

The most open-minded black music ideologists concede that whites can learn to play the music, but because they are not African American, they do not have the blues as a way of life. As a result of not being "blues people," they enter jazz with a world-view that, in Baraka's opinion, is "not consistent with the making of jazz."[43] Even when the talents of white artists are recognized, they are sometimes resented for enjoying the fruits of African-American culture without having to experience racial oppression. This sentiment is encapsulated in the Sounds of Blackness lyric: "Everybody wants to sing the blues / But nobody wants to live my blues."[44]

Much of the estimation of white jazz musicians, especially those who gained fame before World War II, is marked by bitterness over their financial success, itself the result of racist hiring practices. The artists most singled out for condemnation from the decades preceding World War II are Benny Goodman and the Original Dixieland Jazz Band.

The Original Dixieland Jazz Band

The Original Dixieland Jazz Band had the distinction of producing the first jazz recording. As a result of its success, the record industry produced an entire series of recordings by white jazz bands. Since the music was recorded exclusively by whites for the next five years, many whites considered jazz to be "a specialized form of white dance of music."[45]

Jazz histories tend to overstate an otherwise viable point: that the success of the ODJB came at the expense of African-American musicians. It actually could have been a black group that made the first jazz record, since cornetist Freddie Keppard turned down an offer to record before the ODJB's records came out. Keppard was concerned that a recording would give other musicians a chance to copy his music.

In the first two decades of this century, discrimination against African Americans in the music business was not a uniform policy. Although the recording industry undoubtedly gave its better jobs and contracts to whites, it did not neglect African Americans when there was a financial incentive. The black orchestra leader James Reese Europe, who had become famous for his association with Vernon and Irene Castle, a popular white dance team, recorded with Victor in 1914, three years before the ODJB's recording debut. Europe's orchestra played a mix of minstrel, ragtime and orchestral music. By the mid-1920s the record industry had begun to realize that big money could be made by attending to the interests of specific ethnic groups. Along with recordings of the ethnic musical idioms of Germans, French, Irish, Jews, Native Americans, Hawaiians, Bohemians, Poles, Tyroleans, and Scandinavians, there were recordings of blues and jazz for African Americans. From 1922 on, black jazz bands were recorded regularly.

How good was the ODJB? As often as not, its members have been held in contempt for claiming that they invented jazz and refusing to acknowledge the importance of African-American musicians. Nick LaRocca, leader of the ODJB, certainly gained no friends in the jazz community for the racist comments he made in the jazz press. He was also reviled for copyrighting pieces of unknown origin such as "Tiger Rag" that were a well-established part of the standard New Orleans repertoire years before the ODJB recorded them. Although it was dishonest for LaRocca to take credit for compositions that he didn't write, it must be conceded that this practice has not been unknown in the music business. In the 'teens, few musicians were familiar with the nature of copyright laws and contracts.

Most of the top white musicians grew up hearing the ODJB and were impressed by the group's recordings. But after they were exposed to performances by African-American musicians like King Oliver, they changed their views. The white clarinetist and saxophonist Mezz Mezzrow described the ODJB in terms most jazz musicians came to accept:

> They were really a corny outfit, and if they ever had a touch of
> New Orleans it was as frail as a nail and twice as pale, strictly a

white-man's version. But they were fast and energetic and they
had a gang of novelty effects that the public went wild
about—jangling cowbells, honking automobile horns, barnyard
imitations, noises that sounded like everything but music.[46]

Mezzrow's evaluation of the ODJB was distorted by his indignation that
the group was given prominence over performers he considered to be
the best jazz musicians in the world. For instance, consider his comment
that the group featured "noises that sounded like everything but music."
Here he comes close to excoriating the ODJB simply for mixing silliness
with jazz, as if doing so showed disrespect to the jazz tradition. But in
this period of jazz history white bands did not have a monopoly on
comic jazz. There were several African-American bands that also had a
desire to amuse their audience and that had the same battery of noise-
making percussion instruments and sound effects.

Mezzrow was distressed that the majority of Americans preferred a
musical style in which the characteristics of African-American music
were watered down. Like many jazz critics, he was concerned that the
authentic—the "real"—jazz was being passed over in favor of a commer-
cialized version. Although one can, perhaps, accuse the ODJB of being
mediocre, it is unfair to call its members imitators. The story is more complicated. The ODJB came out of an almost-forgotten musical world developed by poor whites, Latinos, and southern European immigrants in
New Orleans.[47] Although some elements of its music were taken from
African-American musicians, the band was never interested in sticking
faithfully to the jazz idiom developed by blacks.

The criticism of the ODJB has been replicated whenever a white group
appeared before the public and met with success. White musicians are
criticized for copying the music of the top African-American musicians of
the day and for benefiting from the preferential treatment given whites in
a racist society. They are condemned for watering down the essential
African-American elements and for drawing attention away from influential styles created by African Americans that had not received widespread
attention and public support. Such criticism of pre—World War II white
musicians was justified up to a point: white musicians were rarely able to
succeed in an African-American style on a level with top African-American
artists. In the 1920s and 1930s the most important and influential music
produced by white musicians trained in jazz came from artists such as
George Gershwin and Raymond Scott, who created music influenced by
jazz but were not dedicated to sticking closely to its stylistic canons.

Before leaving the subject of the Original Dixieland Jazz Band, a few comments from Louis Armstrong are in order. Armstrong's book, *Swing That Music,* advertised in 1936 as "the first published book in English on the new Swing Music," is rarely cited by jazz writers. One of the reasons for its neglect is that it is full of praise for the Original Dixieland Jazz Band and its founder, Nick LaRocca. Jazz archivist Dan Morgenstern, who wrote the forward to the 1993 edition, believes that the praise was offered because 1936 was the year in which the four surviving members of the ODJB got together again. Morgenstern implies that Armstrong was instructed to add a few favorable words. In any case, Morgenstern regards the passages on the group to be "shall we say, politically incorrect."[48] Readers should judge for themselves.

> In 1909, the first great jazz orchestra was formed in New Orleans by a cornet player named Dominick James LaRocca. They called him "Nick" LaRocca. His orchestra had only five pieces, but they were the hottest five pieces that had ever been known before. LaRocca named this band, "The Old [sic] Dixieland Jazz Band." He had an instrumentation different from anything before—an instrumentation that made the old songs sound new.... [LaRocca's] fame as one of the great pioneers of syncopated music will last a long, long time, as long, I think, as American music lives.[49]

Note that in the preceding passage Armstrong did not attribute the invention of jazz to the ODJB, a claim made by LaRocca. He credits the ODJB only for devising a new jazz instrumentation and popularizing the music.

The ODJB started an unfortunate trend in jazz: ascribing the development of new styles to musicians who did not originate them. These popularizers were inevitably white, while the architects of the new style were African-American. In the next generation the role the ODJB played in its own day was taken up by Benny Goodman. Because of his central role in swing, Goodman helped perpetuate the consensus that jazz was an American product, not an African-American one.

Benny Goodman

The King of Swing turned out to be none of the African-American musicians who had formulated the style—Fletcher Henderson, Duke Ellington, Don Redman, or Count Basie. Instead, it was Benny Goodman. At the most, Goodman can be given credit for popularizing his generation's style of jazz, much as the ODJB did for New Orleans jazz. Many members of the jazz community have been bitter about Benny Goodman's lionization. The antipathy is typified by an anecdote in Dizzy Gillespie's autobiography.

In 1955 Charlie Shavers was playing with Goodman at Basin Street East while Gillespie was performing around the corner at another club. Gillespie went down to Basin Street East and waited outside the club for Shavers. While he was waiting, a white man asked Gillespie if he was going to sit in with Benny Goodman. Gillespie replied that he didn't play for free. "Not even with the King?" the man asked.

Gillespie responded, "What King? . . . I played with all the Kings." Gillespie then recited the "kings" he had played with: Coleman Hawkins, Benny Carter, Charlie Parker, Ben Webster, Chu Berry, Art Tatum, Earl Hines.[50]

Goodman was the first prominent white musician to hire African-American musicians for live performances, and well after the Swing Era was under way he was the only major bandleader to hire black musicians on a permanent basis.[51] He was responsible for making stars out of Teddy Wilson, Charlie Christian, and Lionel Hampton. Although his role in opening up the music business for African Americans has been well recognized, Goodman has also been criticized for benefiting from the talents of these musicians, some of whom are considered to be his musical superiors. Perhaps Goodman would not have been in the position of hiring them as sidemen if these African-American musicians could have thrived without being associated with a white bandleader.

Such a view has its merits. White bands made much more money than African-American bands. For instance, the men in Bob Crosby's group "made four or five times as much as those in Count Basie's." And while white musicians had good opportunites outside of jazz, African Americans were not offered the lucrative studio or staff jobs in film and radio.[52] Nevertheless, when carried to the extreme, the view that white musicians gained from the financial hardships of black musicians produces a picture of the jazz world of the 1930s and 1940s in which white musicians play the role of plantation owners and African Americans the sharecroppers or worse. Duke Ellington, Louis Armstrong, and a few other African-American musicians and entertainers were making good money. Involvement of black arrangers with white bands may have been more common, but there was also work for white arrangers with black bands. Bill Challis, Russ Morgan, and Will Hudson wrote for Fletcher Henderson's band. Hudson wrote for McKinney's Cotton Pickers, Erskine Tate, Cab Calloway, and the Mills Blues Rhythm Band. And Morgan wrote an arrangement of *Body and Soul* for Louis Armstrong. Gene Lees claims in *Cats of Any Color: Jazz, Black and White* that "Fletcher Henderson probably played more charts by white arrangers than Benny Goodman played charts by Fletcher Henderson."[53]

Goodman's detractors try to reduce Goodman's big-band sound to the influence of one man—Fletcher Henderson. In *Blues People,* Amiri Baraka goes a step further by implying that Goodman underpaid Henderson. Baraka cites the exact amount: "only $37.50 per arrangement before Goodman actually hired him as the band's chief arranger."[54]

The more important question, of course, is not whether Goodman was underpaying Henderson but whether Goodman's band was merely the Fletcher Henderson Orchestra in whiteface. This point of view was espoused by musicians angered to hear the same arrangements Henderson's own band had played suddenly becoming the vehicle for a white bandleader's rise to fame and fortune. Their anger led them to perceive the relationship between Goodman and Henderson as an example of a recurring complaint in American race relations: the white man benefiting from, and getting the credit for, the black man's labors.

There is much truth to this perception, but it is complicated by an important fact. Henderson's influence on Goodman's big-band sound was not exclusive. At all stages of his career Goodman hired a number of arrangers, both black and white. Fletcher Henderson was not the only arranger, and, in fact, he was not the only Henderson to arrange for Goodman. It was Horace Henderson, an arranger whose work is not always distinguished by jazz historians from that of his famous brother, who wrote some of Goodman's best-known selections.

Yet even if the Henderson sound, with its endless interplay between sections of the big band, became the primary vehicle for Goodman's rise to fame, Goodman cannot be entirely blamed for relying on what had merely become the predominant style of the day. Neither can he be blamed for hiring the best arranger he could find.

Goodman has been criticized for being a second-rate musician. The French critic André Hodeir refers to his style with contempt as "the Goodman type of academic playing."[55] From a technical standpoint alone, however, Goodman was one of the greatest clarinet virtuosos in the history of jazz, and he was most certainly the most influential figure on that instrument during the Swing Era for both white and black clarinetists. But his achievements do not end there. Although his big-band sound can be stiff, his small groups with Teddy Wilson, Gene Krupa, and Lionel Hampton seem above reproach. Outside of jazz, Goodman had a profound effect on twentieth-century classical composition by commissioning important works from Béla Bartók and Aaron Copland. Although his idiosyncratic style as a classical clarinetist at first was not well received, it has had a strong influence on a leading contemporary clarinet, Richard Stoltzman.

While many African-American musicians thought Goodman did not deserve his acclaim, a few thought otherwise. Cootie Williams, who joined Goodman's big band for a year before returning to Ellington trumpet section, was full of praise: "That Goodman band—I loved it. It had a beat, and there was something there I wanted to play with." And here's what Williams has to say about playing with Goodman's sextet: "Each man could take care of himself. The thing would just move, that's what I enjoyed. There was never a let-down. Soon as one guy stopped playing, here came another, right in on top. With Benny no one could sit back—and *he* couldn't sit back, either."[56]

Post–World War II White Jazz Musicians

Bebop was the first jazz style in which African Americans got the credit for being the leaders and creators of the music. This phenomenon is a reflection of the growth in racial pride that was felt in the African-American community during and after World War II. Miles Davis called bebop "an all-black thing,"[57] and his opinion is shared by most jazz writers. Yet the black audience for bebop was smaller than it had been for previous jazz styles. When bebop came into prominence, the black audience, which had grown enormously during the Swing Era, diminished.[58] Despite the concentration of African Americans in the upper echelons of bebop, the music was not important to most blacks, who preferred rhythm-and-blues to bebop. When asked about the significance of Charlie Parker to African Americans, Art Blakey replied, "Hell, Negro people never even heard of Charlie Parker."[59]

Bebop has been described by some as a style that blacks created in such a way that whites would not be able to copy it. Much has been made of Thelonious Monk's comment, "We are going to create something that they can't steal because they can't play it." (Actually, it was Mary Lou Williams who attributed that statement to Monk.)[60] Did Monk mean that he, as a leader of the bebop fraternity, wanted to keep whites from stealing the music? Critic Leslie Rout believed this was exactly Monk's intention, as well as the intentions of other formulators of the new style: "the creation of a jazz form that whites could not play."[61] Yet several white musicians participated in the legendary jam sessions at Minton's. In the beginning, trumpeter Johnny Carisi was the only white musician there. He was welcomed, according to Gillespie: "He'd learned all the tunes. Played all of Thelonious Monk's tunes, all of mine. I'd play a chorus. He'd be right behind me. Roy [Eldridge]? Right behind Roy. Right behind everybody. He was welcome as long as he could blow the way he did."[62]

Carisi got a mixed reception. When he did well he was sometimes given back-handed compliments in which praise for mastering the style was mixed with rebuke for coming up to Harlem to steal it.[63] Later other whites came to Minton's—Kai Winding, Benny Goodman, Tony Scott, and musician-turned-critic Michael Zwerin.

Critic Ron Welburn argues that the white participants were really not welcome at Minton's and had no business being there. He thinks that Gillespie was referring to whites when he said how, along with Monk, he "began to work out some complex variations on chords . . . to scare the no-talent guys." Welburn comments that "given the presence of white musicians at Minton's, they must have comprised a majority of the 'no-talent guys' *for a strictly black musical idiom*."[64]

Although some African-American musicians may have been anti-white or believed that whites couldn't play jazz, the leaders of bebop showed by their hiring practices that they didn't share those feelings. Parker, Gillespie, and Davis all had white sidemen. At times, blacks criticized them for hiring whites when many talented black musicians were unemployed. Davis responded, "I wouldn't give a damn if he was green with red breath. I'm hiring a motherfucker to play, not for what color he is."[65] Gillespie considered these mixed bands to be pioneer efforts in breaking down racial barriers.[66]

All in all, African-American musicians had no problem accepting white musicians into their circle, especially if whites had paid their dues by playing in black-led groups. Lee Konitz, Stan Getz, George Wallington, Al Haig, Red Rodney, Teddy Kotick, Gil Evans, Gerry Mulligan, and many other whites freely circulated in the bebop crowd. It was the white critics, not the musicians, whom the bebop musicians held in contempt. The unkind reviews of early Parker and Gillespie recordings were just the tip of the iceberg. What particularly angered Miles Davis was that, when white musicians became leaders of their own groups in the early

1950s, the critics chose to spotlight them rather than black musicians: "Now, I'm not saying here that these guys weren't good musicians, because they were; Gerry, Lee, Stan, Dave [Brubeck], Kai, Lennie [Tristano], all of them were good musicians. But they didn't start nothing, and they knew it, and they weren't the best at what was being done."[67]

What especially irritated him was the attention given to Chet Baker, who had played with Charlie Parker for several months when Parker was in Los Angeles. Parker was full of praise for Baker and when he came back to New York told Gillespie and Davis: "You better look out, there's a little white cat out on the West Coast who's gonna eat you up."[68] Baker was voted Best Trumpet Player in a 1953 *Down Beat* poll. According to Davis, the critics may have ignored him and Gillespie because they were "old stars," but nothing justified their giving more attention to Baker than to the brilliant trumpeter Clifford Brown, who, like Baker, was a new face on the jazz scene. Davis recognized that Baker was good, but he thought Clifford Brown could play rings around him.

Among all the white musicians of the 1950s Dave Brubeck was the one who reaped the most scorn. Most of it came because he had not paid his dues playing with bebop musicians. When Brubeck opened in New York in 1951, he had already received the attention of the jazz press. At one appearance his group played opposite a band led by Dizzy Gillespie. Gillespie was so angered by what he considered to be the unwarranted attention Brubeck was receiving that he threw eggs up on the stage.[69]

Most of the postwar white jazz musicians were involved in cool jazz. Frank Kofsky, in his Marxist analysis of the jazz community, *Black Nationalism and the Revolution in Music,* is committed to the view that cool jazz was a white conspiracy. He reasons that, since few whites had successfully mastered bebop, they decided to create a style they *could* play, and they did this "under the shibboleth of making the music more 'legitimate.' "[70] He states that Miles Davis was the lone African American to play a prominent role, and that Davis "repudiated" the movement several years later when he recorded the blues composition, *Walkin'*. Kofsky also states that black musicians on the West Coast were "excluded from the cool movement."[71] He seems to be unaware that the African-American musicians John Lewis, George Russell, Art Farmer, and Chico Hamilton were important figures in the cool style, and that African-American musicians on the West Coast jazz scene with a bop orientation such as Hampton Hawes, Curtis Counce, and Leroy Vinnegar were often featured in bands led by cool jazz musicians.

Kofsky dislikes cool jazz. He also dislikes Beat writers and painters. Both supposedly celebrated withdrawal from society rather than the revolutionary activity Kofsky favors. Kofsky claims that "when Beats were gathered in their pads, cool jazz, rather than bebop, rhythm and blues or rock and roll, provided the musical backdrop."[72] What a preposterous statement! Kerouac talks about his admiration for black jazz musicians in *On the Road,* and this book was surely the most influential book of the Beat generation. In *Down and In: Life in the Underground,* Ronald Sukenick describes how bop was the music of the Beats, and Charlie Parker their hero.[73]

Where was the African-American community when these white musicians were, in Kofksy's view, taking over jazz? Somewhat predictably for a Marxist historian, Kofsky explains it in terms of economics. In his view, the black audience was on its way toward a rapprochement with bebop when World War II ended. But it was not to be. The economic downturn in the years immediately following the war was especially hard on the black community, and jobs gained during the war were lost. African Americans no longer had enough money to go to jazz clubs and purchase records. Dance halls closed in record numbers, and some musicians were forced to leave the music field for employment elsewhere. As a result, bop was forced underground. African Americans did not return to jazz until the Korean War. With the new wartime economy, they once again had jobs and the money to spend on jazz records and to attend clubs and concerts.

Even so, Kofsky's economic analysis is not entirely without merit. The closing of dance halls did have a major impact on music. But the dance halls closed down because they could no longer support large dance bands when people lost interest in swing. This shift affected bebop musicians only because the big bands had provided alternative employment. In any case, economic factors do not alone account for people's tastes. Why did bop go under? Both whites and African Americans were probably turned off by this often esoteric form of jazz and were drawn to music that was easier to listen or dance to. Americans no longer empathized with the heated passions of bebop. They were responding to a music that provided them with a more soothing sound. But the quiet romanticism and intimacy of many cool jazz recordings were echoed in African-American popular musical styles of the time. The vocal groups of the 1950s known as "bird groups" such as the Ravens had a similar mellifluence, as did Johnny Mathis's work.

DIFFERENCES BETWEEN AFRICAN-AMERICAN AND WHITE JAZZ MUSICIANS

In 1956 the French critic André Hodeir remarked about the cool style that "modern jazz's opponents won't fail to point out that what we have here is a return to the European conception of 'purity of sound.' "[74] Hodeir correctly points out that there is nothing in the classical saxophone tradition like the tone quality of a Lee Konitz, whose style is 180 degrees from the full-throttled tone of the pre-eminent classical saxophonist, Marcel Mule. Several years after Hodeir's analysis of cool jazz was published, Amiri Baraka in *Blues People* compared the playing styles of Paul Desmond, the quintessential cool saxophonist, and Charlie Parker, the master of bebop saxophone playing. He considers their styles to represent, respectively, the European and African-American approaches to art. In the context of this discussion Baraka describes Desmond as producing "a sound on his instrument that can almost be called legitimate, or classical."[75] It seems inconceivable that Baraka had listened to any classical saxophonists before he wrote this statement. If he had familiarized himself with classical saxophone playing, he would have had to conclude that neither Desmond nor Parker played in a classical style. He could have made a case that Desmond sounded "white" because Desmond was hardly a blues player, but this does not make him a "classical" player. There are more ways of being white than Baraka imagined.

Kofsky attempted to define the differences between African-American and white jazz as follows: African-American jazz is based on "heightening the emotional intensity," while white jazz is set on "incorporating new technical devices into jazz as ends in themselves."[76] A number of writers and musicians have voiced similar ideas. According to Ornette Coleman, blacks and whites have profoundly different attitudes about showing emotion:

> I think black people in America have a superior sense when it comes to expressing their own convictions through music. Most whites tend to think that it's below their dignity to just show suffering and just show any other meaning that has to do with feeling and not technique or analysis or whatever you call it. And this to me is why the black man has developed in the field of music that the white man calls jazz. And basically, I think that word, the sense of that word, is used to describe music that the white man feels is really inferior.[77]

Malcolm X believed that African Americans could spontaneously invent, while whites could only repeat what they had heard before. He spoke on the subject of African-American creativity in his address to the founding meeting of the Organization of Afro-American Unity in 1964:

> I've seen black musicians when they'd be jamming at a jam session with white musicians—a whole lot of difference. The white musician can jam if he's got some sheet music in front of him. He can jam on something that he's heard jammed before. But that black musician, he picks up his horn and starts blowing some sounds that he never thought of before. He improvises, he creates, it comes from within. It's his soul; it's that soul music. It's the only area on the American scene where the black man has been free to create. And he has mastered it. He has shown that he can come up with something that nobody ever thought of on his own.[78]

A few jazz musicians have praised white musicians, yet it is often done grudgingly. Art Blakey had some kind words for white musicians: "If you want them to, they'll do the same thing every night, year in and year out. They'll work together, they won't be late, there's no ego thing going on, and when they come out with something, they make it not because they're great but just because of their togetherness."[79]

Throughout his career, Ornette Coleman has chosen white bassists. Two of them—Charlie Haden and Scott LaFaro—are among the leading innovators on the instrument. During the heyday of black nationalism in the mid-1960s, Coleman felt obligated to justify the presence of whites in his groups, a presence that seemed to embarrass him. He reasoned that white musicians make better bassists than African Americans because there are few African-American players who understand the instrument and can play it expressively. According to Coleman, blacks "haven't taken the string instrument as a part of their high ethnic expression."[80]

Coleman's assessment of the ability of African Americans to play string instruments is both flawed and quixotic. Trained African-American string players are not as rare as Coleman suggests. The violin was the most beloved instrument of black slaves, and bluegrass country fiddling is probably derived from African-American violin technique.

In *Blues People,* Amiri Baraka examines the differences between the white and black approaches to jazz as exemplified by Louis Armstrong and Bix Beiderbecke. Baraka seldom acknowledges the talents of white musicians, but he shows a great deal of admiration for Beiderbecke's emotional and intellectual achievements as a jazz musician.

He sees Beiderbecke as a rebel against white American society. But although influenced by African-American culture, Beiderbecke followed European aesthetic standards. Armstrong, on the other hand, was an entirely different kind of artist whose music fell well within the bounds of the musical traditions of African-American culture and remained almost untouched by European aesthetic ideas. While Beiderbecke did not fit into his own (white) society, Armstrong was "in terms of emotional archetypes, an honored priest of his culture—one of the most impressive products of his society."[81]

Beiderbecke's music, along with the music of nearly all white jazz musicians, was guided by a philosophy that Baraka calls "the artifact given expression." What I think he means is that people with a European heritage and orientation make a separation between the artist and the expression of the art itself. The expression takes on a life of its own, becoming a reified object. The consequence of this is that people of European heritage have established an aesthetic based on "the principle of the beautiful thing as opposed to the natural thing." A singer's voice can be conceived as beautiful, but "mere expression cannot be thought to be."[82] For artists with an African heritage and orientation, however, the artifact is just the means of self-expression, and the musical instrument merely its agent. There is no distinction among "music, dancing, song, the artifact, and a man's life or his worship of his gods. *Expression* issued from life, and *was* beauty."[83]

Baraka's convoluted distinctions between "the artifact" and "the natural thing" found resonance within the avant-garde jazz community, especially as avant-garde musicians and their followers had rejected accepted standards of musicianship and were fascinated with non-Western music. Outside this limited sphere, it gained few adherents. Most musicians had too much respect for the difficulties of mastering "the artifact" and "the agent"—that is, musical forms and standards and instrumental technique—to pay much attention. But Baraka's emphasis on environment as a means of explaining and accepting differences between white and African-American musicians has proven to be one of the most enduring ideas in the jazz community. I have seen half a dozen instances in the literature on jazz (a few predating *Blues People)* in which "environment" is used to explain the differences between white and black musicians. But the musicians and writers who see value in "environment" rarely explain precisely what they mean, leaving the reader uncertain about which aspects of "environment" they are referring to.

The importance of environment as a way of explaining basic differences between African-American and white musicians occurred to Cecil Taylor one night in the early 1950s when he heard Horace Silver playing with Stan Getz:

> That night I dug that there were two attitudes in jazz, one white and one black. The white idea is valid in that the cats playing it play the way their environment leads them, which is the only way they can play. But Horace is the Negro idea because he was playing the real thing of Bud, with all the physicality of it, with the filth of it, and the movement in the attack.[84]

It is easy to read into Taylor's comment that the *right* way to play is Silver's, not Getz's.

According to Lee Konitz, environmental factors played a key role in the music of his teacher, Lennie Tristano:

> He certainly is a direct development, or "white" development, if you will. And I think there's a basis of different environmental experience to make that distinction. That he used all of those materials that were basically brought to their full fruition by black men and he did it from his experiences in Italian-American [*sic*].[85]

Konitz's thinking is fuzzy about whether the "environment" that forms the basis of Tristano's music was white American culture or Italian-American culture. His attempts to explain Tristano's music by means of environmental factors remind me that it in other artistic communities people do not usually give so much importance to environment in order to explain artistic difference. They consider more transitory and idosyncratic events—sociopolitical movements, personal hardships and just plain serendipity—as having an equal or even greater role than environment. There is something damning about the notion that one's entire artistic output is determined by ethnicity.

The theory that environment has had a profound effect on establishing differences between white and African-American musicians is based on the unspoken assumption that musicians of the same race have grown up in the same environment. When exposed to the light of day this argument looks feeble. If one examines the backgrounds of, say, the African-American bebop musicians of the 1940s, one quickly realizes that they came from very diverse regions and economic classes. John Lewis was from Albuquerque, Charlie Parker from Kansas City, Dizzy Gillespie from South Carolina, and Thelonious Monk from Harlem. Miles Davis's and Dexter Gordon's families were well-off, while Art Blakey's worked in the steel mills. It becomes quickly apparent that physical environment had little impact on forming the nucleus of bebop musicians.

In the jazz literature, environment is invariably cited as a factor to explain white jazz musicians rather than African-Americans. But "environment" is just another racial code word, as were "West Coast" and "East Coast" in the 1950s. When Dizzy Gillespie says, "There was no such thing as 'white' in our music, because most of the contributors . . . were black," and then explains that it is "just a matter of environment that makes me act one way and makes a white guy act another way," one understands that "environment" is merely a polite and somewhat pretentious way of asserting the inevitability of African-American dominance in jazz.[86] In effect, "environment" prevents whites from achieving greatness in jazz, while it ensures that *only* African Americans will dominate.

BATTLING THE BLACK MUSIC IDEOLOGY

One of two things is true. Either jazz has evolved into a major art form, and an international one, capable of exploring and inspiring the full range of human experience and emotion. Or it is a small, shriveled, crippled art useful only for the expression of the angers and resentments of an American minority. If the former is true, it is the greatest gift of blacks to America, and America's greatest aesthetic gift to the world.

If the latter is true, it isn't dying. It's already dead.
—Gene Lees, *Cats of Any Color*[87]

The proponents of the black music ideology have written a revisionist history of jazz that overstates the impact of racism on African-American musicians and minimizes the influence of whites. Any books written by whites that stray from these views are subjected to charges of racism. Even the most benign statements are criticized as being racist. For instance, ethnomusicologist Helen Myers singles out the following sentence in Frank Tirro's textbook, *Jazz: A History,* as an example of the thinking of white writers who deny the achievements of African Americans: "Contrary to popular belief, jazz does not owe its existence to any one race."[88] Tirro was simply stating the obvious—that jazz did not spring from African-American culture without the influences of American band traditions and Western harmony, melody, and rhythm. Myers is wrong to accuse him of racism on the basis of one sentence taken out of context.

White musicians have, naturally, not taken kindly to the unflattering views of black music ideologists. Jim Hall responded with the following comment to charges that whites stole the music: "I've always felt that the music started out as black but that it's as much mine now as anyone else's. I haven't stolen the music from anybody—I just bring something different to it."[89]

Bill Evans was appalled by the notion that "only black musicians can be innovative," since he believed that creativity is an innately human characteristic that goes beyond race. He rationalized the black music ideology as the reaction of a group of people who "haven't had much, so they want to make jazz one hundred percent black." Evans wanted "more responsibility among black people and black musicians to be more accurate and to be spiritually intelligent about humanity." He believed that African Americans should consider the consequences of their statements before putting them in print. He warned them that "to say only black people can play jazz is just as dangerous as saying only white people are intelligent or anything like that."[90]

Trumpeter Ruby Braff finds ridiculous the notion that jazz could be called black music:

> What is "black music?" I never saw black music. What is black music? Would you mind telling me? What is black music? Are they referring to jazz? Jazz is an American product made up by all people in this country. . . . It just so happens that great pioneers of jazz, of improvised music, were the black people, the great black artists, who would turn over in their graves if they ever heard the way any of these guys are playing today. It's a horror show. It's terrible. . . .
>
> For years and years black people wanted integration in this society and to get together, and they got all these people to help them—white people, black people. Now are they saying that they want to be separating now? Or do they want to be

separating in music but not in housing, in industry, in politics? Where is it? Where is it?

I never in my life thought of music or anybody's color. We
played with people. If you asked me if there was black cats in
the band, I couldn't even tell you. I'd have to say, "Who's
black here, who's white." That's how little any of us give a
damn.[91]

There is an edge of disingenuousness to the ways these three white
musicians—Bill Evans, Jim Hall, and Ruby Braff—responded to the black
music ideology in interviews between 1974 and 1992. They spoke
about jazz as if they were oblivious to the fact that "white" has been a pejorative term among jazz musicians and critics for decades, going back at
least as far as 1930, when the jazz critic Charles Edward Smith wrote
that Louis Armstrong's playing "succumbs more and more to the white
man's notion of Harlem jazz."[92] In a 1959 article, "Race Prejudice in
Jazz," Nat Hentoff describes how he heard an African-American musician "[curse] one of his sidemen loudly for playing 'too white.' "[93] Jazz
musicians, white and black, have been denigrating for decades the average white musician's ability to swing. Hentoff cites a white pianist who
admitted that he preferred "not to play in an all-white rhythm section, because there aren't that many white groups that can really swing." Hentoff
also noted that Europeans have developed a reputation for believing that
"a Negro musician must be superior to a white musician if only because
he is a Negro."[94] In fact, critic Gary Giddens was told by a few musicians
that European jazz promoters in the 1960s insisted that black-led bands
have all-black personnel. As a result of this quest for authenticity, some
black musicians had to fire white sidemen.[95]

One of the leaders in this backlash against the extremes of black nationalism was Billy Taylor, a noted jazz pianist with a doctoral degree in
education. Although he recognizes that jazz came out of African-
American culture, he believes that the music is no longer solely black
music, having transcended its ethnic boundaries. He calls jazz "a unique
American phenomenon; . . . America's classical music." Jazz artists have
developed "an American way of playing music" that reflects American
values and contributes to the shaping of American culture. Jazz "meets all
the criteria for determining whether a music is classical: it is time-tested;
it serves as a standard or model; it has value; and it is indigenous to the
culture for which it speaks."[96]

Pop music standards provide those who believe that jazz is an American classical music with their best argument. Written by both whites and African Americans, it can only be viewed as American, neither white nor black. The importance of these songs as inspiration for jazz musicians is not often recognized by the musicians themselves or by jazz critics. Irving Louis Horowitz and Charles Nanry wrote in "Ideologies and Theories about American Jazz" that universal recognition of the central role of the popular song repertoire "would signify the end of most forms of racial and ideological disputation concerning the writing, nature and purpose of jazz."[97]

In the last few years two jazz writers, James Lincoln Collier and Gene Lees, have taken upon themselves the task of battling the racist propaganda that has been written over the last thirty years. Collier's views on the excesses of black music ideology are laid out in *Jazz: The American Theme Song* (1993). Lees addresses the topic in *Cats of Any Color* (1994). It is only regrettable that their agenda appears to be not only to correct inaccuracies in the literature but to cast doubt on the premise that African Americans have a culture of their own, distinct from white American culture.

Collier believes that it is historically inaccurate to describe jazz as a product of "black culture." Jazz came into existence at a time when black Creoles, key figures in the birth of jazz, were regarded as culturally distinct from American blacks. The differences between the two groups—Creoles and American blacks—were real and substantial. Creoles were Catholics, blacks were Protestant. Creoles spoke French, blacks spoke English. Creoles had their own songs, American blacks had an entirely different repertoire consisting of work songs and spirituals. These profound cultural differences extended into the economic and social arenas as well.[98] In Collier's opinion, during the formative years of jazz, "black" culture did not include Creole culture. He therefore concludes that "jazz did not arise from some generalized 'black culture' or 'black experience.' "[99]

Collier takes a different approach toward the jazz establishment's tacit acceptance of the black origins of jazz. He points out the disdain many African Americans have felt toward jazz. It was not an art form they were proud of, especially since some of its early development took place in brothels. But Collier ascribes too much significance to African-American antipathy toward jazz, as if the animus itself somehow proved that jazz could not be an integral part of black culture. The disdain jazz suffered was not unique: Popular music in general has always been regarded with negative feelings by many sectors of American society.

Collier's notions about black culture could not have been timed more poorly, for a wide range of African-American artists and intellectuals, cultural theorists and even television writers have been promoting the view that there are many ways of being African-American. Their views are more sophisticated than Collier's and allow for a more flexible conception of black culture that takes into account the diversity of the African-American experience.

Collier treats at length the history of the dance band in America and ties its development to such white musicians as Ferde Grofé and Art Hickman. It is a commendable addition to the literature on American popular music and adds a new dimension to our appreciation of swing. Because Collier's work is so well documented, jazz writers can no longer assume that African-American musicians invented the dance band and formulated the ways in which the ensemble came to be orchestrated. But despite Collier's contribution, the roles of Fletcher Henderson and Don Redman in making the dance band a jazz group remain unassailable.

While most writers divide jazz history according to race, Lees and Collier provide a view of jazz history as a unified stream. They show that jazz has not always been a one-sided affair, with African Americans creating the music and whites copying it. They emphasize that whites also influenced African Americans, a point that black music ideological literature often ignores. Lees points out that Lester Young was influenced by Frank Trumbauer, Rex Stewart was influenced by Bix Beiderbecke, and Henderson learned from Bill Challis. He also reminds us that Gil Evans and Bill Evans were major figures in the development of jazz.

Despite its shortsightedness, the black music ideology makes several valid points. In *Blues People* Baraka successfully proved that change in jazz is closely related to changes of attitude within the African-American community. That is, change is not the result of musical developments per se but of sociopolitical events affecting the African-American community. And black musicians have indeed determined the directions the music has taken over the years. It was New Orleans musicians who originally created jazz out of march music; Louis Armstrong who created the soloist's role in jazz; Fletcher Henderson and Don Redman who took the dance band and made it into a jazz group; James P. Johnson who created stride; Dizzy Gillespie, Charlie Parker, and Bud Powell who made bebop. After World War II, Miles Davis, Ornette Coleman, Cecil Taylor, and John Coltrane developed and brought to fruition free jazz, cool jazz, jazz-rock, and modal jazz. Even when African Americans have not been the first to create a new jazz style, they have invariably become its leading figures.

Black music ideologists are correct in their assessment of jazz as a language that black musicians understand in a different way than whites. For whites, jazz is a means of self-expression and a display of artistry. For African Americans, jazz is certainly that, but in addition it is an assertion of ethnic identity. The philosopher Kwame Anthony Appiah noted in the context of his study of African culture and philosophy that there was a profound difference between the respective goals of European and African writers that could be summarized as "the difference between the search for the self and the search for a culture."[100] The same words could be used to distinguish between white and African-American jazz musicians.

The exponents of "jazz as American classical music" are happily free of the rancor that makes the "jazz as black music" perspective such an off-putting experience. Theirs is an ecumenical vision of the jazz world, a place in which everyone is equal according to his or her ability and one's ethnic background is never a drawback. Yet the "jazz as American classical music" ideology somehow manages to skirt the issue of black dominance in jazz. The blacks who have proclaimed jazz to be a universal language still pay homage to its African-American ethnicity. When Duke Ellington said in his autobiography that jazz was "an international music" he also commended white musicians for growing close to the "black soul."[101] Billy Taylor, a popular exponent of the notion that jazz is American classical music, has some harsh words for white ethnomusicologists and jazz writers that reveal Taylor's mixed feelings about relinquishing the African-American culture's "ownership" of jazz. According to Taylor, books by white authors "are interpreting, from another cultural background, what they have heard from black people. Though they are excellent books, if one reads them all they show emphatically how a subject may be defined in part by what is left out as well as what is included." If jazz is international music, it doesn't need to have a black soul or a white soul. But if jazz is not black music, why do students of the music need to know, as Taylor insists, about "the value system of its creators?"[102]

Such racial paradoxes are what make the music so compelling as a cultural phenomenon. Jazz is somehow able to be both an African-American ethnic music and a universal music at the same time, both an expression of universal artistry and ethnicity. Black musicians lash out at whites, and yet invite them into their bands. Wynton Marsalis refuses to accept white accomplishments in jazz, but proclaims the genius of

Beethoven. Amiri Baraka heaps scorn on the art of the white world, and in the next breath praises Roswell Rudd. There is no accounting for jazz. As Dexter Gordon once put it to jazz critic Gary Giddens, "Jazz is the great octopus; it'll do anything; it'll use anything."[103]

African Music, African Identity

In 1993 construction workers in the Wall Street area of New York City uncovered the remains of an African slave burial ground. The discovery stopped construction on the skyscraper they were building until steps could be taken to preserve at least a section of the historical site. The cemetery, artifacts from which were displayed at an exhibit mounted in a municipal building around the corner from the site, showed that African customs were very much in evidence in the early years of slavery in the American colonies.

For Michael L. Blakey, director of the slave burial project at Howard University, the discovery of the cemetery was significant for African Americans as a group, not just for historians: "A people's identity is largely historical. What we know of ourselves is primarily connected with the past. How we developed here is important to how we believe in ourselves and look to the future."[1]

The advancement of an historical sensibility has been especially crucial to African Americans because much of their history has been forgotten or distorted by racism and ignorance. An understanding of their African heritage has been a vital component.

Nineteenth- and early twentieth-century African-American intellectuals were ashamed of what they considered to be the vulgar habits of their

people. In particular, they shunned the religious practices that were
African-influenced.[2] Their disdain for African culture was in keeping
with the negative picture of that continent portrayed in books. One might
assume that nineteenth-century African Americans who returned to Africa would have disagreed with this view. In fact, the Rev. Alexander
Crummell, one of the leaders of a group of people who made new homes
for themselves in Liberia, painted a sordid picture of the continent:

> Africa is the victim of her heterogeneous idolatries. Africa is
> wasting away beneath the accretions of moral and civil miser-
> ies. Darkness covers the land and gross darkness the people.
> Great social evils universally prevail. Confidence and security
> are destroyed. Licentiousness abounds everywhere. Moloch
> rules and reigns throughout the whole continent, and by the
> ordeal of Sassywood, Fetiches, human sacrifices and devil-
> worship, is devouring men, women, and little children.[3]

In the early twentieth century African Americans began to learn more about
Africa but continued to hold on to their conception of Africa as a unified culture. Leaders of the various back-to-Africa movements played a strong role in
maintaining this image, as is evident in devastating criticism of Marcus
Garvey by Claude McKay, the Harlem Renaissance poet and novelist:

> He talks of Africa as if it were a little island in the Caribbean
> Sea. Ignoring all geographical and political divisions, he gives
> his followers the idea that that vast continent of diverse tribes
> consists of a large homogeneous nation of natives struggling
> for freedom and waiting for the Western Negroes to come and
> help them drive out the European exploiters.[4]

The old negative idea of Africa began to change in the United States in
the 1920s for a variety of reasons. The discovery of African art by
Picasso and other European artists put an aesthetic stamp of approval on
African culture. In the following decades African Americans made first-
hand contact with Africans who had migrated to the United States, and
during World War II the people of the two continents met around the
battlefields of Europe and North Africa. As the anthropological literature
on Africa expanded, African Americans learned that African people had
societies that rivaled the complexity of Western societies.

During the years after slavery, African Americans developed the notion that their culture consisted exclusively of the bitter fruits of their own oppression. Otherwise, it was a tabula rasa. At the same time, African Americans felt a strong identification with Africa as the homeland. But since nearly all the literature of African Americans pointed to America as the sole source of its culture, the African connection was discounted as mere nostalgia. The publication of a single book, *The Myth of the Negro Past* (1941) by the anthropologist Melville Herskovits, marked a real turning point in the way African Americans conceived of Africa and their African heritage.[5] Herskovits laid the groundwork for the concept of an African diaspora—a cultural linkage of people of African descent in North America, the Caribbean, and South America. Partly as a result of his work, African Americans began to consider themselves as an "African" people. They searched with pride for threads connecting them to Africa and to people of African descent scattered throughout the Americas. Much of the writing on the African roots of African-American culture and music is based on the work of Herskovits and his students, notably Alan Merriam and Richard Waterman. Herskovits's work provided Amiri Baraka with the bulk of his information on the African influence.

Since the 1960s an idealized version of Africa has been proposed as a model for African-American culture. Several essays in *The Black Aesthetic*, a collection of essays edited by Addison Gayle Jr. (published 1971), promote Africa as such a model. Critic Ron Welburn advocates the development of a danceable religious music that should depend on "the same strong relationship to our mystical nature and conception of the universe as religious songs of the nineteenth century and our daily life in Africa's past."[6] In this literature the adjective "African" is the ultimate encomium. Welburn commends James Brown for having a music that "resembles Wolof traditional orchestras of xylophones, lyres, and drums."[7] Critic-musician Jimmy Stewart praises the music of Ornette Coleman as a return to African values. More recently, social commentator Greg Tate, in a 1994 *New York Times* article, describes the contemporary rapper as a modern-day version of the *griot*, the traditional historian of West African societies.[8]

Since the early 1970s the holistic view of African culture has been championed in the United States by such Afrocentric scholars as Molefi Kete Asante. An important principle of the Afrocentric philosophy is that African societies, despite their apparent diversity, evolved from a shared Egyptian background. Under this rubric the key to understanding African tradition is to pursue it back to its roots in "classical Africa." Such an approach reconfirms "the unity of African thought, symbols, and ritual concepts."9

The Ashanti philosopher Kwame Anthony Appiah, who has been teaching in the United States for several years, is unimpressed by claims for the centrality of Egypt in African history. He notes that, even if such claims are correct, there is no direct or continuous tradition of Egyptian study in Africa itself, or any feeling of reverence for Egyptian roots. Furthermore, he cannot accept the notion that Africans have a common culture. Appiah is bewildered that, in light of its incredible diversity, anyone could reasonably assume that Africa was culturally homogeneous:

> Compare Evans-Pritchard's famous Zande oracles, with their simple questions and their straightforward answers, with the fabulous richness of Yoruba oracles, whose interpretation requires great skill in the hermeneutics of the complex corpus of verses of Ifa; or our own Asante monarchy, a confederation in which the king is primus inter pares, his elders and paramount chiefs guiding him in council, with the more absolute power of Mutesa the First in nineteenth-century Buganda; or the enclosed horizons of a traditional Hausa wife, forever barred from contact with men other than her husband, with the open spaces of the women traders of southern Nigeria; or the art of Benin—its massive bronzes—with the tiny elegant goldweight figures of the Akan. Face the warrior horsemen of the Fulani jihads with Shaka's Zulu impis [warriors]; taste the bland foods of Botswana after the spices of Fanti cooking; try understanding Kikuyu or Yoruba or Fulfulde with a Twi dictionary. Surely differences in religious ontology and ritual, in the organization of politics and the family, in relations between the sexes and in art, in styles of warfare and cuisine, in language—surely all these are fundamental kinds of difference?10

THE AFRICAN ROOTS OF MUSIC IN AMERICA

What do we know about African musical legacy in the early years of slavery? We have the reports of a few observers who took an interest in the music of the slaves, as well as the remains of a few instruments. A few musicians wrote musical transcriptions, although these have not been especially useful because of the musicians' lack of understanding of African music. Since there were no cassettes, compact discs, videos or record albums uncovered in the slave burial grounds, we can only speculate about the many aspects of the African legacy in African-American music.

African musical instruments or their prototypes survived in the United States and outlived slavery. One of the most important "instruments" of West African drum ensmbles is hand-clapping, which became a feature of African-American church music. One-string instruments that closely resembled West African instruments have been found in the southern United States. Cane fifes, found in savanna and rain forest areas of West Africa, were used in the many fife-and-drum ensembles of the South, still extant in Georgia and Mississippi in the 1960s.[11]

One of the myths of African-American music scholarship is that the drums were taken away from the slaves. It is an interesting fact that drums were brought to the New World on the slave ships. Due to the staggering mortality rate, the slave-ship captains brought drums aboard so that the Africans could exercise. One observer wrote: "In the intervals between their meals, they are encouraged to divert themselves with music and dancing; for which purpose such rude and uncouth instruments as are used in Africa are collected before their departure."[12]

Once in the United States, the drums were banned. Yet despite the strict enforcement of these bans, they somehow survived into the twentieth century. The Federal Writers' Project of the 1930s produced several reports from former slaves in Georgia that indicated that drum-making in the African tradition existed in America without the knowledge of whites.[13]

By far the most common and longest-lived of all African instruments in the United States was the banjo. The instrument has gone through many changes since the days of slavery, but it still bears a close resemblance to the xalam, a Wolof lute. The xalam is often played in an ensemble with a bowed lute and a tapped calabash. This ensemble is remarkably similar to the banjo, fiddle, and tambourine ensemble popular in the United States before the twentieth century. The similarity is especially apparent because the bowed lute in the xalam groups is played country-fiddle style with the instrument pointed at an angle down to the ground rather than being held upright in the classical manner. Both the folk banjo and the xalam are fretless instruments with one or more unfingered strings (sometimes called drone strings). On the xalam, only the two inner strings are fingered, while strings one, four, and five are fixed.[14] The banjo has a short string played by the thumb, which is that instrument's drone string.[15] Both of the instruments "[employ] a technique in which the performer, using the thumb, index finger, and middle finger of the right hand, strikes down on the strings rather than plucking up on them."[16] Although there are similarities between the banjo and the xalam, there are basic dissimilarities as well. The blues scholar Samuel Charters notes that the sound of the xalam is "low and rounded"—not at all reminiscent of the high-pitched, jangling sound of the banjo.[17]

Xalam music is based on fodet, a repeated pattern with a fixed number of beats and several clearly marked phrases within the pattern.[18] Michael Theodore Coolen, who spent two years studying the music of xalam players in the Senegambian region between the Senegal and Gambian rivers, believes that the fodet was the African source of the blues. Like the fodet, the blues is also a repeated pattern with a specific verse form—AAB—and a specific length—twelve measures (less stringently measured in folk blues than in the popular blues form of W. C. Handy). As in the blues, the phrases of the fodet "are marked off through the use of different phrases by different tonal centers."[19] Coolen speculates that the Senegambian slaves took a few aspects of the fodet and used them to create the blues. Since the banjo was probably based on the xalam, it is not too far-fetched to suppose that the fodet form indeed exerted an influence.

Coolen's discussion is refreshing for several reasons. The commonly accepted judgment on the blues is that structure and harmony are the European element of the blues, while tonality, rhythm, and timbre are African. Instead, Coolen found structural and harmonic sources in an African musical idiom. In addition, while most speculations about the African sources of African-American art go no further than to show a generalized cultural unity, Coolen was looking for specific influences.

Coolen based his search for the roots of the blues on the commonly held belief that the slave culture came from West Africa. In this, he was certainly not alone. The idea that African-American culture sprang from West Africa gained wide acceptance through the writings of Melville Herskovits, the leading figure in the field of African diaspora studies. Since the late 1970s, however, researchers have begun to take a second look at the statistics on slave importations. They have found that at several points in the history of the slave trade, about a third of the slaves came not from West Africa but from Central Africa. Scholars such as Philip Curtin, Winifred Vass, Peter Wood, and Joseph Holloway have revealed, as much as the extant historical documents will allow, the African ethnic makeup of the United States in the colonial period. In general, West Africans constituted the house servants, skilled artisans, cattlemen, and cultivators of rice, corn, and millet. They were chosen for these tasks because the slave merchants knew they had practiced these skills back in Africa. Slaves from Central Africa were assigned to the field work.[20]

It was among the Central African group that a relatively homogeneous African-American culture was able to develop. The musical fruits of this culture were field hollers, spirituals, and the blues. According to Vass, a shared Bantu linguistic heritage gave this group of slaves the foundation to establish an African-American culture, while infrequent contact with their European masters protected it from European influences.

West African culture developed in America in a different fashion. Because West African ethnic groups shared little in common linguistically, it was difficult for slaves from this part of Africa to find much common ground. Also, unlike their Central African counterparts, West Africans found themselves in close contact with their European slave masters. As a result, American culture developed as a process of reciprocal acculturation between West Africans and Europeans. Much of what West Africans contributed to the American colonies and later the United States has lost its identity as African. Thus it comes as a surprise that practices one has become accustomed to thinking of as European were contributed by West Africans. For instance, it was the Fulani slaves who introduced open grazing to the raising of cattle in the United States. It has even been suggested that the term "cowboy" was originally used for slaves herding cattle, and that the term is analogous to "houseboy."

Recent scholarship that makes a distinction between West African and Central African contributions to the United States provides the basis for a better appreciation of African-American music. In "The Origins of African-American Culture," Joseph Holloway suggests that the house slaves and skilled slaves who were mostly of West African origin had an entirely different cultural background from the field slaves taken from Central Africa. It seems plausible that their music was also different. The music of the field hands was the field holler, the blues, and spirituals. The music of the house slaves was by and large banjo music sounding similar to the xalam music of the Wolof people studied by Coolen. It is also plausible that the music of the two groups of slaves had entirely different cultural ramifications as well. The music of the field hands was a blacks-only type of enterprise, since it was the product of a distinctly African-American culture practiced far from the eyes and ears of European Americans. The music of West African slaves was regarded in an entirely different light by blacks and whites. Banjo playing, like other African practices of West African origin (such as herding cattle) undertaken by slaves in close contact with European Americans, quickly lost its identification as an African practice, while the blues retained its stature as a product of a distinctly African-American culture.

African music survived in rhythmic devices such as off-beat phrasing in which the stressed beats of a melody fall on the off-beats, producing a psychological effect of two overlapping time schemes. When lyrics are sung with off-beat phrasing, verbal stresses do not correlate with stressed beats. African and African-American singers and instrumentalists share a predilection for distorted tones and a tendency to swoop up or down to a note in a seeming avoidance of exactly defined pitch. Ostinatos predominate in many African-American idioms. This, too, is an African influence.[21]

The Cool Aesthetic

The aesthetic notions that guided the development of jazz and other African-American idioms also have their roots in Africa.[22] These notions have affected the way African-American idioms sounded and the modes of behavior of the musicians who created them. The aesthetics that generated jazz and other black idioms stem from attitudes originating in black culture with reference to awareness and style, glossed by the terms "hip" and "cool," respectively. Before discussing how these concepts have been traced back to Africa, I must first define these oft-used terms.

Richard Majors and Janet Mancini Billson, authors of the first substantial study of "cool" behavior among blacks in the United States, define coolness as "a ritualized form of masculinity that entails behaviors, scripts, physical posturing, impression management, and carefully crafted performances that deliver a single, critical message: pride, strength, and control."[23] This sort of coolness has little to do with the mid-1950s style of jazz called cool jazz, which lacked the "cool" attitude jazz musicians of other styles displayed in their music and lifestyles.

A "hip" person is one who is socially aware and privy to the inside story. Roy Carr, Brian Case, and Fred Dellar, authors of an entertaining study on hipness and hip jazz musicians, writers, movie stars, and comedians, called hip "an understated state of grace that does not necessarily wish the world well" and "an uncrackable code" designed to prevent imitation.[24] Pianist John Lewis noted that Lester Young's dress and his individual way of talking "were a way to be hip—to express an awareness of everything swinging that was going on."[25]

Robert Farris Thompson has fostered the idea that the concept of coolness is a trans-Atlantic African philosophy affecting art, ethics and religion:

> [Cool philosophy] is a matrix from which stem ideas about being generous, clear, percussively patterned, harmonized with others, balanced, finished, socially perfected, worthy of destiny. . . . In Africa coolness is an all-embracing positive attribute which combines notions of composure, silence, vitality, healing, and social purification.[26]

The words indicating coolness in tropical Africa share many of the same meanings as analogous words in European languages: calmness, composure, self-control, and aloofness. But in parts of Africa they have meanings not found in European languages. For example, the Mandingo describe favorable outcomes indicated by divination as "cool." "Cooling" rites are a feature of African religions that deal with violence and social chaos. The Yakö society of the Cross River area where the United Republic of Cameroon and the Republic of Nigeria meet have a ceremony called "cooling the village" using water, a widely used agent of ritual cooling, and herbs.[27]

In "An Aesthetic of the Cool," Thompson attempts to establish the existence of a pan-African philosophy shared by people who in some cases live far apart and share few cultural traditions. He lists the usage of "cool" in thirty-five languages from West Africa through South Africa. For at least a third of the thirty-five languages, Thompson had no ethnographic data and relied on dictionary definitions alone.[28] At times, his claim to find the aesthetic throughout much of the African continent is a little contrived. On closer examination, it turns out that in some languages "cool" is defined as it would be in European languages. Although the presence of the term "cool" may go hand-in-hand with an aesthetic of the cool in the Yoruba and several other ethnic groups, as Thompson compellingly demonstrated, it may not necessarily be related to such an aesthetic in other cultures. Providing evidence that there is a word for the concept of cool does not demonstrate that an aesthetic of the cool exists. But despite its minor flaws Thompson's ambitious project has proven inspirational to scholars studying African arts.

Thompson's observations on coolness in African art and culture resemble those made by jazz writers about Lester Young, the quintessentially cool jazz musician. I will discuss a few of these observations, leaving it to the reader to make the decision as to whether the similarities demonstrate a plausible case for the continuity of an African aesthetic of the cool in the jazz world.

For Thompson, African art is both a product of the aesthetic of the cool and a force to help promote it. He found representations of the cool pose in sculptured figures with a serene, serious demeanor and a closed mouth. The Yoruba call this a "cool mouth" (*enun tutu*) and the discretion and deliberation the pose suggests are attributes of cool behavior.[29] The cool pose is found in the postures of dancers and musicians. Among the Gola of Liberia "somnambulistic movement and attitude during the dance or other performance [are] considered very attractive."[30] Such stony silence shown in African sculpture and in the pose of musicians and dancers represents a cool attitude. Stanley Dance made a similar observation about Lester Young: "[He] wore an incurious, enigmatic expression on a strangely boyish face."[31] Bobby Scott, a pianist who played with Young in the mid-1950s, noted that Young spoke only when he had something to say: "He spoke less than almost anyone I have ever known. I came to read his silences, hoping to see what it was that he wasn't saying."[32]

Thompson observed that in African cultures coolness unites calm with vitality. In this respect, the difference from European conceptions of coolness becomes clear. In Young's music there is the same strange union of calm and vitality: great rhythmic elasticity and strength expressed paradoxically by a a smooth timbre and melody lines that float in defiance of the rhythm section's steady beat. In his dress and demeanor, there was the same quality of calm mixed with stirring brilliance. He presented a carefully maintained image of an unruffled hipster. Pianist Jimmy Rowles noted that when Young got upset he would take out a whisk broom and brush his shoulder.[33] The use of a brush to metaphorically sweep out bad feelings is familiar to the Yoruba; it is an emblem of the *orisha* Obaluaiye, the smallpox deity.[34]

I have suggested a few parallels between the cool aesthetic of African culture and the music of jazz musicians such as Lester Young. But the music of West Africa has a greater kinship with idioms other than jazz in which repetition plays a major role. In some respects, jazz with its emphasis on unpredictibility represents a departure from most African-influenced idioms. For unlike jazz, they are based on repeated musical lines of short duration. Jazz is far less repetitious. In the mainstream jazz style, pianists avoid playing the same rhythmic pattern twice; drummers steer away from rote repetition of the "ride" rhythm pattern played on the cymbals; and bass players add unexpected off-beat accents as a divergence from the quarter-note walking pattern. Even when jazz musicians play Latin music or other dance-based idioms, their performances typically are less bounded by repetition.

John Miller Chernoff, an ethnomusicologist and performer of West African musical styles who is greatly influenced by Thompson's writings, found parallels between Dagomba music and the music of James Brown. Dagomba music stays in one groove and then blends into a related variant. The timing of transitions and the intensity of the music are guided by an aesthetic of the cool, according to Chernoff's teacher, the Dagomba drummer Ibrahim Abdulai:

> What you should have in mind if you are going to make a style or change to another topic on the drum is that you should lower your drumming down before you take your style. If you don't make up your mind or cool your drum before you make your style, you will spoil the whole thing. The one you are playing, you will spoil it, and the next style too that you are getting to, you will spoil that one also. If you are playing by heart or very fast, you will spoil everything. You have to make it *baalim*; you have to be slow before you get to the next style.[35]

Brown's music typically consists of an ABA structure, with A being a long vamp and B being the bridge passage. The way Brown times the transitions from the vamp to the bridge and back again is similar to the timing Ibrahim was describing.

Metronome Sense

Richard Waterman, one of the originators of African diaspora music studies, hypothesized that because people are not aware of their physical responses to hearing and performing music, musical cultural patterns are especially resistant to change.[36] In "African Influence on the Music of the Americas," a 1952 article that has become a cornerstone of African-American music studies, Waterman proposed that people of African descent shared a highly developed "metronome sense." The term, which Waterman coined, refers to the way people sense rhythm through the perception of regularly spaced beats. What varies among the people of the world is the degree to which listeners are able to make sense of the beats without hearing them stressed in the music.

Let's take march music as an example of music in which little metronome sense is required. Not only are the drummers stressing every beat, but the melodic line generally supports the beat structure. The music of the singer Michael Jackson could be a sort of midpoint in the metronome sense. In his music, a drummer clearly stresses every beat, while Jackson sings a vocal line in which the beat structure is suspended for several beats at a time. Rumba percussion music requires more of a metronome sense; the beat is rarely sounded, and the placement of the stresses may suggest an entirely different metrical orientation. Even a trained musician—that is, one who has received years of training in classical music or jazz—would lose track of the downbeat on hearing rumba for the first time. On the other hand, a *rumbero* (rumba player) would have no problem picking up the beat. When the beat is actually sounded in music requiring a well-developed metronome sense, it "serves as confirmation of this subjective beat."[37] In addition, musicians may not be following the beat alone. They may be relating their individual rhythmic lines to a timeline or coordinating their entrance with another line. Nevertheless, what the African music scholar David Locke calls the "constant primary meter ('African 4/4')"[38] is always there.

Ethnomusicologists such as Chernoff who have spent years learning and performing African music have found the concept of metronome sense to be useful. Nevertheless, one must stand back and reflect on the fact that Waterman formulated his idea of a cognitive framework for African and African-American music without having elicited the idea from musicians. In several African and African-derived idioms meter is not the driving rhythmic force. Although salsa musicians may at times allude to the basic 4/4 beat especially in relation to notated parts, the rhythm that rules supreme over their music is the clave, an asymmetrical phrase. In fact, the leader of a salsa ensemble typically counts off the clave rather than the meter:

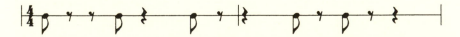

The much-studied music of the Ewe provides another example of music in which an asymmetrical phrase, rather than the pulse of a steady beat, is the primary source of timing.[39] From this perspective, the framework of regularly spaced beats, which for Waterman constituted metronome sense, is not very important in the hierarchy of rhythms.

Composer Olly Wilson was ready to dispense with metronome sense entirely:

Such claims are conceivable, but given the embryonic state of psycho-cultural analysis they remain dubious and, under any circumstance, outside the range of competence of most musicologists, especially musicologists who are not native to the group whose collective psychology they attempt to explain.[40]

The one tradition to which the idea of metronome sense clearly applies is jazz, for it is a tradition in which musicians are always talking about the beat. Waterman exhibited a profound understanding of how jazz musicians describe their music—what ethnomusicologists call a "native" music theory—when he alluded to "the development of a 'feeling for the beat,' so important in jazz musicianship."[41]

The problem with Waterman's beat-oriented perspective on African music is that it brings in the related concepts of being on the beat and falling off the beat as well as the notion of the beat as reference point. Concerning the latter, David Locke believes that "African musicians think of [their musical lines] in terms of two- or four-beat phrases, not beat-by-beat figures."[42] As I have indicated, the beat-oriented perspective makes much greater sense in jazz than in African music, although there is, of course, the possibility that the pulse as an organizing principle may exist somewhere in Africa. Waterman's thesis that Africans and African-Americans share a unique sense of hearing rhythm is unsupported by recent ethnomusicological studies by performer-scholars. Their data, unavailable at the time Waterman wrote his article, indicate that there are several different ways of sensing rhythm among African and African-diaspora people.

Revitalization

Richard Waterman was impressed by the fact that in North America the African concept of music apparently disappeared until it resurfaced with jazz. In many areas it somehow was maintained "without musical embodiment—kept alive, it is true, by other rhythmic interests." The fact that it was revitalized after decades of being dormant or in hiding indicates "the almost incredible toughness of basic musical culture-patterns."[43]

Ethnomusicologist Charles Keil in his study of urban blues singers uses the notion of revitalization in describing the African-American popular music of the 1960s:

It is simply incontestable that year by year, American popular music has come to sound more and more like African popular music. The rhythmic complexity and subtlety, the emphasis on percussive sound qualities, the call-and-response pattern, the characteristic vocal elements (shout, growl, falsetto, and so on), blues chromaticism, blues and gospel chord progressions, Negro vocabulary, Afro-American dance steps—all have become increasingly prominent in American music.[44]

The theme of revitalization is often coupled with the belief that black musical styles develop in order to avoid acceptance by the white majority culture and that the reactive force of this frame of mind brings to the surface non-Western musical traits. In the following passage, Baraka notes the development of these traits in rhythm-and-blues—and, in the process, nearly equates unmusicality with non-Western music:

The point [of rhythm-and-blues], it seemed, was to spend oneself with as much attention as possible, and also to make the instruments sound as unmusical, or as *non-Western*, as possible. It was almost as if the blues people were reacting against the softness and "legitimacy" that had crept into black instrumental music with the advent of swing.[45]

Like religious faith, the revitalization theory is difficult to argue with. How can one prove that a musical concept is there all along, when the existing music may perhaps belie its existence? Without taking away from the possibility that an African aesthetic runs like an underwater stream throughout American history, it appears that scholars who support this belief sometimes ignore more tangible reasons for the changes that have occurred in African-American music. Keil's attempt to explain the jazz of the 1960s comes to mind.

Keil is struck by what he calls "the apparent Africanization of contemporary jazz"—in particular, the use of "the crossed triplet rhythms of West Africa." For Keil, the interest in these rhythms is due to a natural evolution founded on the perpetual search for "a maximum amount of swing."[46] It is noteworthy that Keil seeks an explanation of these significant rhythmic changes in jazz without considering that musicians in the 1960s were fascinated with African music for both musical and social reasons, and that aspects of African and Afro-Cuban music had steadily been introduced into the idiom since the 1940s. It seems more likely that the exposure to African and Afro-Cuban music was a more important factor in the "Africanization of contemporary jazz" than what Keil suggests was an inevitable evolution.

People of African descent have been interested in their African roots for centuries, and it is likely that the African legacy is a reflection of individual choices, not just abstract processes. Some of the aforementioned scholars seem to make a division between the recent past, in which instances of African Americans who have chosen to get closer to their African roots abound, and a distant past, when African values were absorbed by African Americans without their awareness. All I am suggesting is that conscious decision-making played an important part and that the recent past may not be so different from the distant past.

Interpretations of the African Influence in Jazz Studies

To explain the history of jazz, most jazz writers formulate a generalized description of African music culled from the writings of ethnomusicologists. In *Early Jazz,* Gunther Schuller based his understanding of African music on A. M. Jones's study of the music of the Ewe people of Ghana and, like Jones himself, applied the data to all of African music.[47] Such a process of generalizing from attributes specific to one small area to all of Africa has been noted since the nineteenth century, when one observer noted that "writers are fond of selecting the prominent traits of single tribes with which they are best acquainted, and applying them to the whole race."[48] There are many ethnomusicologists who dismiss out of hand the characterization of African music as an "indivisible whole," to use Jones's phrase. Klaus Wachsmann noted that it is very difficult to identify "distinctly African features common to the whole continent" because the data accumulated on African cultures have been variable in quality and orientation.[49] And Gerhard Kubik asserted that "there is no African music, rather many types of African music."[50] Such a perspective influenced a review of Gunther Schuller's book, *Early Jazz,* by Frank Gillis and Pekka Gronow, in which they criticized Schuller's chapter on the African origins of jazz: "Schuller continually refers to 'Africa' as if it exists as a single, unified culture area. Africa is of course composed of many diverse and distinctly different cultural groups representing a wide range of music styles."[51]

Several authorities on jazz do not properly differentiate jazz from other American idioms. By contorting the anthropological and musicological constructs used to show the similarities between African music and American music, they help promote a confused notion of the African legacy in jazz. For instance, consider the usage of "call and response," a term that refers to a musical texture found in much of African music in which an unchanging theme of short duration sung by a chorus alternates with an improvised response by a soloist. Amiri Baraka believed that call and response was displayed in the way jazz pieces are structured with a melodic statement followed by "an arbitrary number of improvised answers or comments on the initial theme."[52] It makes little sense to use the term "call and response" to describe the typical jazz performance in which a composed melody is followed by several "choruses" of improvisations on the chord structure of the melody. Joachim Berendt goes far beyond the bounds of common sense when he said about the jazz solo that "call and response no longer follow each other, but are sounded simultaneously."[53]

As in other areas of interest to jazz musicians and writers, unsubstantiated opinions about African music are cited over and over until they are unquestioned. One source of several of the more flagrant abuses is the writings of Ernest Borneman, a student of the early ethnomusicologist Erich von Hornbostel. Borneman wrote with an authoritative tone about African languages and African music without supplying bibliographic support—a problem in much of the literature on jazz. Marshall Stearns, Amiri Baraka, and Gunther Schuller were all taken in by his assertions and cite him in their own respective tomes. Borneman's *A Critic Looks at Jazz* (1946) is replete with fanciful notions, the most irritating being a theory that Africans singing music in the major scale are uncomfortable with the third and seventh steps and will add "violent vibrato effects until they reach scalar value and become effective as sharps and flats." Borneman proposed that this tendency was responsible for the development of the blues scale.[54]

A Night in Tunisia: Imaginings of Africa in Jazz, by poet Norman C. Weinstein, is the first book-length study of the African legacy in jazz. Rather than dealing with the actual influences of African music on jazz, Weinstein chose to act as a "chronicler detailing the way jazz composers creatively have struggled over time with the African theme."[55] The book is a study of twelve figures: Duke Ellington, discussed through the voice of Madame Zzaj, Ellington's imagined personification of jazz; John Coltrane; George Russell; John Carter; Count Ossie, an early Rastafarian musician who led a jazz-influenced group until his death in 1976; Randy Weston; Max Roach; Pierre Dørge, a Danish avante-garde jazz guitarist who studied with kora player Foday Musa Suso; Archie Shepp; Yusef Lateef; Sunny Murray; and Ronald Shannon Jackson. In addition, there is a chapter on Dizzy Gillespie's *Night in Tunisia,* a piece that has become the vehicle par excellence for jazz musicians to metaphorically explore their African roots. Weinstein evaluates the different interpretations it has been given by the composer and by Art Blakey, Eddie Jefferson, Sarah Vaughan, and Herbie Mann. Weinstein is not interested in making a literal analysis of the song. Whether it is Tunisian, African, or Afro-Cuban is beyond the point. What is essential to Weinstein is the way that the song has become a vehicle for jazz musicians' imaginations.

Giving proper treatment to the artist's work is of paramount importance to Weinstein. Although he explores the question of African identity among jazz musicians, he is primarily concerned with describing the works of the musicians. Because he did not pursue a sociological study of the African influence on jazz musicians as a group, he does not delve into broader issues. However, such an approach would inevitably place the art on a more mundane level with political and social currents and would not have been in the spirit of Weinstein's endeavor.

Weinstein's study is based on a perception of African-American art as "counter-racist."

> African-American artists produce art in the context of combating centuries of racist-constructed imaginations of Africa. Faced with centuries of distorted visual and written accounts depicting Africans as uncivilized ape-men inhabiting a savagely dark continent, faced with the horrors of the slave trade and European colonialism and neo-colonialism, Africans and many African-Americans have developed a counter-racist imagination of Africa.[56]

In the spirit of promoting counter-racism, Weinstein tends to avoid analyzing the veracity of claims of African influence objectively. Nevertheless, he is not afraid to take issue with artists whose statements don't ring true. For instance, he notes that there was "something preposterous, on a literal level" with poet Don L. Lee chanting, "We have come back," to a crowd in Algeria. Weinstein is also critical of Archie Shepp's attempt to blend avant-garde jazz with North African music.[57] Despite his fascination with a metaphorical Africa, Weinstein is quite aware that "there is something potentially pretentious and pompous in attempting to synthesize two cultures as distinct as African-American and African."[58]

A Night in Tunisia illustrates the problems of using ethnomusicological
literature out of context to prove similarities between jazz and African
music. For instance, Weinstein finds close parallels between Art Blakey's
drum style and the Dagomba drummers of Ghana, based on a description of the African drummers' use of silence in John Miller Chernoff's
book, *African Rhythm and African Sensibility*.[59] Weinstein comes close to
suggesting that somehow the Dagomba drummers are the prototype for
Blakey's drum style. But Blakey's use of silence was different from that of
the Dagomba drummers in several respects. The context of the silences is
entirely different. While Blakey customarily played unaccompanied solos, the Dagomba drummers play in a drum ensemble. Blakey's use of silence is purely dramatic, but it is functional for the lead drummer in a
Dagomba drum ensemble. The Dagomba drummer uses silence because
by overplaying he will destroy the integrity of a rhythmically elaborate
pattern.[60]

Weinstein notes the close relation between dance and music in both
West African music and Swing-Era jazz and cites ethnomusicologist J. H.
Kwabena Nketia to support his contention that the interplay in jazz between musicians and dancers originated in Africa. Yet he fails to give
proper weight to part of Nketia's statement, that the interplay is based on
"conventions and modes of interpretation demanded by the particular
type of dance drama or its social context."[61] While it is probable that jazz
dance stems from African prototypes, it is simply not true, as Weinstein
implies, that African and American dance styles adhere to the same "conventions and modes of interpretation."

Weinstein makes a parallel between the coordinated independence of
African drummers with a similar independence as described by Willie
"The Lion" Smith. According to Smith, Harlem stride pianists could perform a different song with each hand at the same time. Nketia spoke of
African drummers who were capable of playing two different patterns simultaneously. Weinstein made the somewhat far-fetched claim that
"Smith has described one of the most central principles in African drumming: the creation of multiple rhythm lines emphasizing the independence of the motions of the right and left hand."[62] However, performing
two percussion patterns that interlock in a cross-rhythmic texture is not
the same thing as the trick of playing, say, Johnson's *Carolina Shout* with
one hand and Joplin's *The Entertainer* with the other.

Weinstein has difficulty dealing with jazz musicians who see jazz and
African music as two distinct and unrelated entities. For this reason Art
Blakey was especially puzzling to him. On the one hand, Blakey was a

major figure in the movement to introduce African elements into jazz. On the other hand, Blakey made a point of distinguishing between African drummers and jazz drummers, saying: "They have nothing to do with what we are doing. . . . You can't mix what comes out of the African culture with what came out of our culture. I play a western-made drum."[63] Weinstein is unwilling to accept Blakey's disclaimers that he and his music, for better or worse, came from an American culture, not an African one. The author believes that in Blakey's music a totally different message, a reaffirmation of African identity, was being given a voice. Weinstein implies that Blakey was denying his African heritage.

AFRICAN MUSICIANS AND JAZZ MUSICIANS

The original link between African music and African-American idioms such as jazz was forged by slaves who remembered the ways they made music in their homelands and adapted them for use in a foreign land. More recently, other links have been forged, as Africans who moved to the United States encountered musicians eager to learn about their music and culture. The list that follows contains biographical information on the first generation of African musicians in the United States.

African Musicians in the United States

Asadata Dafora (1890–1965)

Probably the first African to teach Americans about African culture was the dancer, choreographer, and percussionist Asadata Dafora. Born Austin Dafora Horton, he came from one of the most prominent families in Freeport, Sierra Leone. His great-grandfather was knighted by the queen of England, his father studied at Oxford University and his mother was a pianist who studied in Paris and Vienna. The family belonged to the Temeni ethnic group. As a boy Dafora ran away from home several times to see the seasonal dance celebrations held throughout Africa. To develop his musical talents, he was sent to Italy to study voice. He made his debut in Africa and then sang in the operas *l'Africaine* and *Aïda* to great acclaim throughout Europe. He began his career in 1910 as a dancer specializing in African traditional dances. He presented the first full-length concert of African music and dance in the United States in 1934 at the Little Theatre in New York City.

Starting in the early 1940s, Dafora performed on the same stages with jazz musicians and popular entertainers. Among his papers at the Schomburg Center for Research in Black Culture in Harlem is a flyer advertising a program at the Howard Theatre in 1946 that featured Ella Fitzgerald.[64] Many of these concerts were designed around an African-diaspora theme of continuity with African roots. At times, the concert notices were written in language that today some would find elitist. For example, a 1959 concert that included the Asadata Dafora dancers and Les Jazz Modes Quintet with Charlie Rouse and Julius Watkins was advertised as "a musical program from the primitive to the contemporary." The jazz part of the program included a narration by Bill DuPree with music apparently influenced by the music of Africa, Brazil, Trinidad, and Cuba as well as the standard fare of mainstream jazz—blues, original compositions, and arrangements of show tunes.[65] At the end of the concert, Dafora's ensemble performed with Les Jazz Modes in a show of cultural unity.

Olatunji (1927–)

The Yoruba percussionist and choreographer Michael Babatunde Olatunji originally came to the United States on a scholarship to Morehouse College in Atlanta. Although he had been playing drums since he was a child, he arrived at college expecting to put his drumming aside. Olatunji was startled the first time he heard African-American music because it reminded him of African music. As a result he joined the campus jazz ensemble and made his way back to music.[66]

In the late 1950s he began recording a series of albums for Columbia Records, the most famous being *Drums of Passion*. His song, *Uhuru*, Swahili for "freedom," with lyrics by the Nigerian poet Adebayo Faleti, gained popularity among people closely involved with the African independence movement.[67]

Olatunji has been credited with the dissemination of African music among jazz musicians. His ensembles at times included such musicians as Clark Terry, Yusef Lateef, and George Duvivier. He was especially close to John Coltrane (see below). Shortly before Coltrane's death Olatunji opened a school for African arts in Harlem, the Center for African Culture. He was especially interested in teaching jazz musicians African languages. He believed that, since African music and speech share tonal and rhythmic elements, knowledge of African languages would enhance a musician's understanding of African music.[68]

Guy Warren (1923–)

Another prominent figure in African music who came to the United States was the Ghanaian drummer and composer Guy Warren. Warren

played with Dizzy Gillespie and Lester Young in the 1950s before returning to Africa.[69] His composition *The Mystery of Love,* written for a 1957
show at the African Room in New York City, was recorded by Art Blakey
and Randy Weston, among others.

Warren, Dafora, Olatunji, and many of the African musicians who
came to the United States were not trained in native arts in the indigenous manner of master musicians. It was not until a decade or so later
that musicians recognized as master musicians in Africa came to this
country at the invitation of ethnomusicology programs at UCLA and
Wesleyan University.

Abdullah Ibrahim (1934–)

The pianist and composer (and sometimes saxophonist, flutist, and vocalist) Abdullah Ibrahim came to the United States when American jazz
musicians were adding African elements to their music. As a soloist and
leader of his own groups, he showed a South African way of integrating
jazz and African music.

Jazz was nothing new to South African musicians. Their countrymen
had been hearing jazz since the 1930s.[70] Big-band jazz and singers such
as Ella Fitzgerald were very popular in the cities of South Africa. Abdullah Ibrahim, a Muslim whose birth name was Adolph Johannes Brand, re-
called playing in a dance band in the early 1950s that contained five
reeds, eight brass, and a rhythm section that performed Basie arrangements. He learned about new jazz recordings from sailors and "gang-
sters," who were among the few blacks who could afford record
players.[71] One gangster in particular, named Shaki, used to play Ellington from morning to night every Sunday.

In 1959, Ibrahim formed the Jazz Epistles, the first South African jazz
band to record an album devoted to original material. The group included rising stars of South African jazz such as Hugh Masakela. At the
time, Ibrahim used the name Dollar Brand. Dollar was a nickname given
him by jazz-loving sailors. Shortly afterward, Ibrahim and his wife, the
singer Sathima Bea Benjamin, left South Africa for Switzerland. There
they met Duke Ellington, who was then serving as an artist-and-
repertoire (A&R) representative for Reprise Records. Through Ellington,
Ibrahim recorded the album *Ellington Presents the Dollar Brand Trio.* In
1965, he and his wife moved to New York, where Ibrahim quickly landed
some important engagements, including the Newport Jazz Festival. In recent years he has led a group called Ekaya (Home), featuring alto saxophonist Carlos Ward. His music combines the influences of Thelonious
Monk and Duke Ellington with South African popular music.[72]

Hugh Masekela (1939–)

Ibrahim's most prominent associate has been trumpeter Hugh Masekela. In 1955, Masekela formed the bebop-inspired group The Merry Makers of Spring. Shortly thereafter, he became a star player, first with the African Jazz Revue, the first black show which the South African authorities allowed to perform before a mixed audience, and then with the aforementioned Jazz Epistles. His first album recorded in the United States was *The Americanization of Ooga Booga,* recorded in 1965. Subsequently, Masekela made a hit recording with the Philemon Hou composition *Grazing in the Grass.* Masekela's repertoire has been a mix of his own compositions and other South Africans with soul standards by songwriters like Smokey Robinson and Gamble and Huff. His career has been divided between California and Africa, where he performed with the influential Nigerian songwriter and saxophonist Fela Kuti in the 1970s. In recent years, he has returned to South Africa to record and collaborate with a younger generation of South African musicians.[73]

Jazz Musicians and African Music: The Pioneers

Before African musicians came to this country and introduced Americans to the sounds of Africa, members of the jazz community had a strong political identification with Africa. The Pan-African movement made its way into the Ellington band when trombonist "Tricky Sam" Joe Nanton joined the band in the 1920s. Nanton was deeply involved in the Marcus Garvey movement, and several other West Indian musicians who played in Ellington's band and other black bands were also Garveyites.[74] The identification with Africa was not a precondition for a love of African music, but the two often went hand in hand. The movement to Africanize jazz took place shortly after the hard bop musicians led by Art Blakey and Horace Silver put rhythm-and-blues and gospel elements into jazz. Both of these trends were associated in the jazz community with African-American pride. Few white musicians were involved with either soul music or African-influenced jazz. At the time, it would have seemed odd to hear a white organist playing in the Jimmy Smith mode, as Joey DeFrancesco has been doing in the 1990s without turning any heads. Until ethnomusicology programs began to include performance classes in African music, not many whites were involved in African music. In the 1970s several musicians, notably David Locke and John Miller Chernoff, became expert musicians in African traditional music.

A number of jazz musicians were writing compositions in the 1950s and 1960s that, while not in an African musical style, had titles with an African theme. Some examples are Sonny Rollins's *Airegin* (Nigeria spelled backwards), Jackie McLean's *Appointment in Ghana,* Curtis Fuller's *The Egyptian,* Art Farmer's *Uam Uam* (Mau Mau spelled backwards), and Mongo Santamaria's *Afro-Blue.* Compositions that speak of Africa were nothing new in jazz. There are many early jazz and popular-music tunes with references to Africa such as *Sudan, Zulu's Ball, Ethiopian Suite, Senegalese Stomp,* and *Morocco Blues.*

The list that follows contains biographies of the African-American musicians who pioneered in bringing African music and culture to the jazz community, beginning with Duke Ellington and ending with Malachi Favors.

Duke Ellington (1899–1974)

Ellington's relations with Africa began when Garveyite "Tricky Sam" Nanton joined his band and continued throughout his career. In 1947 he wrote *Liberian Suite* at the request of the Liberian government. In 1966 the Senegalese government requested Ellington to perform at the World Festival of Negro Arts. Here he performed his composition, *La Plus Belle Africaine.* About the occasion, Ellington wrote: "After writing African music for thirty-five years, here I am at last in Africa!"[75]

Dizzy Gillespie (1917–1993)

Dizzy Gillespie, the jazz trumpeter and a founder of bebop, found his way into Afro-Cuban and African music because of the conga player Chano Pozo. On the advice of Latin-jazz pioneer Mario Bauza, Dizzy Gillespie hired Pozo for his big band in 1947. Pozo helped create several compositions that became Afro-Cuban jazz standards: *Tin Tin Deo, Manteca,* and *Guarachi Guaro.* The George Russell-Dizzy Gillespie extended composition, *Cubano Be, Cubano Bop,* featured Pozo leading the band with Afro-Cuban cult drumming and chants.[76]

Gillespie copied a 6/8 rhythm from Chano Pozo and adapted it for the jazz drumset. First, he taught it to Charlie Persip, and then other drummers learned it.[77] The 6/8 rhythm Gillespie copied from Pozo was probably the bembe[78]:

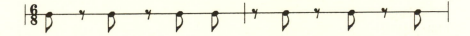

This Afro-Cuban rhythm is identical to what some ethnomusicologists call the standard or "bell" pattern of West African music, a seven-stroke figure played on a metallic instrument such as a hoe blade or an iron bell. The figure has been adapted by many drummers to be played on the bulbous center part of the cymbal, which yields a cowbell-like sound. While Afro-Cuban and African percussionists play the figure over and over without variation, jazz drummers, who tend to avoid rote repetition, play it with variations.

Gillespie played several benefit concerts at the Diplomat Hotel for the African Academy of Arts and Research, a Harlem organization founded in 1943 to disseminate information about Africa and to act as a home away from home for the growing legions of African students studying in the United States. In addition to Gillespie, the performers consisted of Charlie Parker, Max Roach, African drummers, and Cuban drummers. In one concert the musicians accompanied dancer Asadata Dafora. Gillespie regretted that the concerts were not recorded. He found that through participating with African musicians, he and Charlie Parker "found the connections between Afro-Cuban and African music and discovered the identity of our music with theirs."[79]

Gillespie had a strong conviction that whites did not want African Americans to find out about their African heritage:

> They wanted you to just think you're somebody dangling out there, not like the white Americans who can tell you they're German or French or Italian. They didn't want us to know we have a line so that when you'd ask us, all we could say was we were "colored."[80]

According to Gillespie, the white response to the African heritage has always been conditioned by fear, self-protection, and the desire to keep African Americans disunited. Gillespie cited as proof the commonly held but mistaken belief that slave owners had a policy of keeping slaves apart who spoke the same language. In fact, Jessie Gaston Mulira, in "The Case of Voodoo in New Orleans," insists that slave traders made no deliberate attempt to separate slaves who had the same ethnic background and language.[81] Gillespie also described the bans on the use of large drums as attempts by whites to keep African Americans from being united. Since these large drums had the capability of being used for communication, Gillespie is probably correct, but in ascribing the development of African-American music along what he called "monorhythmic lines"[82] to these bans he went a little too far. It is just as possible to maintain a polyrhythmic texture using small drums and hand-clapping, a razor strop, or any other item as it is with large drums.

Gillespie's statements about African music reveal a widespread bias concerning African music and African identity. African music is inevitably equated with multi-drum ensembles—an ensemble type maintained almost everywhere in the African diaspora *except* in the United States. The multi-drum ensemble thus took on the stature of the African heritage denied.

Except for the tone poem *Kush,* Gillespie rarely delved into African music per se. His musical inspiration was Afro-Cuban rather than African. It was Art Blakey who became the principal figure in the incorporation of African musical influences into jazz. Composer and tenor saxophonist Wayne Shorter, who played with Blakey for several years, described how Gillespie's Afro-Cuban jazz led to Blakey's involvement in African music: "Dizzy Gillespie's thing was Afro-Cuban. Then Art Blakey took off the Cuban and said 'Afro' and the whole jazz world understood."[83]

Art Blakey (1919–1993)

Art Blakey is believed to have lived in Africa for several years in the late 1940s. Although some critics claimed he was there to study African drums, he stated that he went there to study religion and philosophy. In any case, Blakey developed an interest in African music through recordings and live performances. His adaptations of multi-drum music for the drumset have become a standard part of jazz drumming. The way he tuned his drums created the effect of a drum ensemble. Blakey pioneered the technique of bending drum pitch. One of his famous solo devices was to play triplets on the floor tom-tom while raising the drum pitch in degrees by applying pressure with his elbows on the drum head. Drummer Roy Brooks used a tube and air pressure to create a similar effect. The sounds these drummers produced are reminiscent of those produced by African pressure drums.

Although Blakey was certainly aware of the African roots of jazz, he was adamant that jazz was an American phenomenon: "Our music has nothing to do with Africa. African music is entirely different, and the Africans are much more advanced than we are rhythmically, though we're more advanced harmonically."[84]

He also said that "to put Africa and jazz together, well, that's the biggest lie ever told."[85] It filled Blakey with indignation that jazz was attributed to Africans because it failed to give credit to African Americans as the originators of the music: "This is our contribution to the world, though they want to ignore it and are always trying to connect it to someone else. It couldn't come from anyone but us. It couldn't come from the Africans."[86]

Although it is a little unclear in the context, Blakey is probably referring to whites when he refers to "they who would rather give credit to Africans than to African-Americans." The irony is that it is African Americans who have been especially vocal in declaring jazz and other attributes of their culture as African idioms.

Blakey's album, *The African Beat*, was a successful blend of jazz and African music in which African elements dominated. Blakey demonstrated that he had internalized his knowledge of African music and was able to play in a manner that, while it meshed with the context, still sounded unmistakably like Art Blakey. In addition to two American drummers who had studied Afro-Cuban and Nigerian music as well as the Jamaican drummer Montego Joe, who performed with Olatunji, Blakey included three African percussion specialists: Solomon Ilori, James Ola Folami, and Chief Bey. Rounding out the ensemble were Yusef Lateef playing oboe, saxophone, flute, cow horn, and finger piano; Curtis Fuller playing tympani (only on one track); and bassist Ahmed Abdul-Malik. These musicians were among the most prominent in the jazz community with a background in African music.

The African Beat demonstrated to jazz musicians the possibilities of integrating hand percussionists into the rhythm section. Several decades after this record came out, the jazz community has become accustomed to rhythm sections with several percussionists. But at one time the multi-percussion concept was problematic for drummers. Adding extra percussion meant that they had to play less than they would in a standard jazz setting. An additional problem is that most of the drummers in multi-drum ensembles play traditional ostinato figures that fit together into a complete web. Unless the jazz drummer blends into this web, he or she is like a fifth wheel.

In more recent years, jazz drummers have been able to listen to new African popular musical styles such as soukous and the newest Cuban style, songo, for inspiration. In these styles, the drumset is seamlessly integrated into a multi-drum ensemble.

Ahmed Abdul-Malik (1927–1993)

Jazz musicians have been drawn to the Middle East since the 1940s. Duke Ellington's *Caravan* and Dizzy Gillespie's *Night in Tunisia* were early reflections of this interest, although these pieces do not really have much to do with Middle Eastern music. If one had to pick a key figure in the fusion of jazz with Middle Eastern music among the musicians who have worked in this area—Randy Weston, Yusef Lateef, and Ornette Coleman are just a few—it would probably be the Brooklyn-born bassist Ahmed Abdul-Malik. Unlike most jazz artists with Arabic names, he grew up in an Arabic environment. Abdul-Malik was of Sudanese descent and spoke Arabic. He had a diverse career that today would be described as multicultural. In addition to the bass, he played oud. Besides playing and recording with jazz musicians such as Thelonious Monk, Art Blakey, Randy Weston, and Coleman Hawkins, he played in symphony orchestras and with the calypso singer Lord Macbeth. His early professional career included playing for Greek, Syrian, and Gypsy weddings.

The Music of Ahmed Abdul-Malik, a 1961 recording, reveals the diversity of his music. He derived his composition *Hannibal's Carnivals* from three sources: highlife, calypso, and the chord changes for the bridge of Monk's composition, *Well, You Needn't. La Ibkey*, named for an Arabic phrase meaning "don't cry," is in 7/4. In addition to recording compositions influenced by music outside the jazz tradition, Abdul-Malik and his ensemble recorded *Don't Blame Me*, a pop standard recorded many times by jazz musicians, but this time featuring jazz cellist Calo Scott. Based on this recording, it seems that at the core of Abdul-Malik's musical interests was a fascination with exploring a variety of musical cultures—Middle Eastern, jazz, African music, calypso, and so on.

Randy Weston (1926–)

Randy Weston has had a lifelong interest in African music. Marshall Stearns and Asadata Dafora familiarized him with African music in the early 1950s.[87] He has traveled and performed in Africa many times. In addition, he ran a nightclub in Morocco for several years. Weston believed that in the traditional music of the African continent we can hear the elements of all modern African and African-American musical idioms.

> I've listened to African music and I've heard everything from old-time blues to avant-garde. . . . I've heard singers who sang things that were rhythmically just like Charlie Parker playing his horn. I've heard cats who sound like Coltrane. The music of the tribes is just unbelievable.[88]

He was convinced that there is a single factor permeating all African music and its descendants but, apart from calling it "a beat," he could not verbalize it. But he was sure that "there is a certain something which identifies you with an African drummer." Weston told Art Taylor, an African American, that Taylor would have no problem playing with an African drummer.[89] Such a statement calls to mind a *New York Times* newspaper article, "Africa and Afro-America," written by Tom Mboya, a political figure in Kenya, shortly before his assassination in 1969. Mboya criticized African Americans who wanted to be granted automatic citizenship in Kenya's new nation without regard to the cultural differences they would encounter if they emigrated: "What is unrealistic . . . is the ease with which some black Americans think they can throw off their American culture and become African."[90]

Weston has long been interested in showing through music that people of African descent are related to one another. In 1960 he recorded the album *Uhuru Africa.* The musicians were consciously chosen to represent Africa, the Caribbean, and the United States. They included Olatunji; two Cuban drummers, Candido and Armando Peraza; as well as several African-American jazz musicians. To show that there was also a connection with African Americans from outside the jazz tradition, he used Brock Peters and the concert singer Martha Flowers for the project. The lyrics for one song, *African Lady,* were by Langston Hughes. A few songs were in Swahili to demonstrate the connection between African language and African rhythms. Weston made the album to celebrate the independence movements that were then in full swing throughout much of Africa.[91]

Weston believed that the destiny of African Americans is to draw all people of African descent together. This Garveyite mission had a great spiritual pull for Weston. He believed that jazz musicians could play a significant role in knocking down the barriers among people of African descent and providing greater contact among them. And, like Garvey, Weston wanted to make a homeland in Africa, "a place where there are people who look like us." In addition, Weston spoke to Taylor about building a cultural center in Africa for black artists, complete with gymnasium and "courses in everything from Arabic to Swahili." He also dreamed of making a jazz museum there: "Why Africa? Because Africa is the source of our music."[92]

One of the best recordings of African-influenced jazz is Randy Weston's *Music from the New African Nations Featuring the Highlife.* Weston's compositions, Melba Liston's arrangements, and the improvisations by Weston and the members of his band, mesh well with the highlife-inspired rhythms. In addition to Weston's own pieces, there is Guy Warren's *Mystery of Love* and a composition by the Nigerian entertainer Bobby Benson,

Niger Mambo, a title that reflects the Cuban influence on West African popular music.

John Coltrane (1926–1967)

Blakey and Weston were the first to study African music in depth and to use African music in jazz in a profound manner. But it was John Coltrane whose music was taken up by black nationalists with a strong anti-European, pro-Third World ideology. Coltrane was influenced as much by Indian music as by African. Although in many ways African and Indian music are very different, they do share a few important traits. Music plays a significant role in the religious practices of both India and Africa, and music is closely tied to mysticism. In addition, percussion is an important element on both continents, although the rhythms are entirely different. Mixing African and Indian influences made perfect sense to black nationalists who saw a commonality between African and Eastern culture, based on the fact that both continents were inhabited by dark-skinned people and colonized by Europeans.

Coltrane recorded two albums emblematic of his interest in Africa: *Africa/Brass,* which featured a big band, and *Kulu Sé Mama,* a recording done with vocalist and percussionist Juno Lewis. Several of Coltrane's compositions refer to African locales or were based on African music. For instance, the melody for *Dahomey Dance* came from a recording of two African men imitating drum sounds.[93] From a rhythmic point of view, the trademarks of Coltrane's style were a triplet-based rhythmic feel reminiscent of West African music, and the use of bass ostinatos for rhythmic counterpoint. The bass lines had the force of a percussion line in a multi-drum ensemble. McCoy Tyner tended to play a repeated accompanying pattern in which the notes of the chords would change but the basic rhythm stayed the same. To a foundation of piano and bass ostinato lines, drummer Elvin Jones added rhythmic excitement by creating ever-changing improvisations on a triplet rhythmic scheme. Jones played the bembe figure in Coltrane's music when the rhythm was African-influenced. In addition, he adapted the figure for a slow, rolling 3/4 beat.[94]

The African influences in Coltrane's music extended beyond the realm of his famous quartet consisting of Elvin Jones, Jimmy Garrision, and McCoy Tyner. Taking a cue from African music, he added hand percussionists to the ensemble and then, in a step that many musicians found unacceptable, used two drumsets—Rashied Ali or Frank Butler with Elvin Jones, and Rashied Ali with Ben Riley. As Coltrane's music developed, the steady rhythm and ostinatos gave way to a music that often lost a sense of pulse. The ecstatic quality, which was there from the start of his quartet, took center stage.

Coltrane developed a strong relationship with Olatunji, and dedicated a song to him titled *Tunji*. Coltrane met the Yoruba drummer when their bands were playing on the same bill at the Village Gate in the early 1960s. When Olatunji was trying to get his Center of African Culture started, he looked to Coltrane for support. Coltrane told Olatunji that he wanted to study African religion, Yoruba, African history, music and dance. He wanted Olatunji to take him to Africa, which he felt was the source of all music. Coltrane's band performed at the opening of the school in April 1967. It was to be one of Coltrane's last performances before his death a few months later.[95]

For Coltrane, African music was an influence he felt comfortable using freely. He was never interested in African authenticity as such. He never made a recording with African musicians in the manner of Blakey's *African Beat* or attempted to play African traditional music. The question remains why black nationalists who expressed an interest in getting back to African roots gave Coltrane so much of their adulation rather than Randy Weston, Art Blakey, or an African musician like Olatunji.

The reason may be that Coltrane was more in the nature of a charismatic figure than Weston, Blakey, or others. As his music became less based on chord changes and more on free improvisation, Coltrane became a leader in the jazz avant-garde. His music was regarded by some as a political statement of black nationalism.[96] Political implications could also be drawn from another name for this style—"freedom music." Coltrane's music had a harshness and projected an attitude that seemed to fly in the face of European aesthetics. He was regarded as an angry man who was using music as a vehicle of protest, despite the fact that Coltrane himself often denied this. What established his black nationalist credentials was the combination of non-Western motifs in his music combined with what drummer Philly Joe Jones (who played with Coltrane when they were members of the Miles Davis Quintet) called "all that screaming and hollering you hear in the music."[97]

In interviews and in the liner notes he wrote for his albums, Coltrane never expressed the Afrocentric beliefs of his accolytes. His response to questions about his political beliefs and the importance of African and Middle Eastern influences were almost invariably equivocal.[98] His entire universe was music and its spiritual substance. He was not guided by nationalistic concerns, but his music inspired Archie Shepp and Malachi Favors (discussed next), who were probably the first musicians in the jazz community to articulate black nationalist ideas and express them in music.

Coltrane recorded *Kulu Sé Mama* in October 1965 in Los Angeles with the quartet, augmented by several other musicians. It was a collaboration with Juno Lewis, a percussionist, drum-maker and vocalist from New Orleans. Lewis played several unusual percussion instruments: the Juolulu, water drums, the Doom Dahka, and the conch shell. His song, subtitled *Juno Sé Mama,* was written in a mix of English and a New Orleans dialect called Entobes. The music begins and ends in a tender mode with rhythmic coloration. Most of the piece is in a medium-tempo 6/8 rhythm. In addition to Lewis, the rhythm section included Elvin Jones and Frank Butler on drums, bassists Jimmy Garrison and Donald Garrett (who also doubled on bass clarinet) and pianist McCoy Tyner. The record is suffused with percussion. It sounds at times as if one of the drum set players is playing hand percussion, because one can hear Lewis's drumming simultaneously with cowbell and jingling bells. *Kulu Sé Mama* is a seamless piece in which rhythmic and timbral concepts influenced by African music dominate. The album came with a poem by Juno Lewis that combined straightforward autobiography and passages in which the author assumes the role of a mythic figure. The poem is an integral part of the music, although it appears to be unrelated to the sung text. In it Lewis spoke about his descent from a family of drummers and his hopes to establish "a first Afro-American art center," "a home for homeless / Future sons of drums." When he wrote about the music, it's not clear if he was referring to the music on the recording or to a metaphysical music called *Juno Sé Mama.* In any case, Lewis attributes many powers to this "ritual," which he dedicated to his mother.

The ritual called "Juno Sé Mama" described in the poem is a metaphor for the quest for African identity. The quest thus becomes a means of establishing an identity for the lost souls in the poem who ask, "Who are we?" The quest for an African identity is a psychic balm for "all those who have suffered the after-effects of slavery."

Malachi Favors (1937–)

The Association for the Advancement of Creative Musicians (AACM) is an organization formed by musicians in Chicago in 1965 to sponsor performances by its members and to provide a forum for musicians to exchange ideas. A number of prominent jazz musicians and bands came out of the AACM, such as Anthony Braxton, Muhal Richard Abrams, Lester Bowie, Roscoe Mitchell, Henry Threadgill, the Art Ensemble of Chicago, and Air. The AACM constituted the first school of jazz musicians to formulate a music based on African ethnographies and Afrocentric literature. The AACM did not originate the use of free jazz. Ornette Coleman, John Coltrane, and Cecil Taylor were the pioneers of that style. But the members of the AACM provided the musical concepts of free jazz with a theoretical foundation based on notions about African community and ritual.

At the time the AACM was being formed, bassist Malachi Favors had already been a devoted reader for many years of the literature about Africa and African Americans. Favors has been credited with disseminating that literature to the members of the organization. He has also been credited with promoting the small percussion and wind instruments musicians in various AACM ensembles played, instruments that Muhal Richard Abrams explained "had a lot to do with our thoughts regarding African instruments." When Favors performed with the Art Ensemble of Chicago he wore facial makeup that expressed his commitment to Egyptian philosophy.[99]

CHOOSING A CULTURAL IDENTITY

Opinions about the influence of African music and culture on the United States have been determined by the racial climate of America, where the attitudes, customs, and habits of African Americans and white Americans are considered to be separate identities. Out of this dualism has sprung up a folk anthropology in which Americans differentiate behavior and other cultural attributes as either "white" or "African-American."[100] In this folk anthropology, theories about the origins of white and African-American cultural characteristics have tended to create two pigeonholes: African influences and European influences. All cultural attributes of whites and African Americans must fit into one or the other. The simplistic nature of the distinction reminds me of the infant toy in which cubes can fit only into square openings and spheres can fit only into round ones.

In reality, there is a cultural continuum in which relatively few cultural attributes are exclusively African and relatively few exclusively European. Most occupy a middle ground, the result of other influences entirely, such as Asia and Native America, or new American inventions born without apparent cultural influences. Nevertheless, when it comes to black culture, the tendency has been to name these middle-ground attributes as "African" or "European." The naming has occurred in a charged atmosphere, with stigma being placed on being called "European" or "African." It has been influenced as much by changing political and social circumstances as by new anthropological findings such as those of Howard University's slave burial project. I am reminded of a recent conversation on a talk radio station in which a white caller stated that he didn't want his children to be forced to attend a black school. His problem was that he did not want them to learn "African values." Unwittingly, this caller had turned the Afrocentrist argument for the superiority of African values on its head. He had surely heard these arguments about Afrocentrism in the media. They received a lot of attention because of their controversial nature. But for him, African values were not a cause for pride but the legacy of an inferior strain of humanity.

By insisting on assigning cultural attributes and origins to two narrowly defined categories, Americans have perpetrated a long list of falsehoods. *The Myth of the Negro Past* was the way Melville Herskovits described the set of myths held by those who believed that African Americans were a people without a history or a valuable culture. But in the last few decades, black nationalists have developed their own myths.

I began this chapter with the image of a burial site of African slaves being uncovered. In a manner analogous to this disinterment, scholars have been uncovering areas of American culture in search of vestiges of African musical practices. Some of these analyses have been highly fanciful, if inspiring. The notion of a "cool aesthetic" is especially inviting, if only as a heuristic device for understanding the personal styles of jazz musicians like Miles Davis and Lester Young. They are problematic because, like religious faith, they are resistant to factual arguments. One can no more disagree with the notion of a "race memory," a Jungian term used by poet Larry Neal in his essay/poem "Some Reflections on the Black Aesthetic,"[101] than argue that Santeros go into a trance state because they hypnotize themselves. There is a place for mysticism and magic. My contention is simply that sometimes there are more rational means of explaining the long continuity of African traditions.

Race and Religious Identity

Religious identity and spiritual discovery have been important themes in the jazz community for half a century. As early as the 1940s several prominent African-American musicians converted to Islam. In the 1950s religious fervor became a strong element in jazz through the music of Horace Silver, Bobby Timmons, Charles Mingus, and other composers. In the 1960s black jazz musicians were attracted to religions in which mystical experience plays a central role.

Race played a central role in forming the religious identities of black jazz musicians. They steered clear of the religious establishment because they believed it to be hopelessly enmeshed in social patterns that have helped to maintain racially oppressive roles and promote materialistic values. Their adoption of religions that were new to this country, like Buddhism, represented both a rejection of America's religious past and a withdrawal from its social norms.

EASTERN RELIGIONS

Islam

Islam has probably existed in the United States since the early days of slavery. A small percentage of slaves were Muslims, and documents written by them in Arabic exist. African Americans have promoted Islam as a superior alternative to Christianity ever since the late nineteenth century, when the pan-Africanist and scholar Edward Blyden noted that Islam had a better record of racial equality. Unlike the Bible, the Koran specifically addresses racial prejudice: "A white man is not superior to a black man, nor a black man to a white man, nor an Arab to a non-Arab, nor a non-Arab to an Arab. But the best of you is he who is most excellent in his morals."[1]

The first Islamic movement in the United States after slavery was Islamic in name only. It was the creation of Noble Drew Ali whose book, *The Koran*, bore little resemblance to the Islamic Koran. Ali established several sites, dubbed Moorish Science Temples, for his followers to worship his idiosyncratic religion.[2]

In 1921, the Ahmadiyya Movement in Islam (AMI), an international organization then based in India, became the first legitimate Islamic group to establish itself in the United States. The vast majority of the AMI's converts were black. The primary aim of AMI missionaries was to present Islam as a tolerant and enlightened religion. In addition, they wished to teach their prospective converts about the writings of the group's founder, Hazrat Mirza Ghulan Ahmad. Ahmad was born in 1833 in Qadian, a small town in the Punjab section of India. In 1889 he developed what he considered a revitalized and modern approach to Islam. He was determined to convert not only other Muslims to his group but Hindus and Christians as well. Toward the end of his life Ahmad claimed to have received revelations and to be able to perform miracles. He also claimed to be an avatar of Krishna and the Second Coming of Christ, claims that helped attract followers from outside Islam, as well as many enemies.[3]

One of Ahmad's goals was to correct the errors of other faiths and to argue for the humanity of their divine figures. He devoted a considerable amount of his writings to the "true" story of Jesus, who Ahmad maintained was still alive when he was taken down from the cross. Subsequently, Jesus traveled east to Iran, Afghanistan, and finally to the Kashmir region of India, where he met up with a tribe of Israelites who had taken up Buddhism.[4] Some hold that the Ahmadiyyans were opposed to Christianity,[5] but Ahmad's writings are filled with praise for Jesus. In fact, his teachings allowed former Christians to continue their devotion to Jesus while still practicing Islam.

For the AMI, music and the practice of Islam are not considered incompatible. In this respect, it differs from Orthodox Muslim sects, whose members are generally forbidden to become musicians. But music has long been practiced in the folk and art music traditions of Muslim people throughout the world. In addition, Sufi sects of Islam actively endorse the performance of music.[6]

Just a decade after the AMI established itself in the United States, a few jazz musicians became Ahmadiyya Muslims. But it was only in the late 1940s that the movement took off. Art Blakey, Talib Dawoud, Mohammed Sadiq, Sahib Shihab, Ahmad Jamal, Dakota Staton (Aliyah Rabia), Yusef Lateef, and Idrees Sulieman were a few of the musicians to convert. The phenomenon attracted the attention of the African-American press in the early 1950s. *Ebony* published an article in 1953, "Mohammaden Religion Appeals to Many Progressive Jazz Men." Up until the 1960s the AMI was the most popular Islamic group among jazz musicians.[7]

Talib Ahmad Dawoud played a major role in introducing musicians to Islam. While in Chicago, he introduced Yusef Lateef to the AMI. In the late 1940s Dawoud and his wife, Dakota Staton, moved to Philadelphia and played a major role in establishing the religion there. In 1959 he started a splinter group called the Muslim Brotherhood. One of the better-known members of the Muslim Brotherhood was McCoy Tyner. Dawoud gave Tyner his Muslim name, Sulieman Saud.

One of the first and best-known converts to Islam in the jazz community was Art Blakey. Blakey came to Islam after traveling to Africa to study religion and philosophy. He said that Christianity had been a religion he was forced into: "When I was growing up I had no choice. I was just thrown into a church and told this is what I was going to be. I didn't want to be their Christian. I didn't like it."[8]

Blakey was especially devoted to his new religion during the late 1940s. He adopted the Muslim name Abdullah Ibn Buhaina. His house was a center for Islamic meetings, according to Yusef Lateef, who attended these meetings after he himself converted in 1948.[9] For an engagement at Small's Paradise in Harlem, Blakey assembled a seventeen-member big band called the Messengers. According to Talib Ahmad Dawoud, the group's lead trumpeter, all of the band's members were Muslims. In "Beliefs of the Ahmadiyya Movement in Islam," messengers are described as people through whom "God has revealed His Will and His purpose."[10] In subsequent groups led by Blakey, the personnel was no longer Muslim, and Blakey changed the band's name to the Jazz Messengers. The original Islamic meaning of the name was thus lost.

For an African American in the 1940s becoming a Muslim carried a bonus: a ticket out of the American racial caste system. A Muslim was not treated as a "colored person" but as a foreigner. Whites saw someone who had adopted a Muslim name as an Arab, and suddenly that person could be served in whites-only restaurants. A few musicians became Muslims for purely social reasons. Dizzy Gillespie attested in his autobiography:

> Musicians started having it printed on their police cards where it said "race," "W" for white. Kenny Clarke had one and he showed it to me. He said, "See, nigger, I ain't no spook; I'm white, 'W.'" He changed his name to Arabic, Liaqat Ali Salaam. Another cat who had been my roommate at Laurinburg, Oliver Mesheux, got involved in an altercation about race down in Delaware. He went into this restaurant, and they said they didn't serve colored in there. So he said, "I don't blame you. But I don't have to go under the rules of colored because my name is Mustafa Dalil." Didn't ask him no more questions. "How do you do?" the guy said.[11]

After the 1960s the Nation of Islam, also known as the Black Muslims, became the dominant Islamic group for the African-American community. The AMI did not make peace with Elijah Muhammad's Nation, and Blakey considered the Nation to be "a disgrace to a great religion. They're just as bad as the Klan."[12] Though probably never as successful as the AMI at capturing the attention of the jazz community, several musicians did become members of the Nation of Islam. One convert was organist Larry Young (1940–1978), who adopted the Muslim name Khalid Yasin. The idea for his composition *Heaven on Earth* came from the title of an article in the Nation of Islam newspaper *Muhammed Speaks* and was influenced by his first experience of seeing Elijah Muhammed at the annual Savior's Day Convention in Chicago.[13]

Islam had an influence that extended beyond those jazz musicians who converted. John Coltrane was fascinated with the religion. Many of his closest associates, including his first wife, Naima, and his longtime pianist, McCoy Tyner, were Muslims. Miles Davis wrote in his autobiography that if he had to state a religious preference, it would be Islam.[14] Max Roach wrote an article about race relations in *Muhammed Speaks* in the early 1960s.[15] A decade later he told Arthur Taylor that he was "definitely a Muslim. To me it's a natural concept, and I fall into it easily. However, I am not as prolific [*sic*] and I don't practice as much as I could, but I do my best."[16]

In some respects, the experience of Islam has had a salutary effect on the careers of many jazz musicians. The religion could make it easier for them to establish contacts with other like-minded musicians and to attract the interest of music lovers who shared their rejection of mainstream American religions. Merely having an Arabic name in the 1950s could attract attention. On the other hand, being a Muslim in the United States has always been difficult because Islam is seen as anti-American. The period during which jazz musicians were converting to Islam coincided with Israel's first conflicts with Arabs. According to Dizzy Gillespie, a number of Jewish booking agents arranged a "semi-boycott" of jazz musicians with Muslim names, but this claim is highly doubtful.[17] Even if the boycott did take place, it had no discernible effect on the successful careers of Ahmad Jamal or Art Blakey.

Did the music of jazz musicians who converted to Islam change as a result of their conversion? A number, including Yusef Lateef, McCoy Tyner, and Art Blakey, became leaders in the Africanization of jazz. When I questioned Talib Dawoud about the African influence in jazz, he asserted that the musicians' artistic interests were unconnected to their conversion to Islam. Certainly the music of at least one AMI convert, Ahmad Jamal, stayed firmly in the jazz mainstream.

Baha'i

Like Coltrane, Dizzy Gillespie became religious at a critical point in his life. He had developed a drinking problem that ruined several public appearances. By 1968 Gillespie was ready to do something about it.

During a performance in Milwaukee, Gillespie received a phone call from a woman named Beth McKintey. She asked if she could come over to his hotel room to talk about a book on Charlie Parker in which Gillespie figured prominently. He agreed to meet with her, but, for reasons of propriety, he suggested that she and her husband meet him at the club where he was performing. It turned out that McKintey was a functionary in the Baha'i religion. Over the next few months, she and Gillespie continued to talk about Charlie Parker as well as about Gillespie's family and childhood. He began to receive Baha'i literature in the mail. What especially interested him was a book by Bill Sears, *Thief in the Night*, in which the author claims to demonstrate that the prophesies of various religions have been fulfilled by Bahá'u'lláh and the establish-

ment of the Baha'i faith. McKintey and other members of the Baha'i faith
arranged to have Gillespie meet Sears. He did and decided to become a
Baha'i. The religion seemed to corroborate long-held beliefs of Gillespie,
such as the unity of mankind, the oneness of God, and the spiritual development of mankind.[18]

Baha'i developed in Persia (now Iran) in the mid-nineteenth century.
Originally known as the Babí' faith, it was based on the teachings of Báb
(Siyyid 'Alí' Muhammad), who predicted that a great prophet would soon
appear. Soon afterward he was executed by the government, and his followers escaped to what is now Iraq. They were led by Mírzá Husayn-Ali,
who declared himself to be the prophet that Báb had predicted. In 1863,
Husayn-Ali adopted the name Bahá'u'lláh, which means "Glory of God,"
and the religion became known as Baha'i.

Baha'is (members of the Baha'i faith) believe that God sent a series of
prophets to help mankind. Bahá'u'lláh was the latest in a chain beginning
with Abraham and continuing through Moses, Jesus Christ, and Muhammed. Bahá'u'lláh declared that God wished to unite all people and that all
religions should honor Him. Bahá'u'lláh wanted to place all the world's
people under one government federation. He was opposed to all forms of
discrimination.

Conversion to Baha'i enabled Gillespie to formalize his beliefs about
the history of jazz. He began to understand history along the same lines
that Baha'is described the spiritual development of mankind in general.
The Baha'is believe that certain individuals arise and become the dominant force of a specific period. Similarly, Gillespie saw the development
of jazz as a series of dominant individuals from Buddy Bolden and King
Oliver through Ornette Coleman and John Coltrane. He therefore concluded:

> The message of our music runs the same way as the message
> of religion. These people that come to bring messages in the
> different ages in the spiritual development of man are similar
> to musicians, the messengers of our music who come to bring
> newer ages in the music.[19]

Buddhism

In the 1970s Herbie Hancock began to practice Nichiren Shoshu Buddhism. This form of Buddhism is based on the teachings of Nichiren, one
of the most controversial figures of Japanese religious history. Nichiren

was a thirteenth-century Buddhist monk who believed that the teachings contained in the Lotus Sutra, known in Japanese as Myohorengekyo, were the only correct elements of Buddhism. All other teachings he considered an abomination. The single practice of Nichiren was to recite the Daimoku, *Nam Myoho Renge Kyo* ("Adoration to the Lotus of the Perfect Law"). In the late nineteenth century, a variety of new religious movements based on the teachings of Nichiren were formed. One of the new religions was called Nichiren Shoshu, meaning "true Nichiren teaching," and it can be considered a purist version of Nichiren's practices.[20] This is the group with which Herbie Hancock became affiliated.

The act of chanting *Nam Myoho Renge Kyo* is the most important part of Nichiren Shoshu Buddhism. Reciting one's praise of the Lotus Sutra is supposed to put one in harmony with the power of the book. In addition, adherents of the religion believe that the chanting has a positive effect on the world. Chanting is not done merely to secure oneself a place in the hereafter. It also produces good effects in the here and now. It is this pragmatic element of the religion that many find appealing.[21]

Nichiren Shoshu Buddhism has had a profound effect on Hancock's life. He says that he chants in order to set goals, overcome obstacles, and find solutions. Chanting has also led him away from jazz and into funk. Funk was a musical style he had secretly admired for years but had been too snobbish to explore: "I was really disappointed in myself for that narrow-mindedness. Since that was the kind of music I really dug, and since I had to do something new anyway [after his sextet broke up], I decided to give it a try."[22]

Several members of Hancock's next group, Head Hunters, formed in the early 1970s, were involved in Nichiren Shoshu Buddhism. I interviewed a woman who was friends with a member of the group's road crew. She remembers that directly before going on stage Hancock, saxophonist Benny Maupin and the other musicians chanted, accompanying themselves by shaking wooden beads. She found the chant to be rhythmically compelling and inspiring.

THE CHURCH OF JOHN COLTRANE

Max Weber has made a distinction between two types of religious figures: the exemplary and the emissary. The emissary is a messenger such as Mohammed or Moses who has been chosen by God to carry His message. Although such individuals may be regarded by the members of their religion as specially anointed, their role is to fulfill the task God has chosen for them. The exemplary figure, on the other hand, has endured an extended period of purification during which he subdued the beasts within and attained a state of sainthood.[23]

John Coltrane was acknowledged by his followers as such an exemplary figure. His music revealed to them an individual who had reached an elevated state of consciousness. For several decades the jazz community had ascribed special importance to altered states of consciousness, either drug-induced or musically inspired. Coltrane showed that religious mysticism could lead someone to such a state without intoxicants. In this respect he was a role model for young musicians who wanted to join the jazz community without becoming alcoholics or drug users. Shortly after his death it was common to see jugs of water on stage, in what was sometimes a pointed display of the performers' sobriety.

Coltrane experienced a religious awakening in 1957. Like other jazz musicians who have reconnected with their faith or converted to a new one, it was his way of escaping drug addiction. Coltrane had been a heroin user, but it was his struggle with alcoholism that finally brought him to religion. His spiritual awakening had a profound effect on his music. While he was undergoing it he had musical dreams in which he heard sounds that he spent the rest of his life trying to recapture. In one dream Charlie Parker told him to keep working on his new approach to harmony.[24] After his religious awakening Coltrane's music grew to become monumentally intense, seemingly created in a state of mystical enthrallment. Like some Pentecostal preacher, Coltrane was the message-giver working himself into an ecstatic trance.

A Love Supreme was the first of a series of Coltrane albums whose titles expressed Christian imagery. The liner notes for *A Love Supreme* consisted of a message Coltrane wrote himself, beginning, "All praise be to God to whom all praise is due." Coltrane went on to describe the album as "a humble offering to Him. An attempt to say 'Thank you God' through our work, even as we do in our hearts and with our tongues." It is difficult to imagine a musician of an earlier generation making a comparable statement. Religion seemed to be the furthest thing from the life of a hip jazz musician before *A Love Supreme.*

Coltrane went on to record compositions with titles like *Dear Lord, Vigil, Ascension, Amen,* and *Attaining.* He also recorded a five-part composition called *Meditations* consisting of *The Father And the Son, And the Holy Ghost; Compassion; Love; Consequences;* and *Serenity.* After *Meditations,* Coltrane told Nat Hentoff that his goal was "to uplift people, as much as I can. To inspire them to realize more and more of their capacities for living meaningful lives. Because there is certainly meaning to life."[25]

Coltrane's followers heard in his music a message of freedom and revolution. Coltrane did not specifically state these sentiments, but his followers heard it anyway. Some of this message came through as a result of the way the group was organized, with the members expressing themselves without restraints. Many musicians regarded Coltrane's band as a model of community interaction, "a collective concept of aesthetic spiritualism."[26]

Coltrane also had a wide interest in religion. Through friends and through his first wife's family he learned about Islam. Later he explored Hinduism, Yoga, and the writings of Krishnamurti. The composition *Reverend King* was composed as a demonstration of how these various religious strains could be combined. Dedicated to the Rev. Martin Luther King Jr., it begins with the Buddhist incantation, *om mani-padme hum* (O Jewel in the Lotus! Amen!).

Shortly before he died, Coltrane and his second wife, pianist Alice Coltrane, talked about setting up a center for music and meditation. They conceived it as a fellowship based on music, because they "thought music was a single universal force and that there could be no dividing lines or categories."[27] Some years after his death a church was, in fact, established with Coltrane revered as its prophet and his music constituting the sole element of its ritual. St. John's African Orthodox Church was founded in San Francisco in 1971 by Franzo King.[28]

Race and Jazz Communities

Sociologist Robert Stebbins defines the jazz community as a status group in which social differentiation occurs at two levels: within the community at large and within the status group. Within the status group are core and peripheral institutions. The core institutions are jazz jobs, jam sessions, after-hours social life, the musicians' union, and cliques of musicians who refer jobs to each other. Peripheral institutions are the musician's family and commercial music jobs.[1] Over the years, the jazz community has distinguished itself from the community at large by a variety of distancing techniques that help maintain the integrity of the group, including use of a private slang, specific modes of dress, drug use, and other eccentric behavior.[2]

Like jazz itself, the nature of its community changes rapidly. It currently includes not only working musicians but jazz educators who teach at universities and conservatories; not only jazz musicians playing the most contemporary style but those devoted to recreating styles of the past, such as ragtime. Also, in a community formerly dominated by heterosexual males, there are now women and declared homosexuals such as Fred Hersch and Gary Burton.

Race has played an important role in the formulation of the jazz community, which was one of the first areas of American society in which African Americans and whites mixed as equals. By the early 1930s the jazz community developed a climate of parity among musicians based on ability. Talented African-American musicians were able to receive the accolades of the public, and a few were well compensated. Black musicians were credited with being able to make a "hotter" style of music, but whites were otherwise considered their equals.[3] White musicians took as their models both black and white musicians; so did a few well-known black musicians. The most notable was Lester Young, who cited Frankie Trumbauer (who was part Native American) and Bix Beiderbecke as influences.

Although African Americans probably resented the intrusion of whites, the times were not right for them to be vociferous about whites barging in on African-American cultural territory. Before World War II, it didn't seem to matter.

In the 1940s profound changes in race relations began to disrupt the jazz community. African Americans were demanding respect and credit for their musical expertise and innovative ideas, and they were acknowledged as the engineers of a new style, bebop. The burgeoning pride of African-American musicians resulted in revolutionary changes in the social conventions surrounding their music's production and dissemination. Audiences and music business functionaries had to become accustomed to the fact that jazz musicians wished to be perceived as serious artists. They would no longer accept the role of the entertainer that had been thrust on an earlier generation of musicians.

HEROIN ADDICT COMMUNITIES

Bebop, as with all truly revolutionary artistic development, was met with a negative response that propelled its makers to establish a feeling of community that insulated them against the public's derision. In the jazz world of the 1940s, heroin was part of the glue that held this community together. The trumpeter Red Rodney attested:

> It became our thing. That was our badge. It was the thing that made us different from the rest of the world. It was the thing that said, "We know, you don't know." It was the thing that gave us membership in a unique club, and for this membership, we gave up everything else in the world. Every ambition. Every desire. Everything. It ruined most of the people.[4]

A surprisingly large number of the leaders of bebop either toyed with heroin or were full-fledged addicts. The long list includes Charlie Parker, Miles Davis, Gerry Mulligan, Red Rodney, Wardell Gray, Dexter Gordon, J. J. Johnson, Tadd Dameron, Art Blakey, Sonny Rollins, Jackie McLean, Sonny Stitt, Bud Powell, John Coltrane, Fats Navarro, Gene Ammons, Stan Getz, Chet Baker, and Jimmy Heath.[5] Heroin use in the 1940s seems to have been biracial and largely confined to musicians and their acolytes. It existed in jazz circles several years before it hit the general black community in the early 1950s.[6]

Heroin was not the only drug popular among musicians. Marijuana was already a favorite before bebop and Dexedrine was the drug of choice for Thelonious Monk when he was a young man.[7] Cocaine was also available. It was called "girl," as if it were less manly than heroin.[8] According to Miles Davis, cocaine was the drug of choice of Latin musicians.[9] Although alcohol was mostly associated with earlier jazz styles, many bop musicians were heavy drinkers. But heroin more than any other drug had a seminal influence on the music. The music was the aural equivalent of the hip attitudes of a group of musicians who, if not actual users themselves, found themselves very much at home in places in which heroin use was flourishing.

Being a heroin user did not automatically secure one a place in the world of bebop—only talent did that. Several of the music's innovators, including Dizzy Gillespie and Thelonious Monk, were not heroin users, and a number of prominent musicians, such as Clifford Brown, steered clear of drug use entirely. Nevertheless, heroin was a means of making social contact with many prominent musicians. Pianist Herbie Nichols believed his career suffered because he was *not* a junkie: "It seems like you either have to be an Uncle Tom or a drug addict to make it in jazz, and I'm not either one."[10]

Of course, heroin did not begin with the bebop musicians. The morphine derivative caught on with Americans soon after it was first synthesized in Germany in 1898, and was widely lauded as a non-habit-forming drug. Before the first Pure Food and Drug Act became law in 1906 it was possible to buy, in stores or by mail order, medicines containing heroin without their being so labeled. But less than a decade passed before the tide of opinion against heroin and other opiates had shifted. In 1914 the Harrison Narcotic Act was enacted, controlling the sale of opium and opium derivatives as well as cocaine. The manufacture of heroin was outlawed in 1924.

When did heroin find its way into the music world? Charlie Parker began to use heroin in the 1930s in Kansas City. The drug found inroads into the world of white musicians at around the same time. The Georgie Auld band gained notoriety as a haven for junkies. Trumpeter Manny Fox is often cited as one of the first musicians to become a heroin user, and the one who introduced it to other musicians.[11] Drummer Lou Fromm was arrested and then made a statement that he couldn't play jazz without drugs.[12] The Woody Herman bands of the 1940s were full of heroin users such as trumpeter Sonny Berman, who died in 1947 at the age of twenty-three from a drug-related heart attack.

Drug Use in the 1950s

In the 1950s sociologist Charles Winick undertook a little-known study of drug use among jazz musicians in New York City. The musicians he interviewed were asked only about the drug use of others, who were identified only by race, age, and the instrument they played. At times, some volunteered information about their own usage. Winick ended up with 357 usable interviews. Almost 300 other musicians refused to talk. Winick believed that those who would not talk to him may have been more familiar with drug use than the ones who did. About a third of the musicians he interviewed were African American; the rest were white. Winick claimed to have interviewed "representatives of sixty-six of the eighty-nine important jazz bands of the area."[13]

Slightly more than half of the participants of Winick's study had tried heroin at least once. About a quarter were occasional users, and 16 percent were regular users. The musicians told him that drug use had been much more extensive several years before the interviews took place.

Winick found that drug use among musicians was not disproportionally higher among African Americans. In fact, in light of the high use of heroin in the black community at large, drug use among black musicians was comparatively low. Winick believed that drug use in the black community was tied to low social status. Black musicians were turning away from it because of their high degree of self-esteem and pride in their musical achievements. Prominent musicians like Miles Davis stopped using it by the end of the 1950s. Claude Brown, author of the autobiography *Manchild in the Promised Land*, described a shift in opinion about heroin among aspiring jazz musicians of the time:

The attitude had changed about drugs. These guys didn't believe that drugs had anything to do with playing good jazz. Many of the cats did when we first started out. But it seemed as though the guys who felt that drugs had something to do with it didn't make it as musicians. The cats who were still hanging in there were just good jazz musicians, damn good.[14]

Perhaps heroin use became a rite of passage for some black musicians; the ex-junkie had developed a greater status than non-user. In any case, heroin use was something that everyone in the black community was familiar with. It was ubiquitous there, not merely something one found within the esoteric circles of jazz musicians. Brown maintained that jazz musicians as a group, along with black artists and theater people, were the most upstanding citizens of Harlem.

They didn't want to be a part of street life. Some of them had just awakened to this fact. They were the same cats who had lived according to the code of the street. Now they were the only young people in the community who were doing anything worthwhile. They were married, they had good jobs, and they were always dressed presentably. They had to stand out, because most of the young people in the community were junkies. Anybody who wasn't a junkie stood out.[15]

Drug Use Since the 1960s

As the 1960s progressed, the drug habits of jazz musicians shifted even further away from heroin. Some even practiced abstinence from both alcohol and drugs, especially those who adopted Islam. The jazz musician lost his unenviable status in the popular imagination as the quintessential addict. The rock musician now held that dubious honor. It was a time when prominent stars of the rock world—Jimi Hendrix, Janis Joplin, and members of the Rolling Stones—became well-known junkies, and suffered the consequences in the form of jail sentences and death from overdoses. The hedonism of rock musicians scared many Americans. In contrast, jazz musicians appeared to be harmless artists devoted to mastering their art. Nevertheless, there were still prominent jazz musicians addicted to heroin, such as Woody Shaw.

Heroin's Appeal

Many musicians who began their careers in the 1940s and early
1950s have said that they became heroin addicts because they idolized
Charlie Parker. They thought heroin had something to do with his genius.
Miles Davis remembered: "The idea was going around that to use heroin
might make you play as great as Bird. A lot of musicians did it for that. I
guess I might have been just waiting for his genius to hit me."[16]

Several musicians have pointed out that some young performers suc-
cumb to the bad influence of more prominent musicians, or take up
drugs to alleviate the pressures of the fast-paced and insecure lifestyle
they have chosen. Jackie McLean found that heroin steadied his nerves
and helped him with his stage fright. The possibility that heroin had a
real productive influence on the music of the late 1940s cannot be discounted. As Red Rodney claims:

> I think that a lot of the *good* things in the music were because
> of drug use. The tempos where the guys really played on
> them. . . . The tunes with the great changes in it. The intellec-
> tual part of it. Guys were always experimenting, and the drugs
> had something to do with that, too. When a guy is loaded and
> at peace, he shuts everything else out except what he's inter-
> ested in. Being interested in music, he could turn out the honk-
> ing of the world. And, "Hey, man, I just figured this out," and
> we'd try it that night, and it was great.[17]

A participant described in Winick's study as a "very successful" musician compared heroin use to "going into a closet. It lets you concentrate
and takes you away from everything. Heroin is a working drug, like the
doctor who took it because he had a full schedule so he could concentrate better. It lets me concentrate on my sound."[18]

Despite its destructive effects, heroin found a secure niche in the mystique of jazz. No doubt the first time some musicians used it they saw
themselves becoming inextricably linked to the music's history and to the
music's spirit. An important part of this mystique is the image of the irre-
sponsible, undisciplined, and tragic black genius of jazz. In an art form in
which an idiosyncratic approach to playing an instrument, a personal
mode of dress, and a bizarre mode of behavior are appreciated almost as
much as the music itself, heroin use was just another facet of the jazz life.
For years, the excesses of heroin use seemed outweighed by the great
emphasis placed on individual expression, which heroin seemed to en-

courage. The musician was expected first and foremost to be a unique personality, valued for his nonconformity as much as his art. In a sense, what the audience yearns for is a freak. As Ornette Coleman pointed out:

> Everyone expects the musician in some way to be just naturally out of his mind, whatever it is. I mean some people say, "Well, man, you might not smoke or drink or nothing, but music is your high." You know. Even if you haven't had nothing, not even a drink of water, they'd say, "Well, baby, you know, even if you ain't high on nothing, just that shit you're playing is high."[19]

The Stigma of Heroin

Musicians have been offended by the attention given to heroin use—especially black musicians. Jackie McLean claimed that, because of greater access, "there are more people in the medical profession using drugs than there are jazz musicians."[20] This view has gained wide currency among the musicians of McLean's generation. How true is it? Winick tells us that in England "approximately seventeen percent of the small number of known addicts [were] physicians," making them the largest addict occupational group in that nation in the 1950s.[21] But in the same period of time in the United States, physicians taking narcotics were regarded by the Federal Bureau of Narcotics as constituting a very small number, no more than half of 1 percent of the addict population. Although it may be argued that physician drug use is largely unaccountable, it seems inconceivable that physicians in the United States would become addicted to a street drug like heroin when prescription drugs were so much more readily available to them.

Since the 1950s, the perception of jazz musicians as clean-living, upstanding citizens has been encouraged by several jazz musicians who were well aware that their older image as junkies was bad for business. Concert promoter George Wein asserts that after the drug habits of jazz musicians were revealed in the press, the established nightclubs were reluctant to hire them.[22] It took the tuxedo-attired Modern Jazz Quartet, the business-minded Dizzy Gillespie, and jazz musicians with college degrees to clean up their image. But the truth behind the new image was problematic. Several members of the Miles Davis Quintet were heroin addicts, and well into the 1960s the Ornette Coleman group had drug problems. Heroin continued to be associated with jazz clubs. One prominent Philadelphia club owner/manager was reputed to be an addict. Slug's, an important jazz spot of the 1970s in New York City's East Village, initially gained its reputation as a place where African-American drug dealers did business. According its owner, Robert Schoenholt, the drug dealers and their bodyguards "pulled in the musicians."[23]

JAZZ COLLECTIVES

So far I have described several communities with which jazz musicians have been associated, from religious institutions such as the Ahmadiyya Movement in Islam to casual social groups whose members share drug habits. It would seem unlikely from the standard picture of jazz musicians as diehard individualists that they would have any interest in organizing their own organizations. But in fact, since the 1960s, a surprising number of institutions have been established in the jazz community, ranging from the National Jazz Service Organization in Washington, D.C., and the Jazzmobile in New York City to collectives of musicians sharing similar aesthetic directions and interested in working toward a common goal.

Most of the jazz collectives were started by black musicians who, under the influence of the civil rights movement, were trying to secure a dignified place for black artists and respect for their art form. But in other ways these collectives followed a long tradition of dissident artist associations and had much in common with them. Like them, they were guided by progressive political beliefs and dissatisfaction with the job market. They provided a meeting place for like-minded individuals alienated from the mainstream who could then establish artistic and personal identities through their participation.

Although they were sometimes criticized for being little more than groups of bitter, under-employed, anti-white artists seeking an organization to help jump-start their careers, the collectives have had much of substance to offer. Several afforded poor, inner-city audiences with their only opportunity to hear jazz and gain access to educational programs that provided instruction by working jazz artists at a time when few schools offered such training.

Jazz Composers Guild

In the fall of 1964 trumpeter Bill Dixon and filmmaker Peter Sabino organized a successful series of avant-garde jazz concerts at New York City's Cellar Cafe, which they dubbed the October Revolution in Jazz.

Inspired by the success of this concert series, Dixon and Cecil Taylor got the idea of forming a sort of union for avant-garde jazz musicians. The charter members of the Jazz Composers Guild were, in addition to Dixon and Taylor, Roswell Rudd, Sun Ra, Archie Shepp, Carla Bley, Paul Bley (husband and wife at the time), Mike Mantler, Jon Winter, Burton Greene, and John Tchicai. The guild began with concerts held at Judson Hall and continued with weekly concerts in a loft above the Village Vanguard.

In an interview with Bill Dixon titled "The Jazz Composers Guild: An Assertion of Dignity," the guild's statement of purpose was described:

> The absence of representation of the most vital elements in the main stream of America's contemporary musical culture has made it necessary for the composers and performing musicians most affected to unite for the following purposes: to establish the music to its rightful place in the society; to awaken the musical conscience of the masses of people to that music which is essential to their lives; to protect the musicians and composers from the existing forces of exploitation; to provide an opportunity for the audience to hear the music; to provide facilities for the proper creation, rehearsal, performance, and dissemination of the music.

The Jazz Composers Guild was beset by personality conflicts almost from the beginning. Dixon believed these were inevitable in any association of jazz musicians, since "jazz represents the epitome of individualism." The group was biracial at a time that many black musicians were seeking their own identities apart from whites. As a result there was a continuous state of racial conflict. Dixon had invited white musicians to join because he believed they were badly treated, although not as badly as African Americans were being treated by club owners and record companies. But he was still not comfortable with their presence in the guild and frequently complained about the racial animosities of white members of the collective:

> Even in the Guild, which is comprised of some very intelligent people, there has been a subtle, but apparent, indignation on the part of the white members (and this is something I think nearly all white men have in them) that a black man ... myself,

> Cecil . . . could conceive and execute an idea that would be in-
> telligent and beneficial to all.[24]

Racial animosities were not the only source of conflict. The eccentric
Sun Ra was opposed to the admittance of Carla Bley to the guild. At
meetings he often repeated the old seaman's belief that having a woman
on a voyage will sink the ship.

Financing for the guild's ambitious plans, which included legal services for members and the founding of a music school, was to come from
record companies interested in establishing a recording contract cover-
ing all guild members. In order to pressure record companies to do business with the guild exclusively, members were encouraged to no longer
negotiate individual recording contracts.

Dixon did not figure on the desperation of some of its members to become recording artists at any cost. A few months after the Jazz Composers Guild came into being, Archie Shepp commenced negotiations with
Impulse Records without the guild's knowledge. This action infuriated
the membership and led to the guild's dissolution several months later.
Attendance at the regular Monday meetings began to fall off. Finally
Dixon himself quit, although the other members continued meeting
without him for a few more weeks.[25]

The Jazz Composers Guild died but its spirit lived on in the Jazz Composers Orchestra Association, formed by Carla Bley and her new husband Mike Mantler, whom she married after divorcing Paul Bley. Rudd,
Shepp, and other former members of the Jazz Composers Guild participated in the JCOA's performances and on its recording label.

The Association for the Advancement of Creative Musicians

The AACM was formed in Chicago in May 1965 by pianists Muhal
Richard Abrams and Jodie Christian, drummer Steve McCall, and trumpeter Phil Cohran. Several months later Abrams took over leadership of
the group. Many of the members were recruited from a rehearsal band
he led called the Experimental Band. The AACM helped establish a
number of prominent jazz artists including Muhal Richard Abrams,
George Lewis, Roscoe Mitchell, Anthony Braxton, Henry Threadgill,
Lester Bowie, Joseph Jarman, and Malachi Favors. Mitchell, Bowie, Jarman, and Favors constituted four-fifths of the famous Art Ensemble of
Chicago (drummer Don Moye was never an AACM member).

The following was a list of the association's goals:

1. To cultivate young musicians, and to create music of a high artistic level for the general public through the presentation of a program designed to magnify the importance of creative music.

2. To create an atmosphere conducive to artistic endeavors for the artistically inclined by maintaining a workshop for the expressed purpose of bringing talented musicians together.

3. To provide a source of employment for worthy creative musicians.

4. To set an example of high moral standards for musicians and to uplift the public image of creative musicians.

5. To increase mutual respect between creative artists and musical tradesmen (i.e., booking agents, managers).

6. To uphold the traditions of elevated cultured musicians handed down from the past.[26]

The AACM presented regular concerts and held open rehearsal twice a week. Each Saturday a big band met with the entire AACM membership to perform original compositions. These who wrote for the band were obliged to write a part for everybody.[27] Abrams expected all members to give at least one unaccompanied solo concert, since he believed that doing so would educate them to an awareness of musical organization.[28] Newcomers to the AACM had to be voted in by the general membership. In all AACM-sponsored affairs at least half of the performers (in groups of four or fewer) and 60 percent (in groups of more than four) had to be AACM members.[29]

The collective was financed solely from membership dues and revenue from ticket sales. The members of the AACM vetoed the idea of seeking outside financial support. They didn't want to take any money from the government or from the black bourgeoisie lest they attract influences that might corrupt the association's integrity.

History professor and musician Leslie B. Rout first met Abrams in 1952 when both of them were playing in a local band. In an article he wrote in the late 1960s, Rout explored the AACM's strengths and weaknesses. The AACM performances he had heard at the University of Chicago failed to impress him, and he found laughable the general anti-bourgeois attitudes expressed by members of the group and its followers.

But he praised the AACM as a unique organization that had survived without the encouragement of jazz celebrities or prominent black leaders, and noted that AACM members were proud to have started an organization that supported the work of important new talent. Roscoe Mitchell, one of the most famous AACM members, told Rout, "Chicago will be the new music center. This is the only place with a real organization. Musicians in New York [are] just walking the streets."

The AACM began with an all-black membership. For a while there was one token white member, Gordon Emmanuel, and his participation caused great discord. Eventually he left the group, which had always been intended as a self-help organization for black artists. Abrams addressed this topic in a report on the AACM originally published in 1973 in the black literary journal *Black World*:

> The Black creative artist must survive and persevere in spite of the oppressive forces which prevent Black people from reaching the goals attained by other Americans. . . . For years the mass-media scavengers have stolen and feasted on Black creativity, literally forcing ersatz art on the total American community in general and Black community in particular. . . . The AACM is attempting to precipitate activity geared toward finding a solution to the basic contradictions which face Black people. . . . [It] intends to show how the disadvantaged and the disenfranchised can come together and determine their own strategies for political and economic freedom, thereby determining their own destinies. This will not only create a new day for Black artists but for all Third World inhabitants; a new day of not only participation but of control.[30]

The theme of self-help extended into the AACM's educational programs. Abrams expressed his "keen desire to develop within our students the ability to value *self,* the ability to value *others* and the ability to utilize the opportunities they find in society [emphasis in original]."[31]

The Black Artists Group

BAG was founded in St. Louis in 1968. Its founding members were drummers Charles Bobo Shaw and Abdullah Yakub, trumpeter Floyd LeFlore, and saxophonists Oliver Lake and the late Julius Hemphill. (For many years Hemphill and Lake constituted half of the World Saxophone

Quartet.) Eventually the collective grew to include not only musicians but actors, dancers, poets, and visual artists. In marked contrast to the Jazz Composers Guild and the AACM, BAG was well funded, with grant money from the National Endowment for the Arts and the Missouri Arts Council. Before the funding dried up, the group had its own building with rehearsal and performance spaces. The end of grant support marked the complete dissolution of the group, but the feeling of kinship engendered by the collective had a profound and long-lasting effect on its members.[32]

The Jazz and People's Movement

The Jazz and People's Movement of the early 1970s was a protest group whose aim was to open up television to jazz musicians. Using the element of surprise, the group, led by Rahsaan Roland Kirk, created disruptions during the tapings of television variety and panel shows. On signal, the group's members, nearly all prominent jazz artists, began playing noisemakers, displaying placards, and passing out leaflets. The group especially singled out the shows of Dick Cavett, Johnny Carson, and Merv Griffin. Lee Morgan summarized the group's point of view:

> The airwaves belong to the public and we're here to dramatize that fact. Jazz is the only real American music, but how often do you see jazz musicians in front of the camera? And we're not talking about jazz musicians in the house band![33]

These surprise attacks on the networks succeeded in getting the members of the group some airplay. Dick Cavett invited the group on for a panel discussion. Appearing were members Cecil Taylor, Freddie Hubbard, Billy Harper, Andrew Cyrille, and Kirk's wife, Edith Kirk. There was also a "Dialogue of the Drums" between Rashied Ali, Andrew Cyrille, and Milford Graves on the NBC program "Positively Black." An all-star group led by Kirk appeared on the Ed Sullivan Show, the only major variety show that the group had not yet disrupted.

Collective Black Artists

The CBA was formed in 1969 with the aim of providing artistic services to the black musician. One of the main tenets of the organization was that black artists were the spokesmen for the black community and, as such, must be supported by it:

It's time for us to be real. The African community in America
must strengthen its convictions. And the strength must truly
come from our art forms (culture). Our Musicians/Artists are
the spokesmen of our community. They are not different, or
separate from their community. We are all working together,
collectively.[34]

CBA members were well-known musicians with a mainstream-jazz
orientation, in significant contrast to the generally avant-garde orientation of other jazz collectives in which many of the members were
amateurs.

The core of the CBA was an 18-piece orchestra called the CBA Ensemble, which included prominent musicians like Frank Foster, Jimmy
Owens, Stanley Cowell, Reggie Workman, and Charlie Persip. The CBA
Ensemble performed at a variety of top-notch concert halls and clubs in-
cluding Town Hall and the Village Vanguard. Its concerts often featured
guest stars like Dizzy Gillespie. In addition to the CBA Ensemble, the
CBA sponsored the CBA Institute of Education, which offered the fol-
lowing courses: Business Aspects of the Music Industry, Philosophy of
Practice Techniques, Improvisation, Electro-Acoustical Composition and
Notation, and Black Music in the Americas. Instructors included Jimmy
Owens, Charles Tolliver, Stanley Cowell, Youseff Yancy and Dr. Leonard
Goines. The CBA had a radio program on WNYC called "Anthology of
African-American Music" and began the Composition Reference Li-
brary, a repository of compositions by famous black jazz musicians. The
group was funded by the New York State Council on the Arts and other
groups. In 1974 it hired its first executive director, Cobi Narita.

By the 1980s the CBA folded but was reborn in a series of smaller
collectives under the care of Narita and Barry Harris. By this time there
was less need for jazz collectives. The National Endowment for the Arts
and other major arts organizations began providing steady support for
the music, jazz education became incorporated into most music
programs and conservatories, major cultural organizations such as
Carnegie Hall and Lincoln Center started jazz concert series, and, finally,
African-American culture became accepted in academia. The collectives
had served the purpose of bringing the needs of the jazz community to
public attention.

Asadata Dafora, the Sierra Leonean choreographer, percussionist, and opera singer whose 1934 concert of African music and dance at the Little Theatre in New York City was the first of its kind in the United States. Used by permission of Photographs and Prints Division, Schomburg Center for Research in Black Culture, The New York Public Library; Astor, Lenox and Tilden Foundations

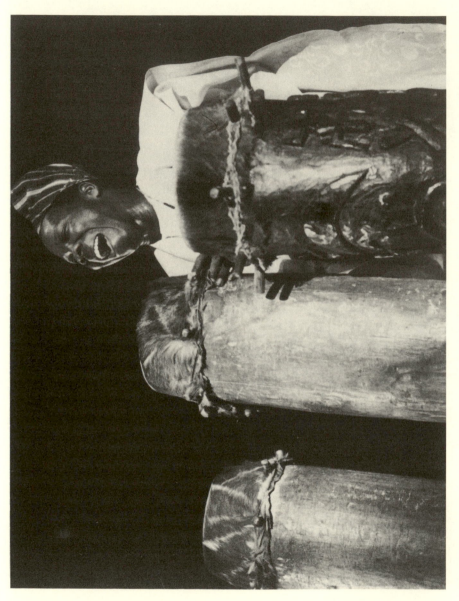

The Yoruba percussionist and choreographer Michael Babatunde Olatunji. Used by permission of Photographs and Prints Division, Schomburg Center for Research in Black Culture, The New York Public Library; Astor, Lenox and Tilden Foundations

The Art Ensemble of Chicago with Egyptian-inspired makeup. Courtesy of the Institute of Jazz Studies

Mezz Mezzrow believed he had cleansed himself of his Jewishness and remade himself into an African American. The renowned New Orleans soprano saxophonist Sidney Bechet appears in the photo. Courtesy of the Institute of Jazz Studies

Johnny Otis, who proclaimed himself to be "black environmentally, psychologically, culturally, emotionally, and intellectually." Used by permission of Photographs and Prints Division, Shomburg Center for Research in Black Culture, The New York Public Library; Astor, Lenox and Tilden Foundations

Songwriter Dan Penn ("Do Right Woman, Do Right Man," "I'm Your Puppet"), "No blacker than the next white guy." Used by permission of Jim Estrin/NYT Permissions

Composer Raymond Scott (1934), whose programmatic works found a natural home in Warner Brothers cartoons. Photo by Paul Gordon. Used by permission of The Raymond Scott Archives

Black Music, White Identity

THE BLACK MYSTIQUE

After studying medicine in Washington, D.C., for five years, the radiologist and novelist Rudolf Fisher returned to his home in Harlem. Going to his favorite cabaret, he had the odd experience of being one of the few African Americans in a crowd of whites where formerly he had rarely seen any whites at all. Subsequently, he went to the Nest, Small's, Connie's Inn, the Capitol, Happy's, and the Cotton Club, where he also found few, if any, African Americans in attendance. As he explained in his amusing 1927 article "The Caucasian Storms Harlem," Fisher had discovered that, in the years he had been living in Washington, whites had taken over Harlem nightlife.[1]

The white cultivation of the black mystique began more than a century before "The Caucasian Storms Harlem." At first, blackface entertainers took on the job of satisfying white people's cravings for the unruly spirit of African-American music. From the middle of the nineteenth century, the blackface entertainers were gradually replaced by African Americans and by white musicians with a sincere interest in and respect for African-American music.

Central to the cultivation of the black mystique is the notion that African Americans are different from whites. Under this assumption, whites latch on to the extreme features of African-American culture that set blacks apart from white America. By extracting these features from less sensational ones, they help fortify the belief that African Americans are the wielders of almost mythical abilities and bearers of numberless flaws, by turns enviable, pitiable, and despicable. The black mystique has historically been cultivated by whites whose contact with blacks has been peripheral at best. The majority of the slumming whites who invaded Dr. Fisher's night spots were there for an exotic night on the town. After slumming went out of fashion, the stream of white visitors to Harlem shrank to a trickle. Except for serious students of African-American culture, most whites rarely came in close contact with the musicians and the environments that created them. Their contact primarily came through recordings, and consequently they felt free to imagine what African-American life was like. Recordings gave whites who mythologized black musicians the chance to form a close, imaginary "soul" relationship with their favorite artists. Thus, author Norman Weinstein, whose own forebears were from Eastern Europe, writes that many years of listening to jazz has led him to consider African Americans like John Coltrane and Duke Ellington his " 'ancestors' . . . if only artistically and spiritually."[2]

Throughout the twentieth century the cultivation of the black mystique has been supported by followers of social movements who saw aspects of their own political philosophies reflected in African-American culture. In the 1920s the followers of an anti-Victorian movement, whose ideas had a tremendous influence on new developments in the arts and humanities from psychoanalysis, the realism of Theodore Dreiser to the Ashcan school of painting, celebrated the frank and rebellious spirit of jazz.[3] Between the world wars a polyglot community of African-American artists, American Jews, and rebellious bluebloods like John Hammond found in jazz an expression of their own anti-elitism. In the 1940s and 1950s the artistic underground discovered in African-American culture the basis for a lifestyle that gave birth to a new American character. The hipster was a "rebel without a cause" with an aversion to conformist behavior and an overriding devotion to pleasure. Norman Mailer described the hipster as a "white Negro," whose mode of behavior came from African Americans.[4]

Since the 1960s white radicals who have seen aspects of their own utopian philosophies in African-American culture have embraced the pariah status of the African American. During the 1970s there was a pamphlet making its way around college campuses called "The Student as Nigger."[5] When feminism became the cause of the moment, John Len-

non revealed that "woman is the nigger of the world."[6] Recently, Noel Ignatiev started a magazine called *Race Traitor* whose goal is to encourage
whites to renounce their racial privileges. It offers six ways "to fight being
white," beginning with: "Identify with the racially oppressed; violate the
rules of whiteness in ways that can have a social impact." The magazine
propagates the belief that the white race is a social construction spawned
in the early days of American slavery to repress African Americans. Its
theme is the phenomenon of white people crossing over into black culture, a phenomenon Ignatiev calls "black assimilation." In one autobio-
graphical sketch a contributor writes how, after most of his whiteness
was washed away, he discovered that he had "plenty of black" inside.[7] Ignatiev is aware that there is a thin line between giving up one's racial
privileges and co-opting African-American ways, but he believes that the
latter is an unfortunate but necessary side effect to the dissolution of the
social order.

Negrophilia and Negrophobia

White admiration for the African American may accompany a profound hatred. The emotions endlessly see-saw from one extreme to the
other according to Bernard Wolfe:

> With us, Negrophilia and Negrophobia are not, or are not *just,*
> polar opposites. We may have to see them . . . as the two sides
> of one coin, a coin we're forever flipping. We can't help our-
> selves. By the law of averages, it comes up heads, now tails. By
> the law of association, every time one side shows up, we're
> acutely aware of the presence of the other just below.[8]

For most whites, this ambivalence arises whenever a group of unfamiliar
African Americans confronts them, or when a conversation with (or
about) African Americans occurs. These are what could be called the
normal expressions of white ambivalence. There are much more bizarre
forms as well. Bluesman Michael Bloomfield remembers meeting white
people in the early 1960s who hated blacks yet "who spoke with a
pseudo-black accent and wore black clothes and drove big pimp cars." [9]
  In an article titled "Ecstatic in Blackface: The Negro as a Song-and-
Dance Man," Bernard Wolfe compares the relationship of the Brahmin
and the Untouchable, respectively the highest and lowest members of
Hindu society, with that of the white and the African American. Accord-

ing to Hindu mythology the Brahmins stem from the Brahma's forehead, while the pariah castes emanate from the lowest anatomical parts. The Untouchables are not allowed to mix with Brahmins, because the Brahma's lowest parts are not worthy of associating with his loftier ones. But in *sakti-puja,* an orgy celebrating the goddess Sakti in which members of all the castes participate, the taboos against the mixing of the castes are temporarily ignored.

In the United States, there are similar practices that, like the *sakti-puja* ritual, provide whites with the opportunity to vent taboo urges:

> Jazz, jitterbugging, zoot, jive, Negrophilia in general—these are daily street-corner and hangout *sakti-pujas* taking place in the open because we have no techniques for draining off our all-at-once emotions about the beckoning Untouchable in private.[10]

A peculiarly American phenomenon is that the pariah-elite exchanges can take place on a purely symbolic level. Rather than meeting the pariah (African American) in an orgy, the white American in the process of dancing African-American-inspired dances, singing or playing African-American-influenced songs, or simply adopting African-American slang experiences *sakti-puja*, without having to experience the actual presence of the pariah.

In the American version of the Brahmin-Untouchable relationship, the white contempt for the African American is influenced by a contradictory phenomenon: The African American is idealized as the incarnation of the free soul, the pre-social being untethered by the constraints of civilization, possessing both innocence and powerful emotions that whites, because of the pressures of modern civilization, no longer possess.[11] In this guise, the African American fulfills the need of providing white America with a way out of its emotionally unsatisfying daily grind.

Wolfe, who wrote his essay in the late 1940s, sees the African-American entertainer as the pawn of white masters who maintained a view of his art as spontaneous and free while disregarding or trivializing the pressure he is under to present unthreatening entertainment. What whites consider to be black self-expression Wolfe sees as "a composite portrait which the white world has slapped together haphazardly out of its own emotional leftovers and flung over the Negro."[12] To present a truer self-portrait, one inevitably filled with anger and bitterness, African Americans had to camouflage their departure from the servile role whites assigned them. Even then, their creative endeavors were constricted by white expectations:

> A socially produced anxiety spread-eagles over his entire existence, negating in advance every attempt at a genuine plunge into the subjective. And the Negro produces unique sounds and movements of anxiety, rituals of tension and malaise; but social reality is their springboard, and social reality their target. Negro song and dance are, in their innermost frames, laments for the *smothered* subjective.[13]

By and large, African-American artists are no longer beholden to white expectations. Surely they never were as responsive to white needs as Wolfe thinks they were. But Wolfe is right in pointing out that whites who have made a cult out of the spontaneity and primitiveness of African-American art fail to see the skill and calculation of the African-American performer. Moreover, these same whites fail to take offense when the African-American artist turns on them. In fact, there are plenty of whites who thrive on the art of angry African-American avant-garde jazz artists—enough to form the bulk of their audience. But this is an old story, an updated version of the slave owner who wants to know what his slaves "are thinking, wanting to be loved and understood by black people."[14]

Wolfe's essay paints a one-dimensional picture of white response to African-American art. He suggests that there is little real substance to black art in itself, that it is mainly a figment of white people's racially twisted imagination. Wolfe is not entirely wrong, but he is not entirely right either. Whites are not so trapped by their racist imaginations that they fail to see the *real* spontaneity and power of African-American art. The way we respond to popular culture, whether it be white, black, or orange, is full of contradictory notions. The best example of how these notions can coexist in the same person is the subject of the autobiography Wolfe helped write: Mezz Mezzrow. Even while holding a conception of African Americans that closely resembled that of a racist, Mezzrow nevertheless had a real understanding of racial oppression. And at the same time he praised the "natural" artistry of African Americans, he showed a profound awareness of the technical skills of the best musicians.

Prestige From Below[15]

The American national character has been derived from ordinary people rather than from royalty or other people in high social positions. Its archetypical figures, the Yankee, the African American, the backwoodsman, have all been outcasts from accepted society:

> Each in a fashion of his own had broken bonds, the Yankee in the initial revolt against the parent civilization, the backwoodsman in revolt against all civilization, the Negro in a revolt which was cryptic and submerged but which none the less made a perceptible outline. As figures they embodied a deeplying mood of disseverance, carrying the popular fancy further and further from any fixed or traditional heritage. Their comedy, their irreverent wisdom, their sudden changes and adroit adaptations, provided emblems for a pioneering people who required resilience as a prime trait.[16]

An important feature of twentieth-century America is that prestige comes both from above and from below. Prestige from above is indicated by the praise someone receives for adopting the values of the ruling class, while prestige from below comes from adopting those of the bottom of society. But it is not the values of the hard-working poor that seem so irresistible but those groups or individuals whose values represent an inversion of the accepted social norms. Puritanism is replaced by pleasure-seeking. In place of merely making a living, the goal of living well becomes paramount. Style replaces substance. And forbidden emotions and taboo activities replace accepted morality. Members of the American middle class—especially its youth—gain prestige among their peers by adopting the habits, ideas, and values of the African-American underworld or the independent backwoodsman. In the 1950s the search for prestige from below became no longer the aspiration of just a small community of disaffected whites but of a movement whose membership has continued to grow exponentially up to and including the present decade:

> Facing a choice between the sterile and homogeneous suburban cultures of their parents or the dynamic street cultures alive among groups excluded from the middle-class consensus, a large body of youths found themselves captivated and persuaded by the voices of difference. Mass consumer culture

had become so hegemonic that middle-class young people flocked to the cultures of the dying industrial city for connection to the past, for emotional expression, and for a set of values that explained and justified rebellion.[17]

The adoption of African-American and lower-class values is what distinguished these white rebels of the middle class from the slumming whites who invaded Dr. Fisher's Harlem in the 1920s. Unlike the latter, they showed a real commitment to African-American culture, but it was not the real African-American culture to which they developed such a strong attachment but to one transmogrified and conditioned by their search for prestige from below. In their rebellion against middle-class values, they adopted role models from the lowest rungs of society. Among the most prominent members of their role models were a junkie (Charlie Parker), a cross-dressing dishwasher (Little Richard), and a truck driver (Elvis Presley).

About that truck driver: Although he occupied a low rung of American society, his pursuit of African-American music nevertheless represented a search for prestige from below. In some respects, African-American culture was even more of a forbidden territory for the Southern white proletariat than it was for the Northern white middle class.

The search for prestige from below by middle-class youths and by members of the Southern working class can easily be dismissed as nothing more than a fatuous rebellion against normal society. Yet one must respect the fact that in African-American culture or even just a version of African-American culture based on phonograph recordings, the white middle-class rebels and the rebels of the Southern working class found a missing piece of themselves.

Jews and the Black Mystique

Jews have developed their own conception of the black mystique that differs in important ways from that of other Americans. Because both African Americans and Jews became city-dwellers and, in some instances, neighbors, Jews got to know African-American music first-hand. George Gershwin became friends with some of the leading African-American pianists of the day, artists like Eubie Blake, James P. Johnson, and Luckey Roberts, several of whom Gershwin met while he was still an impressionable teen-ager.[18] These early experiences of Jews with African-American culture found their mirror opposite in conversions to Judaism by African

Americans like pianist Willie "The Lion" Smith, who was cantor in a Harlem synagogue and wrote Jewish religious music.[19]

Jews considered African-American music emblematic of American culture, and Jews latched onto it as a way of discarding their old-world Jewish identities. Like the cantor's son who chose to become a blackface vaudeville singer in the Al Jolson movie *The Jazz Singer*, Mezz Mezzrow used a career in jazz as a means to make a complete break with Jewish culture. Born Milton Mesirow, he came from a middle-class Russian Jewish family in Chicago and spent his youth and early manhood in the company of other Jews. By the time he met his co-author Bernard Wolfe, Mezzrow had married a black woman and had spent several years living in Harlem, where he attained fame not as a musician but as a dealer in top-grade marijuana. According to Wolfe, Mezzrow was convinced that by spending so much of his life among blacks he had cleansed himself of his Jewishness and remade himself into an African American.[20]

Mezzrow hated to be reminded of his Jewish roots. He disliked the famous popular Jewish entertainers of the day—Ted Lewis, Sophie Tucker, Benny Davis, Eddie Cantor, Dolly Kaye, and Al Jolson—and resented having his Jewish friends asking him not to criticize them:

> The boys had the feeling that we should all stick together and not knock the big names of "our" race. I didn't go for that jive at all; being a Jew didn't mean a thing to me. Around the poolroom I defended the guys I felt were my real brothers, the colored musicians who made music that sent me, not a lot of beat-up old hamfats who sang and played a commercial excuse for the real thing. I never could dig the phony idea of a race—if we were a "race"—sticking together all the way, even when it meant turning your back on what was good or bad.[21]

After the 1950s many cosmopolitan Jews were all too familiar with the embarrassing sight of other Jews like Mezz Mezzrow pretending not to be Jewish. Bluesman Michael Bloomfield reflected their anti-assimilationist attitudes when he remarked that, although he played the blues, he was comfortable with both his Jewish heritage and surname: "I was always an urban Jew, a very well off urban Jew, and I never wanted to be anything but that. I didn't want to be a white black guy. That wasn't my scene at all."[22]

For some Jews black musical idioms have been regarded as a platform for exploring their own Jewish music and Jewish spiritualism in an

American idiom. Jewish musicians heard in the blues the American equivalent of the microtonal dirges of Yiddish music and felt a spirituality reminiscent of their own religion. Jews have been noting the commonality between jazz and Jewish music since the 1920s. In *The Jazz Singer*, an intertitle that follows the movie credits reads, "Jazz is prayer." In the background mournful, East European music plays.[23] Recently, pianist Ben Sidran, whose CD *Life's A Lesson* is a jazz interpretation of synagogue songs, noted that "jazz opened up many of the same spiritual questions" as Judaism. His return to Judaism was marked by an awareness of the connection between jazz and Hebrew liturgical music.[24]

WHITE JAZZ MUSICIANS: IDENTITY IN A BLACK WORLD

How do white jazz musicians come to grips with living artistically in a black world, using the blues and African-American rhythms as the basis of their music? For some, a fascination with African-American culture is a central part of their involvement in the music, while others have little connection to black culture. Some white musicians are aware of the irony involved, while others rarely question their life in a black world playing blues licks. Some white musicians have dedicated their careers to imitating African-American artists or writing in an authentically black idiom, while others have taken the styles of African-American musicians as the springboard for the development of a music with white and African-American influences.

The Mystique of Black Creativity

White musicians have ascribed vast creative powers to African Americans. There was no higher praise among the white Chicago jazz musicians of the 1920s than to say that a group of musicians "played like niggers."[25] Several white musicians have even expressed the notion that white artists are incapable of attaining the level of vitality, sincerity, mystery, flair, and emotional strength reached by the best African-American artists. On hearing the first recordings of white Chicago musicians, Mezzrow said: "It was just an imperfect reflection, like you get in a distorting mirror, of the only real jazz, the colored man's music." The drummer and disk jockey Johnny Otis condemns white jazz musicians who "enter the field with a mathematical and 'intellectual' approach, rather than an emotional and cultural one."[26] For Frank Zappa, African-American rock 'n' roll made white rock 'n' roll puny by comparison.

In my days of flaming youth I was extremely suspect of any
rock music played by white people. The sincerity and emotional intensity of their performances, when they sang about
boy friends and girl friends and breaking up, etc., was nowhere when I compared it to my high school Negro r&b heroes like Johnny Otis, Howlin' Wolf and Willie Mae [Big
Mama] Thornton.[27]

Note that one of Zappa's heroes was the aforementioned Johnny Otis,
a white man who spent his life being mistaken for an African-American.

Because black creativity is esteemed so highly in the jazz world, being
accepted as a member of a prominent African-American jazz group be-
stows upon white musicians a badge of authenticity that their other white
colleagues lack. They are respected by members of the jazz community
for being allowed into the realm of a group of musicians who, because of
their cultural background, are considered to be the arbiters of the idiom,
the figures who have defined where it came from and where it is going.
Nearly all acclaimed white musicians have had close associations with
African-American musicians that brought them recognition from the jazz
community. Bill Evans received renown as a sideman with Miles Davis,
Jim Hall gained the recognition of the jazz community after playing with
Sonny Rollins, and Joe Zawinul became known through playing with
Cannonball Adderley. For Roswell Rudd and Charlie Haden, their associations with African-American musicians gave them clearance to fully
participate in a community of black nationalists in which white musicians
were customarily condemned as musical thieves. By playing with Archie
Shepp and Ornette Coleman, respectively, they were regarded as exceptions to the rule of white expropriation.

Black Like Me

Oh, we're Negroes too. We get to feeling like that's what we are.
—Buddy Holly[28]

Some white musicians have adopted a state of mind that places great
value on the ability to "act black" musically and socially. Mezzrow wrote:
"If you want to play real jazz, go live close to the Negro, see through his
eyes, laugh and cry with him, soak up his spirit."[29] Undoubtedly, few
white musicians would state as baldly as Mezzrow that they became acquainted with African-American society in order to be better jazz musi-

cians. Nevertheless, the desire to make a home for oneself in African-American society and copy African-American habits has been an important factor in the lives of very different kinds of musicians from different eras of jazz. Mezzrow was extremely proud of his friendships on the South Side:

> When I stood around outside the Pekin, beating up my chops with Big Buster, and he put his arms around my shoulders in a friendly way, I almost busted the buttons off my vest, my chest swole up so much. Any time I breezed down the street, cats would flash me friendly grins and hands would wave at me from all sides, and I felt like I was king of the tribe. I was really living then.[30]

Artie Shaw and Chet Baker have both spoken with pride about being welcome guests in African-American neighborhoods. Chet Baker used to go uptown to buy drugs and get high, usually with fellow trumpeter Lee Morgan: "I used to go up to Harlem a lot. At one point I knew everybody. I could go alone anytime at night and walk down the street and everyone would say, 'hey,' . . . you know."[31]

Before he started his own band, Shaw spent his time uptown in the company of musicians such as Willie "The Lion" Smith: "I was actually living the life of a Negro musician, adopting Negro values and attitudes, and accepting the Negro out-group point of view not only about music but life in general."[32]

While Shaw's immersion in black culture ended after just a few months, a few white musicians have been so strongly attracted to blackness that they have almost entirely renounced their racial identities. Most of them have passed into history unnoticed. Fortunately, we have the autobiographies of two, Johnny Otis and Mezz Mezzrow, to document the extreme cases of individuals who, motivated by a complex mix of sentiments—a heartfelt identification with African-American culture, ambivalence toward their own ethnicity and "white culture," and a profound empathy with the underdog status of African Americans—no longer consider themselves to be white. Although their transformations were entirely attitudinal, the racial transformation was no less real to Otis and Mezzrow than if, like John Howard Griffin, author of *Black Like Me*,[33] they had undergone a procedure to darken their skin color.

Johnny Otis was born in 1921 with the name John Veliotes to a Greek-American couple and grew up in the racially mixed community of Berkeley, California. From an early age most of his friends were black. By the age of ten he was dismayed by racial prejudice and remembers wanting not to be white. By the time he was a teenager, it went beyond being ashamed of having the same skin color as the racists; he wanted to *be* black. These sentiments arose before he became a musician and before he married a black woman. Otis identified completely with African Americans and their culture, and proclaimed himself to be "black environmentally, psychologically, culturally, emotionally, and intellectually."[34] Apparently, he considered his own transformation into a white African American to be natural and inevitable, while the attempts of others to adopt the codes of the opposite color to be contrived and artificial. He scorns both white teenagers who try to act black and African Americans who strive to live and act white. He counts himself out among those white jazz musicians who, along with African-American jazz musicians confused by white values, have ruined jazz by their intellectual approach to the music.[35]

As a youth Mezz Mezzrow hopped a freight train down to Missouri with a bunch of friends for an adventure. These dark-complexioned Jews were mistaken for African Americans and given the Jim Crow treatment. Returning home, Mezzrow decided that the Southern racists were right: He *was* an African American, if not by birth, than because of his soul. Mezzrow made a commitment to himself: "I was going to be a musician, a Negro musician, hipping the world about the blues the way only Negroes can."[36]

Unlike Otis, Mezzrow was always aware that, since he was born white, he needed to work extra hard to become black. He credits his abilities as a jazz musician to perseverance and the recognition that he had to learn the music from the "source"—African-American culture.[37] Mezzrow's autobiography contains several statements in which he portrays himself as a wannabe black, but no outright declaration that he had actually crossed over into negritude. It is only in Bernard Wolfe's afterword to *Really the Blues* that we discover that Mezzrow believed he had been physically transformed into an African American. Whether Mezzrow was serious or was only making a joke when he told Wolfe to look at his face for telltale signs of a racial transformation is impossible to decide with certainty. In the text of his autobiography, it is only in the previously cited statement—"I wanted to be a Negro musician, hipping the world about the blues the way only Negroes can"—that Mezzrow admits to wanting to become an African American. But the statement can be read another way. In the 1920s musicians preferred not to call the music they played "jazz," but they had not yet decided on another name. To become a "Negro musician" at that time meant something other than a racial transformation. In fact, Mezzrow tells us that "in those days our music was called 'nigger music' and 'whorehouse music.' "[38] Since he identifies the music of Sidney Bechet, Louis Armstrong, Earl Hines, and others as "Negro" music, it follows that someone who plays that music, regardless of his race or nationality, could be called a Negro musician. Thus, perhaps, Mezzrow was calling his intended profession Negro musician because he was going to play Negro music. He was using the terminology in a sense analogous to calling the prominent non-Latino arranger Marty Sheller a Latin arranger.

I'm White, But My Music Is Black

A few whites have mastered the ability to create music and lyrics in an African-American style so well that it has fooled everyone about their racial identities. Unlike Otis and Mezzrow, most of these artists do not fit the profile of the wannabe blacks. Dan Penn notes that despite the strong influence of African-American music, he is "no blacker than the next white guy."[39]

Probably the first white to study African-American music with any seriousness and use it for his own creative expression was Joseph Lamb, a ragtime composer whose work was written in the first two decades of the twentieth century. So thoroughly did he learn the ragtime style of Scott Joplin that it was not until after World War II that people became aware he wasn't African American.[40]

More recently, the team of pianist Bob Telson and dramatist Lee Breuer created *The Gospel at Colonus,* a brilliant version of the last days of Oedipus set in a black Pentacostal church. Telson's music is so completely immersed in the gospel vein that one is amazed to find it was written by a white man. In the face of America's contentious racial climate and a huge literature viciously attacking white musicians for copying African-American music, it is startling to be confronted with a white man commited to writing gospel music—and so capable of doing it.

In rhythm-and-blues above all other genres, whites have succeeded in writing idiomatically correct black music. One such artist is songwriter and singer Dan Penn, whose songs *Do Right Woman, Do Right Man; I'm Your Puppet;* and *Cry Like a Baby* were sung almost exclusively by black artists. In addition to Penn and Johnny Otis, there were white blues singer Doc Pomus and his partner Mort Shuman, Jerry Leiber and Mike Stoller, and Carole King and Gerry Goffin. As a group, these songwriters produced a large number of the black hits of the 1950s and 1960s for artists like the Coasters, Ray Charles, the Drifters, LaVern Baker, Big Mama Thornton, Charles Brown, Percy Sledge, Aretha Franklin, and Cissy Houston.

Is there anything wrong with whites making a career out of writing authentic black music? In 1994 Amy Linden wrote a *New York Times* article on Dan Penn. Accompanying the article was a photograph of the songwriter leaning against a graffiti-covered wall in Harlem. In the middle of the photo session a car drove by and a passenger leaned out of the window to shout, "Go home, whiteys!" The event was an epiphany in the life of the musician who made "A Career Made of Being Where He Doesn't Belong"—the title of Linden's article. It was not until he attended a music conference in 1969, the year after the Rev. Martin Luther King Jr.'s death, that Penn found out that African Americans in the music industry felt he had no business being where he was. Penn's eyes were opened by a meeting during which white rhythm-and-blues producer Jerry Wexler was hanged in effigy, and speakers demanded that African-American artists work only with African-American musicians and producers.[41]

"A Career Made of Being Where He Doesn't Belong" suggests that Penn had no right to be in the world of African-American music. If Penn were interested in rebutting this point of view, he would only have to point to the success of his work. The article indicates that Penn has no guilt about writing black music. He believes that the artistic achievements of rhythm-and-blues came about as a result of "black singers with white record producers and songwriters or a mixture of them both."[42] He sees no problem with the rhythm-and-blues collaboration between whites and African Americans as long as his black associates got an equitable share in the money. For him, there was nothing strange about singing like an African American or writing in an authentically African-American style. His only mistake, if it can be called a mistake, was in failing to consider the irony of a white man writing black music.

Some white musicians do not see idioms like the blues as a distinctly African-American expression. They consider the blues to be a feeling that anyone can get, and the technique for playing it something that must be learned, regardless of one's ethnicity or race. They believe that peer acceptance is the only viable test of a musician's ability to play the blues. Whites can point to a number of white musicians and Asians who have been accepted into the African-American blues scene: Jesse Edwin Davis in Taj Mahal's early bands; Tim Kaihatsu, a Japanese guitarist in Robert Cray's band; Albert Gianquinto, James Cotton's pianist for many years. In a related scene, there is Billy Peek, a guitarist who performed with Chuck Berry for several years and who recorded a blues album with a song he wrote called *Can a White Boy Play the Blues?*[43]

In the contemporary arts world, voice, or cultural, appropriation is a hot topic.[44] An example of voice appropriation is provided by whites who create art as if they are a member of an oppressed minority group, or who make the lives or images of the members of that group the focus of their art. Voice appropriation is condemned because it places the art of an oppressed minority in the hands of individuals who, despite being culturally and racially linked to historical oppressors, act as if racial politics had no meaning in the context of artistic expression. The act of whites becoming blues singers alters the African-American cultural landscape. Whites thereby make the blues just another form of expression, rather than one tagged as the marker par excellence of African-American identity.

It was the British blues groups of the 1960s and 1970s that, in interviews that questioned their ability to play the music, insisted that the blues is neither black nor white, but simply human. "What is *black* music?" John Mayall asked. "There's no such thing as *black* music."[45] In the years immediately following the success of the British blues groups and the praise bestowed on them for their selfless promotion of the African-American blues artists they admired as well as their efforts to secure them fair treatment, any charges of voice appropriation were considered pure maliciousness.

Several years after the white blues groups had become fixtures on the music scene, a few blues festivals became affairs with few, if any, black musicians in attendance. In his book *White Boy Singin' the Blues,* Michael Bane notes that during one of the regular blues "revivals" in Memphis, black soul musicians, a numerous contingent in what was at the time the locale for a successful soul music industry, were "shunned." Bane commented ironically: "Music has no *color,* man. Don't come telling us about how black you are."[46]

Being True to One's Self

Most white jazz artists have an almost worshipful respect for African-American artists. In this respect, they differ profoundly from their more lowly relatives in the music business, the Southern working-class musicians who call their favorite music "nigger music." But despite their deep respect for the African-American ethos and its artists, only a few whites have chosen the path of near-complete identification with African-American culture, in the way of Otis, Mezzrow, and Penn. Although some white jazz musicians begin their musical education by imitating black musicians and sometimes adopting black speech and behavior, they eventually leave these aesthetic boundaries behind to make an art better reflecting their own backgrounds. Indeed, they are inspired to the quest for achieving an original voice by the black musicians they so admire.

White musicians tend to have a better chance of achieving artistic success when they do not confine themselves to areas in which African Americans have proven themselves superior. Raymond Scott is a brilliant example.

Before the release of *The Raymond Scott Project: Volume One* (Stash) and *Reckless Nights and Turkish Twilights* (Columbia), his music was almost forgotten. His compositions could be heard only in Warner Brothers cartoons, where they had been appropriated by the brilliant film composer, Carl Stallings. Scott's music in the 1930s anticipated innovations that arose several decades later. Predating John Cage's famous *4' 33"* composition by more than a decade, Scott's group once played something called *Silent Music* at the Blue Note back in 1949 in which the musicians pretended to be making sounds on their instruments.[47] Like Frank Zappa, Scott was fascinated with making an art out of performance. Sometimes he marched his band into the audience and conducted with the musicians scattered throughout the auditorium. Or he would instruct the band to play quieter and quieter, while making broader and broader conducting motions as if he were signaling a crescendo. Although his comedic touches and eccentricity point to Cage and Zappa and artists like John Lurie and John Zorn, Scott's work also predates Charles Mingus's work. Both were programmatic jazz composers in an idiom in which programmatic content is rare. Mingus's *A Foggy Day* [48] with its automobile sounds resembles Scott's *Confusion Among a Fleet of Taxicabs Upon Meeting With a Fare*. There are also similarities in the way both composers approach harmony. In a few of his compositions Scott stays on the same chord for long stretches in a manner typical of Mingus's forays into modal jazz.

Scott was born with the name Harry Warnow. He changed his name to avoid charges of nepotism after his brother, Mark Warnow, conductor of the CBS house band, began playing his compositions. He picked the name Raymond Scott out of a Manhattan phone directory because "it was a nice sounding name, it had good rhythm to it."[49] Scott was apparently intrigued with making up humorous names. He called his six-member group the Raymond Scott Quintette and gave the name Eric Hoex to the group's saxophonist Dave Harris, because he thought Harris was too ordinary a name for such a talented musician.

Scott was Jewish. Joel Lewis, who wrote a 1993 article about him in the Jewish weekly, *The Forward,* believes that Scott, unlike his Jewish contemporories such as Gershwin and Goodman, was unaffected by the desire to fit in:

> As a Jewish popular composer, he seems to be the missing link between Gershwin's attempts to be accepted as a "serious" composer and Benny Goodman's and Artie Shaw's desire to be accepted as "serious" jazz musicians, not white imitators. Mr. Scott, at his best, sought neither route; he pursued neither vision, producing a body of music that still defies categorization.[50]

Scott had little interest in sticking to the stylistic constraints of jazz. He turned away from jazz solos unless they were supported by orchestrated accompaniments. Although members of his group played solos, they were painstakingly rehearsed. As a jazz composer, he was alone in his mistrust of improvisation. In contrast to others in the jazz community, he thought that improvisation rarely fulfilled its promise of creating good music. He believed it had put jazz in a rut, with the routine precluding any ingenuity.

Innovation in jazz does not have an impact unless it quickly becomes the common property of many musicians. The evolution of jazz styles progresses less from one great artist to another than from generation to generation.[51] As a result, innovations that do not come out of an entire generation's style do not become anything more than a footnote to jazz history. This is what happened to Scott's music. He failed to make any converts to his ideas about jazz. Although other jazz musicians respected him, they did not consider his music to be jazz. Consider the remarks of Johnny Williams, the Quintette's drummer (and father of *Star Wars* composer John Williams):

> We really didn't want to do any of it. So there we were, doing what he called descriptive jazz and which we thought was descriptive all right but not jazz, because jazz is right now, not memorized note for note. And after all this compulsive rehearsal, suddenly it all caught on and we were making more

money than anybody else in town, all thanks to him. We were doing records, public appearances, making movies, everything.[52]

Williams' statements remind me of a remark Jimmy Giuffre once
made—that his sidemen would rather be playing bebop than Giuffre's
music. Such is the nature of most jazz musicians: They prefer to play the
music of their own generation rather than that of an original composer
without cachet in the jazz community.

Scott's unwelcome reception in the jazz community was not unique.
There were several white musicians and a few African Americans, such
as Herbie Nichols, who have gotten a similar response. But rather than
blaming the jazz community for its excessive purism, it is better to take a
closer look at the relationship between Scott's music and that of the only
other contemporary for whom he had complete respect, Duke Ellington.
In a 1937 article Scott wrote for *Billboard,* he acclaimed Ellington for
"singularly [carrying] through musical ideas, theories and innovations in
jazz despite the barriers that often confronted him because of lack of musical appreciation in the masses, petty prejudices and a general lack of
comprehension of what he was trying to accomplish in jazz."[53] Both Ellington and Scott were pianists, but Ellington had developed a real jazz
style on the keyboard. Scott's style was a pastiche of modern classical music and jazz. Ellington's music, even when he strove toward newness, was
permeated with a unity between his own musical conceptions and that of
his generation. Musicians were ambivalent about playing with Scott; everyone wanted to play with Ellington. Ellington, as Scott noted, "had a firm
belief that a soloist should be given absolute freedom," and the experience of playing with Ellington provided his musicians with the opportunity to establish a distinctive voice. In Scott's group the musicians' own
voices were subsumed by Scott's. Clarinetist Pete Pumiglio said: "We so-
loed, but you got to know what to do so he'd like it."[54]

The typical response within the jazz community is that if the musicians
enjoy playing the music, it is good. If they don't, then it is not. While they
may respect a musician like Scott, they do not love him in the same way
that they love an Ellington. With the ethos of personal freedom stamped
indelibly into the soul of the jazz community, a musician like Scott with
another, perhaps more sophisticated, sensibility is nevertheless branded
an outsider.

Although Scott was one-of-a-kind, some facets of his approach to jazz
are shared by most white innovators. Their interests in jazz are primarily
aesthetic, since their music does not play a part in establishing a group's

social cohesion, as African-American music does for African-American culture. Whites have a strong interest in expanding the technical aspects of jazz by introducing elements from modern classical music. They are less interested in making their music sound like jazz than in expressing themselves. A comment by Chick Corea to an interviewer's question about the limitations of the jazz idiom underlies an attitude shared by many white innovators:

> You have one aspect of this backward, to my way of thinking. The style doesn't dictate the use [of orchestration and improvisation]. The user is the one who creates the style. I don't ask myself, "Does this work as jazz?" I'll create the music I need without thinking about style.[55]

Because compliance with stylistic concerns is less important than personal expression, elements closely associated with the jazz idiom fall by the wayside, especially swing. As a result, one must listen to the music of white innovators with different ears than one uses to hear jazz that falls within the parameters of established styles. In a community in which personal expression is worshipped, it is ironic that a successful performance of standard jazz fare requires that all of its traditional ingredients be present in order for it to be considered authentic. This is especially apparent when white innovators play standard material in an idosyncratic manner. It is difficult to play a convincing rendition of a bebop favorite like "All the Things You Are" without staying close to the bebop style. This is the reason Lennie Tristano's music was so unsatisfying: He tried to play such tunes with a slightly different feeling from Charlie Parker's. Since the Tristano version was close enough to Parker's to warrant comparison, the differences sounded like shortcomings. The reason that the music of such originals as Raymond Scott and Jimmy Giuffre (in particular his trio recordings of the 1950s and 1960s) is so much more satisfying than Tristano's is that there is nothing within the jazz tradition to which it can be compared.

6

Colorless Swing

I have become colorless. I have clear speech and non-ethnic characteristics.
— Bryant Gumbel, former host of NBC's *The Today Show*[1]

Becoming part of the mainstream is essential for any group to succeed in
America. Nelson George, author of *The Death of Rhythm & Blues,* an in-
sightful study of postwar black popular music, believes that African
Americans, overly impressed with assimilation, have exchanged racial
unification "for an American identity of dubious value."[2] Although he
concedes that integration has given them a better life, he argues that it
has disconnected them from the roots of black culture.

George's subject is "crossover," the efforts of minority artists to appeal
to a wider audience by making their music more palatable or by market-
ing it in wider channels of distribution. Although the word is of recent
coinage, it is an old phenomenon.

The ragtime musicians were the first crossover artists. Their strategy
was to gain admittance to the popular music industry by writing songs
that white music lovers would want to buy. Few blacks were able to read
music or could afford to purchase sheet music, so the market was driven
by white tastes. In the drive to reach commercial success, ragtime be-

came a race-neutral style. Both whites and blacks wrote "coon songs" with racially offensive lyrics.

Black swing musicians constituted the next generation of crossover artists. During the advent of swing, the doors to American success were pried open. African-American musicians seized the opportunity to reach white audiences by playing fewer blues compositions and expanding their repertoire of popular songs.

The bebop musicians rejected crossover, perceiving it as a threat to artistic integrity and a reprehensible pandering to white mainstream tastes. Future generations of African-American jazz musicians maintained the beboppers' antipathy toward crossover. Although the hard bop musicians came close to starting on the crossover path by making a rapprochement with popular music, the styles they looked to for inspiration—gospel, soul, and rhythm-and-blues—were created by and for African Americans, not the white mainstream.

It was the fusion musicians who brought crossover back into jazz. Developed in the countercultural 1960s, fusion appealed to a wide, racially mixed audience. The style, based on a variety of influences including Brazilian music, popular African music, black gospel music, rock, and funk rhythms, allowed for a wide range of musical approaches, from the avant-gardisms of Frank Zappa to the sultry, rhythm-and-blues-infused light jazz of Hubert Laws, Grover Washington, and Spyro Gyra.

Fusion musicians brought integration back to the jazz community, which had been racially polarized in the 1950s and early 1960s. Apart from fusion the jazz community continued to be polarized. Whites were rarely found in black nationalist avant-garde circles and in the black neighborhood jazz scene still alive in places like Philadelphia and Detroit, and few blacks played in the big bands accompanying network talk shows. Meanwhile, white and black fusion players played together in the same groups to an extent unparalleled in the history of jazz. There was a sense of fair play in the jazz community, with white and black musicians going through the same black-led bands before they started out on their own. Keith Jarrett played as a sideman with Charles Lloyd and Miles Davis; Joe Zawinul was with Cannonball Adderley and Miles Davis; John McLaughlin, with Tony Williams and Miles Davis; Chick Corea, with Mongo Santamaria and Miles Davis; Randy and Michael Brecker, with Horace Silver; and Dave Liebman, with Elvin Jones and Miles Davis.

Fusion was colorless swing, the music of assimilation. White saxophonists like Lenny Pickett and Dave Sanborn "testified" with gospel fervor, and the Brecker Brothers took pages out of James Brown's book of rhythmic tricks. Meanwhile black musicians like Tony Williams and Billy Cobham explored white rock and Miles Davis added non-Western percussionists to his groups such as Brazilian percussionist Airto Moreira and the tabla player Badal Roy.

Miles Davis, Tony Williams, Herbie Hancock, Wayne Shorter, and other important African-American fusion musicians were inspired by the lifestyles and music of two black rock musicians, Sly Stone and Jimi Hendrix, whose careers reflected both the promise and curse of crossover.

Stone and Hendrix embraced white counter-cultural fashions and values and associated with white hippy "soul brothers." They had roots in black culture but discovered their musical identities in white hippy enclaves. Stone, raised in a Sanctified church, started his career in San Francisco playing white rock clubs and auditoriums. The Seattle-born Jimi Hendrix had years of experience under his belt on the "chitlin circuit" as a rhythm-and-blues sideman with Little Richard before he found his identity as the pre-eminent rock guitarist of modern times while living in London. Even before then, Hendrix had drifted far from the stylistic borders of rhythm-and-blues.

Hendrix's and Stone's music effortlessly flowed from black musical idioms to white ones. Over black funk grooves Sly set lyrics espousing white counter-cultural rhetoric. Hendrix sang Bob Dylan songs like *All Along the Watchtower* and then old rhythm-and-blues standards like *Let the Good Times Roll*. Both musicians led integrated bands to fame and fortune. The Jimi Hendrix Experience was a trio, with the guitarist accompanied by two white English musicians: bassist and songwriter Noel Redding and the superb drummer, Mitch Mitchell. Sly and the Family Stone was racially and sexually mixed, with its members defying status quo expectations. As rock journalist Dave Marsh pointed out: "The women played, the men sang; the blacks freak out, the whites got funky; everyone did something unexpected."[3]

Black America's response to Hendrix and Stone was different. African Americans rejected Hendrix, but loved Stone because he "always gave up the funk." Stone's career demonstrated that it was possible to be a crossover artist without losing the black audience. Hendrix "damaged his connection with black audiences because of his innovative brilliance on the electric guitar, an instrument that, with the declining black interest in blues, fell into disfavor."[4] Hendrix was unhappy and bewildered with his inability to gain a large black audience, as he indicated in a *Life Magazine* interview:

Black people probably talk about us like dogs, until we play. I see some of them on the street, they say, "I see you got those two white boys with you." I try to explain to them about all this new music. I play them some records. I might play them some of what we do. Sometimes they still think we're crazy.[5]

Shortly before his death from a combination of pills and alcohol, Hendrix became involved in black political causes and formed an all-black band, Band of Gypsies. These activities invite speculation that the guitarist was trying to re-create his image to make himself more acceptable to blacks.

The crossover experiences of Hendrix and Stone were replayed in the jazz community, with Miles Davis following Hendrix's example and Herbie Hancock that of Sly Stone.

Davis learned about Hendrix's music through singer Betty Mabry, who became Davis's wife in 1968. Mabry, who performs under the name Betty Davis, was acquainted with Hendrix. Hendrix wanted to meet the trumpeter to learn more about jazz. Subsequently the two became friends. Their friendship continued until the guitarist's death, even after Davis learned that Mabry and Hendrix were having an affair. The trumpeter and guitarist made plans to record, but Hendrix died before the two musicians could meet in a studio.

Hendrix had a strong influence on Davis. Davis stopped wearing suits after becoming friends with the guitarist and began wearing the flowing garments favored by Hendrix. He bought clothes from the same designers Hendrix liked and had his hair styled by Hendrix's hairdresser. Whether Hendrix exerted much of a musical influence is an open question. Davis's music bears scant resemblance to Hendrix's. There are no Miles Davis compositions that in any way sound like Jimi Hendrix's, no Miles Davis solos containing Jimi Hendrix riffs. But bassist Dave Holland, who played with both musicians, believes that Hendrix had a strong musical influence on the trumpeter.[6] Davis himself wrote that he and Hendrix exchanged musical ideas.

With the help of Columbia Records, Davis went after Hendrix's young white audience. To reach them, Davis performed at the Fillmore and other large halls and arenas that usually featured top rock bands. His group appeared on the same bill as such rock headliners as Laura Nyro, Neil Young, the Band, the Grateful Dead, and Steve Miller. Although at first the audiences at these concerts were dumbfounded by the abstract instrumental music with its lengthy improvisations, eventually they were won over. The records were packaged to present the trumpeter as an ally of the rock audience who shared their vision of racial harmony. *Bitches Brew*'s cover art portrayed a black head on the front cover, a white one on the back, and black and white hands intertwined over the record jacket's spine.

Like Hendrix, Davis was attacked for associating too closely with whites. Saxophonist Eddie Harris berated Davis for having a "new white image" and for developing white talent that would take jobs away from black musicians. *Jet,* an African-American magazine, criticized Davis for lowering his dignity by accepting the opening act slot to rock acts.[7]

After Hendrix's death, Davis realized that if he continued recording albums like *Bitches Brew* he, like Hendrix, would never gain a large black audience. Davis turned to Sly Stone and James Brown for inspiration. Davis wrote in his autobiography:

> It was with *On the Corner* and *Big Fun* that I really made an effort to get my music over to young black people. They are the ones who buy records and come to concerts, and I had started thinking about building a new audience for the future. I already had gotten a lot of young white people coming to my concerts after *Bitches Brew* and so I thought it would be good if I could get all these young people together listening to my music and digging the groove.[8]

After the 1970s Davis repeatedly spoke of his strong desire to reach black audiences. In an interview for *Melody Maker,* Davis stated: "I don't care who buys the records as long as they get to the black people, so I will be remembered."[9]

Although Davis worked hard at achieving a sound that had black appeal, several obstacles prevented his success. The music industry had not yet discovered that fusion had a potentially huge black audience. According to Davis, Columbia Records treated *On the Corner* "just like any other jazz album and advertised it that way, pushed it on the jazz stations."[10] Since young blacks tuned in to rhythm-and-blues and rock stations, they didn't hear it.

Davis had difficulties finding the right musicians. When Davis decided to "give up the funk," most of his band members had one foot in the avant-garde. During Davis's solos they played funk; afterward they played in an abstract vein. They were new to funk and electric instruments. Pianist Keith Jarrett disliked playing electric keyboards, and bassists Dave Holland and Ron Carter preferred the acoustic bass to the electric bass guitar.

For the rest of his life, Davis hired few jazz musicians, except if they enjoyed playing funk all night. Holland left Davis in 1970 to play avant-garde jazz, and Davis replaced him with electric bassist Michael Henderson. Henderson, who was playing in Stevie Wonder's band before joining Davis, was the first non-jazz sideman Davis had hired. Drummer Jack De-Johnette left in 1971, also over musical differences. After a series of drummers floated in and out of the band, Al Foster took over the drummer's chair. Although Foster was a jazz drummer, he was prepared to follow Davis's musical direction.

Even after Davis had put together a band of musicians who knew the funk idiom and enjoyed playing it, his own musical sophistication got in the way of fulfilling his desire (in biographer Ian Carr's words) to "be accepted by black audiences on the same terms as the Temptations."[11] Davis's new sound was funk driven by a Stockhausen-derived avant-garde sensibility.

> Through Stockhausen I understood music as a process of elimination and addition. Like "yes" only means something after you have said "no." I was experimenting a lot, for example, telling a band to play rhythm and hold it and not react to what was going on; let me do the reacting. In a way I was becoming the lead singer in my band, and I felt that I had earned that right. The critics were getting on my nerves, saying that I had lost it, that I wanted to be young, that I didn't know what I was doing, that I wanted to be like Jimi Hendrix, or Sly Stone, or James Brown.[12]

With his music creating a dissonant gouache of funk bass lines, electronics, trumpet splatters, percussion, blues guitar, and organ note clusters, Davis was clearly no ordinary musician, and the black audiences looking for simple funk did not buy his records.

To Davis's dismay, they turned instead to his longtime pianist, Herbie Hancock, whose interests in funk were triggered by Sly Stone's music. Herbie Hancock had Stone's gift of appealing to both whites and blacks. *Head Hunters,* with its integration of funk rhythms, call-and-response rhythmic layering, and jazz improvisations, became the best-selling jazz record ever, outselling several times over Davis's best-selling album, *Bitches Brew.*

After recording several chart-breaking funk-oriented records, Hancock helped start V.S.O.P. (Very Superior Old Pale, the name given to high-grade brandy), an acoustic jazz group devoted largely to the musical style of the Miles Davis Quintet of the 1960s. Its core members included Ron Carter and Tony Williams, Hancock's colleagues in the Miles Davis Quintet. Wayne Shorter, another Miles Davis Quintet member, played in the first V.S.O.P. tour along with trumpeter Freddie Hubbard. Miles Davis himself had lost interest in playing anything but his most current music.

V.S.O.P. provided the next generation of jazz musicians after fusion with a model of a musically and financially successful acoustic jazz group. Wynton Marsalis, leader of the movement to bring jazz back to its acoustic roots, performed with V.S.O.P when his career was just getting off the ground. Around the same time Hancock produced Marsalis's first record.

Although Marsalis and Hancock related well musically, they had opposing views on the state of black culture, as a 1984 interview made clear.

Marsalis believed that black culture was being diluted by white imitators of black music and black behavior, and by blacks who modeled themselves on these whites. Real black music was being buried under the weight of crossover rock.[13]

Hancock, unlike Marsalis, had faith in the continuity of black culture in the face of assimilation:

> I understand what you mean about a certain type of groove, like this is the real R&B, and so forth. But I can't agree that there's only one way we're supposed to be playing. I have faith in the strength in the black contribution to music, and that strength is always going back to the groove, anyway. After a while certain things get weeded out. And the music begins to evolve again.[14]

He saw nothing wrong with black musicians who chose to play rock instead of funk:

> It doesn't bother me one bit that you hear more rock and roll in black players, unless it's just not good. The idea of doing rock and roll that comes out of Led Zeppelin doesn't bother me. I understand it's third-hand information that came from black people to begin with, but if a guy likes it, play it.[15]

Less than five years after the Hancock-Marsalis interview, crossover was edged out by rap. Michael Jackson and Prince, the leading crossover stars of the 1980s, lost favor with many African Americans for crossing over too far, according to Nelson George:

> The two greatest black stars of the decade, Michael Jackson and Prince, ran fast and far both from blackness and conventional images of male sexuality. . . . Michael Jackson's nose job, often ill-conceived makeup, and artificially curled hair is, in the eyes of many blacks, a denial of his color that constitutes an act of racial treason. Add to that a disquieting androgyny and you have an alarmingly un-black, unmasculine figure as the most popular man in America.
>
> Prince is similarly troublesome. Where Jackson's androgyny was like that of an innocently unaware baby, Prince preached sex as salvation in explicit and often clumsy terms. . . . No black entertainer since Little Richard had toyed with the heterosexual sensibilities of black America so brazenly.
>
> Prince's most irksome trait was that, like Jackson, he aided those who saw blackness as a hindrance in the commercial marketplace by running away from it. Unlike the many black stars who altered their face to please "the mass market," Prince didn't have to; his features suggested he was a product of the interracial marriages so popular in Minneapolis. But he really wasn't. Both his parents were black. Yet in the quasi-autobiographical film *Purple Rain,* Prince presented his mother as white, a "crossover" marketing strategy as unnecessary as Jackson's tiresome claims to "universality."[16]

A new generation of jazz musicians and fans shared Marsalis's concern with purity. Hard bop and 1960s-style Miles Davis music came back into fashion. These neoconservatives equated fusion with artistic and racial compromise. Neoconservatives were on a mission to preserve jazz as the official African-American high art. They led mostly all-black groups, recruiting young African-American musicians to ensure that blacks were the music's keepers. Saxophonist James Carter remarked in a recent *Jazz Times* article on racism: "It's really about us being able to deal with our own music. To preserve the art amongst the rank of our people. It's my own inclination to deal with my own people, to make sure there's always representation towards them."[17]

There is another musical community operating in the fringe borders of jazz, classical music, and punk that is beyond the scope of this book. This world, occupied by non-categorizable musicians with a jazz background or merely a strong interest in jazz, is considerably more integrated and racially harmonious than mainstream jazz. Henry Threadgill, Don Byron, Bern Nix, and other black musicians who play in Manhattan's downtown arts scene have all led integrated groups, as have several prominent white musicians.

But outside of these fringe areas, today's jazz community is once again racially polarized, with few integrated big-name bands. Young white musicians tend to play in a wide variety of styles, while young black musicians concentrate on the new, bebop-oriented mainstream jazz.

Saxophonist Dave Liebman believes that the jazz community is segregated not because of racial animosity but because people tend to play with their own kind, and follow in the same musical directions as others of their race. Blacks go into mainstream jazz because of Marsalis's success. Liebman believes they excel over white musicians in this area, and offers the following explanation:

> If you look into playing bebop, more black cats will be playing bebop-oriented music than white guys because whites have more opportunities and because of background. . . . Black rhythm sections are more interested in general in playing straight-ahead jazz. The more you do it the better you are at it. That's why black guys swing more; they're more interested in it.[18]

The history of jazz has already experienced several swings between periods of assimilation and racial self-sufficiency, and there is no reason to believe it won't swing once again in the direction of assimilation. The neoconservatives' desire to establish a separate black identity will eventually run its course, and African-American jazz musicians will once again want to experiment with non-black influences and develop artistic partnerships with whites.

Racial Identity and Three Lives

Good bassists are in demand by a variety of artists. If they can read as well as swing, they play everything from rock to symphonies. For many musicians the experience of working with people of different races, economic backgrounds, and sexual orientations is a lost opportunity. They stick to the music at hand and pay scant attention to anything else. But for bassist John Loehrke, playing with musicians from all types of backgrounds has enriched his life and made him attentive to the impact of race in jazz. After playing around Detroit he moved to New York City in the 1970s, where he currently resides. He has performed with a number of prominent jazz and cabaret artists including Chet Baker, Oliver Lake, Henry Butler, Dakota Staton, Margaret Whiting, Pony Poindexter, Horace Parlan, Lee Konitz, and Karen Akers in addition to show and symphonic work.

CG: Do you think the racial climate in jazz is different now than it was when you started playing?

JL: Absolutely. It's much worse. In the 1970s I'd be playing in these after-hours clubs in Harlem and the Upper West Side that were 75 percent black, 25 percent white. And it was very cool. A lot of the musicians had adopted African and Islamic names and wore dashikis. But they were very warm toward white musicians. It was very friendly in spite of all that black nationalism. There was this underlying belief in working things out, in the possibility of things leading to a better society. I think today people have no hope in there being a better society. It's much more cynical now. You know, this is a gross generalization. There are always exceptions. But I think there is much more hostility toward whites. I know a white guitarist who has been working in organ groups in Harlem for years and years. Only in the last couple of years has he started getting hostility from people. It just breaks my heart to see this happening.

I was in Bradley's to hear Tommy Flanagan and there was this up-and-coming young black saxophonist there. He came in and threw his coat down on the piano. The bartender comes up and asks, "What would you like to drink?" It was a white bartender and the saxophonist just went *out* on the guy. He says, "I don't have to drink! What are you talking about? You wouldn't even *have* this place if it weren't for *us*. This is *our* music." This type of hostile shit. There's a lot of hostility, a lot of problems compared to what it used to be.

CG: I'd like to get your response to a statement Ornette Coleman made in the 1960s:

> I think black people in America have a superior sense when it comes to expressing their own convictions through music. Most whites tend to think that it's below their dignity to just show suffering and just show any other meaning that has to do with feeling and not technique or analysis or whatever you call it. And this to me is why the black man has developed in the field of music that the white man calls jazz. And basically, I think that word, the sense of that word, is used to describe music that the white man feels is really inferior.[1]

JL: I think that's basically nonsense. Black musicians use that word "jazz" all the time, especially older ones. I've heard Milt Hinton talk about "jazz." And it's strange hearing Ornette Coleman talk about white musicians in this way, since he has several whites in his band now, and has had whites in his groups since the beginning of his career. So what's he talking about? Jazz is obviously black, and most of its innovators and geniuses have been black. But not *all* of them. You couldn't write a history of the piano without talking about Bill Evans. You couldn't write a history of the bass without writing about Scott LaFaro or Charlie Haden. To me, Coleman's statement is just wrong. It also shows a lack of understanding of white cultural forms. A lot of people who are brought up ignorant of black musical expression don't really know what it is when they hear it, and don't know what black people are doing when they do it. In the same way, maybe Ornette is not really hip to what Pablo Casals is doing when he plays the cello, or what Hank Williams is doing when he sings because it comes from a different set of aesthetics, a different cultural background than Ornette's own. Any time you say any race has an inside track on any means of expression, any road to beauty, you're on very dangerous ground. I take a lot of offense to that. I think it's really silly.

CG: But why dangerous?

JL: Because it leads to notions of racial superiority, which leads to notions of racial *inferiority*. You can't have one without the other. Now we're talking about slavery and ovens, and shit like that. I mean, really, I think it's that serious.

CG: Do you think that when you're playing jazz, you have almost like a switch in your head, like, "Now I'm playing black music?"

JL: I don't think there's that much difference—especially as a bassist. There's not that much difference between what the bass does in a Brandenburg Concerto and what the bass does in a 12-bar blues: It outlines harmonies and supplies a rhythmic pulse. And, no, I don't have a switch in my head. Generally speaking, most of the musicians I really love to play with or listen to are black. I don't consciously think of it as being black music. Any time you play any kind of music there's a certain aesthetic that makes the music beautiful.

A lot of these of the avant-garde musicians like Ornette actually employed more musical techniques and attitudes associated with white music, things like the dominance of tone color, than more mainstream jazz musicians do.

CG: When you said "white music" now you meant classical music?

JL: I guess that's what I mean—European music.

CG: It's really weird to slip in and out of calling something "white music" and then thinking, is that a different body of music than black music? I think when we're talking about black music it's almost an ethnic-type thing. But when we talk about white music it starts to be a little confusing. We think of white as a skin color rather than as an ethnicity and distinguish between, say, flamenco, classical music, and Hungarian folk music—all music performed by more or less white-skinned people. Yet almost without hesitation we call all the varieties of music performed by more or less black-skinned people "black music."

JL: I have a friend in the neighborhood who's a violist. He's black, and he's a *bitch*, he's very, very good. He's been through the music schools—Peabody—and he's played with a lot of B- and C-level symphony orchestras. A couple of years ago there was an opening for a violist in the New York Philharmonic. So I said, "Carl, why don't you audition, man? You don't have to leave town. Send in a tape. They'll accept you for the audition anyway. See what happens." He said, "Oh, no, I would never even bother. "Why not?" I asked. As an answer he pulls the skin on his cheeks. I said," You're kidding me!" He knows New York has one black guy and Boston has an oboe player but he's so light-skinned that you can't . . . He went down the list of the major orchestras and named [them]: "Chicago's got one, Philadelphia's got two"—whatever. And I asked, "Why do you think this is?" and we talked about it. Now, the auditions are behind screens *until* you get to the end. And then for the final thing they look at you. And his feeling—and I agree with him—is that although they're not going to say, "We don't want no niggers in this orchestra," the problem is that by the time you get to the finalists in an audition at, say, the Chicago Symphony, the last five musicians are motherfuckers. They sound fantastic. They play like *angels*. You don't even get into the audition unless you're a *monster*. Anyway, by the time they weed them out through a few listenings behind the screens they look at them. They've got, say, four or five violists who are fuckin' fantastic. Best in the world, right. So what it comes down to is subtle psychological things. And somehow, somehow, their image of a Baltimore Symphony violist is not a black guy. They're not deliberately being racist, but for some reason they look at a black guy and in some subtle way in the back of their brain they think that's not what a Baltimore Symphony Orchestra violist looks like.

Obviously, there are not that many black musicians who are qualified to be in an orchestra because many of them are not following that line of work. But certainly there are enough for every symphony orchestra to have a handful if it were racially blind. So obviously there is some kind of racism at work. That's the only plausible explanation.

And in jazz music it's the same way. I think some jazz musicians say, "We don't want any white guys in the band."

CG: Black or white musicians?

JL: Well, I think a lot of white musicians actually would rather have a black guy, too. White drummers suffer with this stereotyping more than musicians who play other instruments. Somehow the image of a great jazz drummer is a black guy. Maybe this is why there are very few white drummers who have risen to any level of prominence in the last few years. White bassists have a much easier time being accepted in jazz. People have an image in their minds that a great bass player can be white. There are a lot of white bassists that have risen to the apex of the profession and have been very successful—and playing with black guys, like Dave Holland, Charlie Haden, George Mraz, Miroslav, Dennis Irwin, Cameron Brown. It doesn't really make any sense that the bass is considered OK for whites, but not the drums. The bass is as much a rhythm section instrument as the drums. It does that primitive beat kind of thing like the drums. It isn't an intellectual head instrument like piano, saxophone, or guitar. Yet because the bass is associated with being a symphony orchestra instrument, people can see a white bassist in a jazz group more easily than any other instrumentalist. That kind of racism really pervades our society, and it's not something you can legislate out. It isn't just music. I think that's a really big problem and it makes me pessimistic about the future of the nation.

I have a cool story I've got to tell you. When we were talking about this I remembered it. I had a gig with Mike Longo, a white pianist who played with Dizzy Gillespie for years and years. We were talking about racism in jazz. One time they were in New Orleans. He was the only white guy in Dizzy Gillespie's band. There was this woman who was painting the band, and she wouldn't let any of them look at the painting. All week long she was sketching. Finally when the gig was over she showed them the painting. She left him out, everybody was in the painting except for Mike. Isn't that something?

I remember when I was in Germany playing with saxophonist Pony Poindexter, who is best known for playing with Lambert, Hendricks, and Ross. I was the only white guy in his quartet. A couple of times I found out after the fact that the promoter was apologizing that there was a white guy in the band. Some foreigners love watching jazz because it's exotic: Let's watch the niggers go wild, do their tribal bullshit.

CG: What do you think of British blues musician John Mayall's take on black music? "What is *black* music? Music isn't black or white. There's no such thing as *black* music."[2]

JL: That's obviously not true. There are certain forms that have come from the Afro-American community. There are certain musical aesthetics, certain musical forms, certain ways of approaching music that are fundamentally different. I think ultimately any art form touches on universal human truths. That's why we cherish and love it. But this *is* black music. There's no getting around it. It's ridiculous to deny that.

I have a friend who took drum lessons from Elvin Jones. Here's what the lessons were. He went to the lesson and Elvin said, "Let's hear you play." He starts to play. Elvin gets out a piece of music paper and starts writing on it, walks over and puts it on a music stand. "Let's hear you play this." He's written out something in correct drum notation, a polyrhythmic pattern. So my friend starts playing it, works at it awhile. Elvin says, "No, no." Motions him off. "Here's how it goes." He sits down at the drumset, starts playing the figure. "And then you can do this," and he starts adding to it, "And then you can do this," and then he's *off.* He plays for twenty-five minutes straight, drenched with sweat. Hands him the drumsticks and says, "Work on this for next week." OK. That's the lesson. My friend comes back the next week. He has practiced the figure a million different ways. He starts playing the figure and then improvises on it the way Elvin did. And while he's doing it Elvin is getting out a piece of music paper and writes on it. Elvin stops him, puts the paper on the stand. It's the same fuckin' thing. And my friend says, "This is what you gave me last week!" "No. This is how it goes." And the same thing happened. That's either Elvin ripping him off or a really great drum lesson depending on how you look at it. But it's a different way of communication. It's a different way of imparting knowledge than the guys who went to the Berklee School of Music who insist that this is the way that you do this, this is the way that you do that. This is how you run this chord change and this is what happens. It's a different attitude toward what being a musician is and what playing music is. It's that oral tradition that is quintessentially black. B. B. King didn't learn the way he plays—*John Mayall* didn't learn the way he plays—by taking lessons from somebody and having a book on a music stand, using a metronome. And that's one of the differences between black and white music. Black music comes from that oral tradition. Which means that rhythm is a more primary interest because you can't really teach someone rhythm. You can cover a blackboard with harmonies, orchestration, and so on. But how can you teach someone the difference between one *two* three *four* and having it swing, and one *two* three *four* and having it not. That's a lot of what makes this music black music as opposed to white music.

CG: Now you have all the books out.

JL: I use them too.

CG: But when we started being interested in playing there were a couple of books out. Most of them were *shit.*

JL: They were awful, they were completely wrong—John Mehegan, all this weird shit. When I was in college—University of Michigan, which now has a jazz program—they had a jazz band that met one night a week, and they hired a local guy named Louis Smith who had played with Horace Silver and had some recordings on Blue Note in the '50s. And that was it for jazz. He would write out charts for the band, and then guys would try to figure out how to play solos. There was no instruction at all how to do it. It's like yin and yang: Some things are good and some things are bad about how jazz is learned and taught now.

CG: This is Art Blakey from the 1970s: "The only way the Caucasian musician can swing is from a rope."[3] Do white jazz musicians as a whole play a different sort of music than black musicians play?

JL: Most white musicians don't swing as much as most black musicians. But Art Blakey's statement is obviously wrong. It's simply not true. Mel Lewis is a great example of a white musician who could swing. Zoot Sims had more swing than most of the tenor players who ever played with Blakey. In his last band he had a white piano player, Benny Green. For several years he had trumpeter Valery Ponomarev. If these guys don't swing, why was he stupid enough to hire them?

CG: So why did he make that statement?

JL: I think a lot of it is out of hostility. A lot of these black guys of that generation they feel—probably correctly—that they would have made more money if they had been white, that the business end of the music favored white musicians, that white musicians got breaks they didn't get. It's the general racism of our society, the million racial slights and humiliations that black people have to endure that makes many of them bitter and hostile toward white people in general. It isn't all about music. It's about people's lives.

On the whole, most black musicians seem to feel swing deeper and swing harder than white musicians. By swing I mean generating that deep pulse. I think swing is more important to black musicians. It has to do with the way they're brought up—the oral tradition. If you really listen to music, rhythm is more prominent in what comes into your ears than if you think about music intellectually and read it on blackboards and in books. You listen to a Beethoven symphony and the rhythmic component is much more prominent how it affects you than it is if you study it in theory class and you look at it written out in notation.

Some of the great white musicians, you don't think of their rhythm as the main thing they bring to the show. Bill Evans, Lee Konitz, Gil Evans. Anthony Braxton is often accused of being a white-sounding guy. What they mean by that is that there is a certain intellectualism to his playing. Given the dominance in his mind of a note choice or an exact note placement to a microlevel that makes it swing or not, the note choice is going to be a little higher in his consciousness than exactly how he plays it.

CG: You must have noticed that it's a pejorative: "He sounds too white."

JL: Exactly. It is a pejorative. What they mean by "too white" is not being idiomatic to the jazz style. I myself think in those terms. Usually what I mean is that it sounds *tight*. There is a looseness in the black aesthetic. The beat is wider and deeper in a black band like Duke Ellington's than, say, in Buddy Rich's band, where the beat is in a razor-sharp place. In a white blues band it's: *bn-ti chk-i bn-ti chk-i.* In a black blues band it's got more of a rolling sound: *zoo-ka za-ka zoo-ka za-ka.* That's why a lot of this rap music sounds very white too me. It's very sharp, there's no depth to the beat and a lot of the aesthetic seems to be artificial. It's not natural, flowing-out-of-the-dance rhythms the way jazz music is. The way Elvin Jones plays the drums, for example. A lot of what makes it sound so good is that even though he's doing a lot of complex things, they physically flow in a natural way from his body. A white drummer trying to play complex rhythms might intellectually come up with a whole bunch of complex shit and then figure out a way to play it. You get the feeling listening to Elvin Jones that it's something that flows naturally out of a bio-mechanically fluid thing. As he explored the limits of being able to do this little dance with his drums, then it became more complex—as opposed to dreaming up a bunch of complex shit and then figuring out how to play it.

I think that jazz is getting less black now. It's taught in universities, people can buy books by people like Charley Gerard. As this is happening, it's leading to an increasingly closed-minded concept of the music. This kind of rigid idea: "In a *real* jazz band the bass plays down low and plays mostly quarter-notes and walks"—not running over the bass and playing counter-rhythms the way Gary Peacock did with Albert Ayler. This retro hard bop attitude: "Jazz is *this*. In a jazz band the drummer does mainly *boom chucka doom chucka doom chucka doom.*" As jazz has become more academic it's losing a lot of its black aesthetic—ironically, at the same time that these people are becoming more conscious of it being black music.

A lot more intellectualism has crept into the black bands. A lot of Ornette's music now is very European, very intellectual. It's heavy on theory and heavy on ideas. That's one of the reasons these avant-garde guys work in Europe so much. Europeans can hear certain elements they can relate to in their background—these grand romantic gestures. I listen to Steve Coleman, Greg Osby and those guys; there's a lot of very white shit that they do. There's a lot of very intellectual, worked-out, self-conscious things that they do. You listen to the Art Ensemble of Chicago, on the other hand. Their music is also complex, but you get the feeling that it evolved slowly over time. They would hear something and then try to incorporate it, instead of working something out intellectually and then try to make it heard.

Here's another story. I played this gig with a guitar player out on Long Island. He was a white guy who had played with James Brown. There were two white guys in the band at the time. When they first joined the band they were out on stage jamming, and they were trying to play as funky as they could. And James Brown says, "Hey, you guys. I don't want you to play that shit. Why do you think I hire you white boys? I want to hear some of those *College Chords*! That's why I hire you white guys."

I have known both John Loehrke and Alva Nelson, the next interview subject, for over fifteen years. While John is a white Midwesterner, Alva is an African American from Houston, Texas. Since they knew me well they could speak on a familiar level on a subject that strangers would be hesitant to address. Both of these superb musicians have interacted with a wide variety of musicians from jazz, classical music, and popular music, experiences that have given them an enhanced view of culture and race. In Houston Alva studied classical flute with Jan Cole at the same time he was playing piano with blues musician Lightnin' Hopkins and tenor players Don Wilkerson and Arnett Cobb. Alva has performed throughout the United States, Japan, and Europe with Kirk Whalum, Hubert Laws, David "Fathead" Newman, Billy Harper, and Fred Ho and the Afro-Asian Ensemble, and recorded with Lonnie Plaxico, Robin Eubanks, and the Boys Choir of Harlem. *African Suite,* his debut solo piano CD, is a collage of improvisatory styles exploring the synthesis of traditional African rhythms and contemporary piano technique. In it he pays tribute to the African-American holiday Kwanzaa, with several segments dedicated to the seven principles Nguzo Saba.

AN: Jazz is the musical manifestation of the African-American experience. Distinctly African-American. It's not America's art form. You can't take the African out, and that's being done. I've been studying African drums and I want to go back to the so-called roots. [Alva objects to the notion that jazz is a combination of African rhythms and European harmony.] What is that saying? Africa had no harmony? It's not even a question of what's best to call it—African-American or American. Culturally you can't take the African out, even though it's distinctly African-

American. I think that causes problems with a lot of people in terms of cross-cultural whatever. Everybody knows Phil Woods can play. He can play music, he can play the saxophone and he can play jazz, but you can't compare him to Charlie Parker. Charlie Parker is an icon. He's the exception, not the rule. Duke Ellington was an icon. Louis Armstrong *was* jazz. It doesn't make Africans better at anything. So we've overachieved in music and overachieved in athletics. Well, that's all we had. I don't have a problem being American. I went to white colleges, and I recognize what I missed by not going to black colleges, but I made my choice. I was just as interested in Western European music as the next guy, and it's still wonderful music to me. I'm not anti-anything. I'm just very much pro-artist, very much pro-African. But I don't know everything I need to know about Africa, and I've never been there, so I try to put it in perspective.

CG: I want to get your response to this statement by Art Blakey: "Our music has nothing to do with Africa. African music is entirely different, and the Africans are much more advanced than we are rhythmically, though we're more advanced harmonically."[4] He also said that "to put Africa and jazz together, well, that's the biggest lie ever told."[5]

AN: With due respect to Art Blakey, everybody on this planet has to do with Africa. Like it or not, that is where humankind began. As far as we know. Until Dr. Leakey or some other anthropologist comes up with some other theory or finds some other bones wherever.

CG: You're talking about that we're all derived from a common source. Blakey's talking about African-American music in its wide variety in relation to African music of 300 years ago and perhaps as it's happening now. This is an interesting statement to come from the first modern jazz musician to really delve into African music, to learn about it and have African musicians in his band. Yet he makes a statement: "Our music has nothing to do with Africa. African music is entirely different." He's actually annoyed that people say that jazz is African music. The context of the quotation is that he thinks that African Americans are not getting credit where credit is due, that this is something that was made in America and is dissimilar from African music.

AN: OK. We're still talking about apples and oranges. Forget music. Before you get to music you have to have a culture. Music is a product of a culture. It comes about perhaps through oppression, or through the celebratory aspects of whatever culture you're in. Jazz is a product of the African's experience on American shores. Sure, it's different now, because we're in a different place. We were brought to America and the slave masters took the drums from us so the music could not evolve the same way as it would have evolved when certain Africans went back to Liberia and formed that country. Before you can even talk about the nature, the very soul of the music, you need to talk about who created it and why. I would hesitate to say that *this* has nothing to do with *that*.

What Blakey said was wrong. He's entitled to his opinion, and I'm trying to be open-minded. What he said is a closed statement. Everything has to do with something! And if you want the music to grow you need to look at it from another perspective. You have to know the evolution of it. That's all we do in life—I don't care if it's a musician or a research scientist or a politician. If you want to know where you're going, you have to know where you've been.

CG: Is there a connection between your interest in African music and identifying with a worldwide African culture?

AN: That's easy. It's always connected. I think it has a lot to do with my growth and development. But I am still fond of the symphonic form and my instrument, the piano, is not what you'd call an African instrument. In getting to know who I am, where I'm from, then I decided to look at it to find out who I am as an artist—as an African-American artist because it's all one thing. But it doesn't keep me from enjoying all the other music that has come out of America.

CG: You said before that they're taking the African out of African-American.

AN: When you say "American" you don't think black. I don't care who you are. Now, I don't have a problem honoring the flag, the national anthem and all that. I'm talking about what I am, and me being proud of something that came out of my heritage.

CG: This is kind of what Blakey was saying in a sense. He was saying, why does does it always have to be American or African, but not African-American? In other words, giving credit where it's due. They'll say anything (whoever "they" are) to avoid giving credit to African Americans.

AN: And that makes me take another look at his quote, because I do agree with him on that.

A lot of the music was based on oppressive conditions. But if you study Eastern European music you'll see the same thing! The same oppressed conditions. You'll find the same thing in China in respect to the Japanese mistreatment of the Chinese people earlier in this century.

CG: Was there a difference as a musician being down there [in Texas] and being up here [New York]?

AN: I would say that the wonderful thing about New York is that it really is kind of like the land of opportunity. I really believe that if you can do something—whatever that something is—you will get your chance. Now, I may or may not be at a disadvantage because I'm black or whatever. But, see, I've never looked at it like that. You'll never hear me say, "It's because I'm black," because I don't even acknowledge that, because I don't have a problem with it. I went to school with black people, I went to school with white people. I knew when I was at Sam Houston State University it was a racist institution. At that point I was all into my militant thing. I would tell a student or teacher, "I'm here to get an education." And I graduated *cum laude*. I'm not going to be a party to the nonsense I see happening. Now, I got an opportunity to do a lot of things there just because I was interested in getting an education. I was oblivious to all the overt racism that was going on around me. You have to get to a point inside yourself where it doesn't faze you. First of all, I'm not afraid of it. I mean, nobody's going to hurt me. It's not like it was fifty years ago. I did not disrespect the president of the school when I had an interview with him, I didn't disrespect the head of the music department, I didn't disrespect my teachers. I didn't even disrespect the highway patrolman who pulled me over. I don't care if it was for no reason. The kind of things that you hear couldn't happen to me. Rodney King—that could not have happened to me, because I'm protected; I'm above that. I'm not saying that Rodney King is not. . . . Don't get the wrong idea. It has to do with your environment, and who is your teacher.

I had a wonderful high school band director, Conrad Johnson, who taught me everything I needed to know in terms of how to deal with people. I've dealt with white people who are racist and black people who are racist. Because I'm black I understand why the black person does it. I may not understand why the white person does it. What I do is put myself in the situation where I can learn why. So what I did when I was at Sam Houston State University, I went to see my friend's grandmother—a ninety-year-old white woman in Huntsville, Texas. We just sat around and talked.

Everybody's not a racist, even though the term doesn't mean anything—it's one of those sound bites. I'm pro-black. I'm so pro-black it's disgusting. But *we* [Alva and the author] don't have a problem; we've never had a problem. Why? Because we're linked artistically? It had to be more than that. Is it because of our academic pursuits? I don't know. The arts have always transcended those negative things that mankind has come up—like racism. I don't care how far back you go. So that's the beauty in it. So it's up to us artists to teach the politicians—or the would-be politicians—the business persons, the clergy, academia, and whomever. Because we end up being exposed to a lot more than the average person. I haven't been around the world but I've been half-way around the world. It's because I look at music as a profession and how when I'm in some foreign country where I can't communicate, I can still communicate through something that I'm giving. That's how I look at it, as giving of something.

I'll go back to racism in terms of New York and Texas. This is America. It ain't that different anywhere you go in this country. It ain't that different. In New York there's tolerance because of sheer numbers. It has to do with the design of the city, even the subway system. You're never going to go to a place where you're not going to see any black people, any white people, any Asian people, any Latinos. They're going to be there. They might not live there but they're there. Once you grow up seeing all these people, then your acceptance of them, your tolerance of them—however different the culture is—becomes OK.

CG: Have you experienced an anti-black reaction in jazz or in other forms of music?

AN: I have not led a sheltered life. But I cannot remember any situation musically—and most of it has been in music education—where an opportunity eluded me because of race. It may have happened. Even if it did happen right in my face, I might have been naïve. Once I recognize that this ain't going to happen I'm moving on to the next thing. That's the only way I was taught. I will say this. As a flute player in Houston, after a while I was pretty good, when I began grad school. I got a letter to go down and audition for the Summer Symphony. I didn't do it because I got a grant and I went to California. I came back and I was going to audition. I called my teacher, Jan Cole, and another gentleman. I would say that I probably would have gotten that job. Through the grapevine it got around that I was a black man.

CG: And that stopped it.

AN: Well, I don't know because the process never really began. I got a formal invite to come down and audition. The audition music—I knew all of it, and I may have been recommended by Jan Cole. As far as I'm concerned I would have enjoyed that job. I felt bad that I didn't get to play, but after it was over it was over.

Now, I know people, friends of mine, who in my opinion have held themselves back from just looking at: "Everything bad that happens is because I'm black. I can't do this, I can't do that." Well, I worked with white society bands when I was there. Not a lot, but I did it. I've worked with a whole bunch of white people. I worked in Spring Branch school district, I worked in Aldine and Deer Park giving private lessons. Having a degree from Sam Houston State didn't hurt, and knowing people who went on to teach at those schools didn't hurt. But my point is that I needed to do what I needed to do when I was living there. Those were the opportunities that were afforded me.

CG: Makanda K. McIntyre, founder and chair of the American music department at SUNY at Old Westbury, wrote a letter to the editor of *Jazz Times* in which he states that after several decades of teaching he believes that blacks respond to rhythm differently than whites do. He notes a parallel with basketball: "In the old days, the object was simply to put the ball in the basket. Now, it's about the moves you make along the way. Black musicians have moves in their music—within the pulse."[6]

AL: We *do* do things in *our* rhythm. We walk a certain way. It's not better or worse—it's just *how . . . we . . . walk*. Because we're walking to our music. Now, to say that a white musician, or white performer, or white person does not have rhythm, it's an individual thing. You cannot say that white people don't have rhythm the way they dance. If they're dancing to [black] music and they're not seeped in the culture, why would they be able to? At least they're sharing, though.

I never learned to dance. So when we got to a party I'd probably dance like a white guy. I'd do the "mashed potatoes" like James Brown and just embarrass everybody.

I met the poet Ron Welburn when our sons were friends going to the same school. I never mentioned to him that I had read the essay "The Black Aesthetic Imperative," which he contributed over two decades ago to Addison Gayle Jr.'s *The Black Aesthetic*. In fact I wasn't at all sure he was the author. Except for his extensive knowledge of jazz he seemed to have little in common with the hot-headed black nationalist who wrote "The Black Aesthetic Imperative." Adding to the confusion was the fact that his name was consistently misspelled with an extra "l" throughout the Addison Gayle collection.

Ron Welburn is part American Indian. Although as a child he identified with his Indian background, by the time he graduated from high school his identification as an African American had intensified and eclipsed his Indian identity. Since the 1970s Welburn has begun to return to his Indian roots. When I met him in the early '90s, he had established and integrated his identity as a mixed-blood American Indian. At present Ron Welburn is a professor of English at the University of Massachusetts at Amherst, where he teaches Native American literature and literary criticism. He has published several volumes of poetry and his work has been widely anthologized.

Music and musicians have been a profound influence on his writing. In his entry in *Contemporary Authors*, he declared that poetry was "a means to fulfill a musicianship beyond my limited instrumental training and experience." In the poem "In a Crepuscular Mood" he describes his poetry as follows:

> I am not of the imagist school.
> I am not a symbolist.
> I am not a surrealist.
> I am not Beat.
> Music disengages my poems.
> Music disqualifies my editors, but turns on my readers.
> I am of the school of Monk.

An amateur saxophonist and composer, he co-led a jazz group while an undergraduate at Lincoln University and rehearsed the songs of freshman Gil Scott-Heron. He has had a long career as a music critic. In 1975 he was elected a fellow of the Smithsonian Institute and Music Critics Association. The following year he cofounded *The Grackle*, considered to be the first jazz magazine run by African Americans. For several years he worked at the Institute of Jazz Studies at Rutgers University.

CG: I'd like you to respond first by telling me how you felt about these statements that you made over twenty-five years ago when you were asked by Addison Gayle Jr. to contribute an essay to *The Black Aesthetic*. I'm also interested in learning if your ideas on the topics we'll be discussing—the influence of an Afro-Asian worldview, religious identity in the jazz community, and so on—have developed. "The Black Aesthetic Imperative" was an angry political statement. Its venom was directed at European culture and the encroachment of rock in jazz and it encouraged African-American musicians to keep black music within the black community, safely out of the hands of whites. You seem to have changed course since writing the essay as a young man in your twenties. In *Contemporary Authors* you describe yourself as "not very political," and the influences you listed run wildly independent of cultural boundaries, from Twain, Cicero, Levertov, the *Anthology of Negro Poets* on Folkways, Aiken, Faulkner, Eliot, William Carlos Williams, to the Congolese writer U'Tamsi. I believe that was in the mid-1980s. Finally, when I wrote you to arrange an interview, you wrote back: "The essay in Gayle's anthology won't die."

RW: Let's begin at the beginning, when I was an undergraduate from 1964–'68 at Lincoln. I had been listening to jazz in earnest for perhaps a good two and a half years. I was curious about what was going on with the music and being sort of this child of the early '60s I began to look at the issues of how, let's say, race and players are concerned. I had known that Ornette Coleman had used white musicians—Scott LaFaro and Charlie Haden. I had known that Cecil Taylor and a number of other musicians had also done this. And yet surrounding so much of the music was the rhetoric of a nationalist position. There seemed to be this contradiction of what some individuals were saying about the music and what it should be like, and what the musicians were doing. My experience over the next seven or eight years exemplified some of these very contradictions.

I'd talk to musicians when I went to New York. I made friends with Cecil Taylor, Archie Shepp, Marion Brown. I would see them on the street and introduce myself. A lot of times you're in a fishbowl when you're talking to musicians. You realize the kind of fishbowl they may be in. You have these instances where musicians are trying to get their gigs together, and sometimes they can't do those gigs because of the competition. There's a kind of annoyance if the competition comes from white musicians, especially where the people who created the musical form can't really get a chance to play the music.

One of the questions that I asked Cecil was concerning what had been said about the black musicians and black music, and the presence of white musicians in this music. I gained the formulation of the idea that there are these two perspectives: there's the rhetorical one and then there's the musical necessity. What I began to notice more was that it was people like Amiri Baraka who were in the position of playing the culture critic as nationalist, or nationalist as culture critic. And then there were the musicians. And a lot of times the twain didn't meet. I asked Cecil about Mike Mantler. He said, "My music is not that easy to perform. I'm looking for people who can play my music. Dewey Johnson has rehearsed and played my music; I've also used Mike. In a way, Dewey can get inside my music quite well. But the problem is that Dewey doesn't read very well, and a lot of my music is written. Mike Mantler reads my music very well. His interpretation may lack some things I'm looking for. If I could have a situation where Mike did the reading and Dewey did the playing that might be ideal." But he was speaking speculatively in terms of the plausibilities of the settings and so on. In a conversation I had with Archie, Archie said: "There are three trombonists I like to work with: Curtis Fuller is the fastest; Grachan Moncur III is the most melodic; Roswell Rudd is the strongest." And so he used these musicians interchangeably, and at times he used two tandem trombones.

So the question was still left to me to decide for myself. And it was unsettlingly resolved.

Now by the time we get to the writing of "The Black Aesthetic Imperative," the tenor of the music in the broadest sense—say, pop music in the United States—had begun to change. This essay expresses a frustration and a bitterness that jazz was being derailed from an economic and political standpoint by those in a position of power in music culture—not musicians—who were able to dictate a changeover. One of the things that I noticed in *Down Beat* was what Jim Stewart called a "retooling." You no longer saw advertisements for acoustic instruments. You saw advertisements for guitars and for electric pianos. There was that insistent metallic wall of sound that seemed to be encroaching and replacing the jazz sound. All the time I was trying to wrestle with such phenomenon as occurred with the bossa nova craze of 1962. It really wasn't the musicians that you could pick at because I think that Stan Getz and various others who may have been a part of that were being *used* to create a cultural and social kind of condition. I'm not quite sure how to pinpoint where the promoting of the musicians that perhaps the majority of jazz listeners can identify with, at least from a racial standpoint, is going on or if it is something else.

CG: You mean like Joe Lovano as the Great White Hope like they have in boxing.

RW: Yeah. That's the sort of thing that happens. We're talking maybe two generations ago with Stan Getz. When the bossa nova came out, it was as if they threw away everything else. It was like the child that drops that toy and goes over here to get something else.

At the time I was writing the essay in certain ways I didn't have that sophisticated a view of the process [of trends and fads]. I could see it happening, but as far as the compulsions within a cultural economy and the politics of culture there was kind of a gap [in my understanding]. My response was more toward the *effect* upon the aesthetic. I think that I recognized that jazz is still, no matter who plays it, an African-American expression or mode that develops out of a particular mindset or cultural response, or cultural activities. And it has been contributed to by—from the beginning—not only the elements of but also the peoples who represent various European cultural backgrounds, people of color and Native Americans.

I suppose I've given a capsule summary of how this essay came to be. In other respects I re-read it and shook my head and said, "Wow!" I don't know if I'd repudiate it all. It's informed by romanticism and of being in my mid-20s and looking for certain kinds of things that eventually manifested themselves in my life, that all go to make up who I am. So I take it in stride. But I think that the kinds of things that go on in this country in terms of expressive culture and cultural artifacts, particularly created by native peoples and by African Americans, stand the chance of being manipulated for the kind of financial gain that is at least disturbing. It's one thing to be a musician and try to get a gig no matter who you are and what your background is. But when the promoters come along and they make the recordings and they do this and that, and they run away with the money as they used to do, especially in the 1930s, those are disturbing. And I know that in the aftermath of seeing this essay in print and trying to look at myself, the realization was apparent that it's not the musicians—let's say, the white musicians. It's the industry that creates this certain distance between the communities of musicians and sustains it. And then the person of color says, "Where are the musicians of color?" That becomes an automatic response.

CG: In "The Black Aesthetic Imperative," you make the case for an East-West cultural split, with the West representing instability and revolutionary changes guided by a desire to "conquer the universe, not blending with it as you are, as one finds in the Eastern world." You also describe "the African homeland" as "only a part of the Afro-Asian world," suggesting that African aesthetics find their counterparts in Asian culture, and refer to "the music of the Afro-Asian world as a whole."

RW: I'm not so sure about that now. I think I used the term "Afro-Asian" because there were a few black intellectuals who were using it. I don't know whether I would use it now. I think that so much has changed in the international venues and possibilities for jazz music. Some people might call it African-American classical music, great black music. I say jazz by any other name is still jazz. And I know Max Roach doesn't like the term, but it's jazz as far as I'm concerned.

I think that what happens is there is the adoption of philosophical and metaphorical concepts [after the fact]. Jazz came about before the people who were making jazz understood anything about ragas. But then we wake up in the '50s and as Ravi Shankar and Ali Akbar Khan and others came into the States, talked with various musicians and recorded with

Bud Shank and a few others, the nature of the work gains a certain similarity [with Indian classical music] in terms of a performance ideal. But that's something that comes about later. It's not something that you can say, well, it comes from a particular Afro-Asian whatever. It's something that might be imagined, but it's not something that's directly bearing from that. Anytime that you're dealing with something like the African beginnings of jazz, it's there because it's in the imagination of the people who may have been predominant in creating it, but it's not there in terms of something going on musicologically.

In the States, the performance of music having to do with something that was believed to be, and expressed to be, African came about more from touring African groups like Olatunji, Guy Warren, and the dance groups.

CG: Jungian sentiments were popular in the '60s and '70s. In "The Black Aesthetic Imperative" you announced that "the riffs on 'Cold Sweat' evoke racial memory. . . . Timbre and sensibility come closer to Wolof traditional orchestras of xylophones, lyres, and drums." Could you talk a little bit about racial memory, whether that is something you think about particularly in terms of your American Indian background—in other words, if there is some unexplainable connection back to Africa.

RW: [Ron Welburn spoke of feeling an inexplicable identification with Virginia, which he visited annually as a child. Virginia was the land where his Cherokee ancestors lived.] There were certain images that came to my mind even before I understood what images were and had the sophistication of being a poet that gave me a sense of being in Virginia. I looked at it and I articulated it as the kind of racial memory that causes a person to remember places and perhaps having to do with childhood experiences that can't be articulated and that are perhaps in parallel realities, archetypal realities than factual, physical, tangible. Thinking of it in terms of what cannot be articulated except that you *know*.

I think I expanded this idea into something that I didn't know a damned thing about! And that is having to do with, let's say, the memory of something African. Speaking personally—and this is where the romanticism came in—I can't remember [Africa]. I always felt the connection to this country, or this space, and a connection that was older than Columbus. I always felt rooted here. This is one of the reasons I had some difficulty with some of these questions philosophically for that thirteen-, fourteen-year period. Because it was something that wouldn't go away. Everywhere I turned someone would tap me on my shoulder and ask me if I was Indian. That's part of it. But I do think that the statement [of an African racial memory] probably holds true for the possibility that there are people who recognize it and who, at least, without pretense develop a kind of thesis culturally about something known as race memory that has to do with a host of responses that are archetypal, philosophical, physical, visceral, and otherwise.

Some of the ideas were informed by what I understood as notions having to do with negritude. My interpretation was based upon the ideas of a man who was kind of a mentor to me by the name of Wilmer Lucas.[7] He lived in Brooklyn and was teaching at the New School in 1965 when some of us from Lincoln went to a conference that he had coordinated. We were instrumental in Lincoln hiring him in 1966 to teach Negro literature. He used to talk about individuals who exemplified negritude. The idea here was there was a kind of unabashed and nonconfrontational acceptance and enjoyment of oneself racially and a lack of psychological hang-ups, or debilitating social hang-ups.

CG: There was a recent exchange on the Internet newsgroup rec.music.bluenote that began when a Japanese jazz student asked the newsgroup's readers whether they knew the race of certain West Coast musicians. This simple request exploded into a discussion about the relevance of race in art. One participant claimed that art "is color-neutral" and that the tendency of many jazz people to divide the music along racial lines serves only to satisfy a political agenda. The next participant in the "thread" answered: "Would you bridle if I were to describe klezmer as 'Jewish music'? Jazz is black music (or African-American) in the same way. Doesn't say anything about who can play it better, just records the facts about who started it and what culture it's most characteristic of."[8]

RW: I agree. It's the music that would be identified as black as opposed to the matter of who plays it. Jazz music has become an international language. And given that, in a sense if you look at it in terms of a cultural continuum it is likely to ascend to a principal position over European-style classical music. If orchestras in Indonesia, Japan, and South America have been performing Beethoven and Haydn, there also are people [from those places] who have been performing jazz.

One of the things that mellowed me back in the early 1970s was that I was finding that this music had such an international reputation, and it was being adhered to, followed, and so forth on such a grand scale internationally, that the questions of race and culture—people saying that white musicians are stealing from black musicians and all this brouhaha—I won't say that they may be minimized, but the platform has changed to an international scope. This is where the fishbowl [mentality] is no longer tolerable. [Jazz] has become an international form whether anybody likes it or not. It's there; it's happening.

As I studied further the history of jazz music being performed around the world, I came to realize how profoundly glib and presumptuous we all could be about jazz and race on the domestic American scene. By this I mean that James Reese Europe's "Hellfighters" orchestra and Bennie Payton's small orchestra (with Sidney Bechet) performed in France before 1920; Sam Wooding's Chocolate Kiddies toured Berlin, Moscow and Argentina in the mid-'20s—Doc Cheatham, an Indian, was in that band. Jazz got to Japan in 1926 when relief workers took records there while they helped in the aftermath of a major earthquake. Cricket Smith, a trumpeter, went to India with a band and died there in the early '40s; Harry Lim, whom I interviewed for my dissertation, edited a jazz magazine from the Dutch East Indies in the late '30s.[9] See how we've barely gotten to the modern jazz era?

All this activity made it clearer to me that the racial issues involving jazz rest more on the onus and shoulders of promotion, production, journalism, and advertising than on the musicians outright. As a result, as I learned more about the impact of jazz on musicians in the rest of the world, the convenient paradigms for lashing out at white musicians I increasingly deemed as self-serving if not altogether superficial. The old nationalistic arguments about jazz and race, even as I'd contributed to this discourse in Gayle's anthology and on one or two other occasions, I could see being rendered to superfluity. The counter-festivals in New York during the Newport-on-New York years (say, 1972–78), the tightening of jazz-rock fusion's grip on the musical consciousness, the Creed Taylor stylings, and disco were all interesting to watch, because musicians were divided into all sorts of argumentative special-interest camps and no one was making any real money unless they played to a homogeneity of approved style. At least under the Newport auspices some closed session forums of critics from India, Chile, the States, and elsewhere led by Joachim Berendt and John McDonough convened to discuss the larger picture.

And remember, the 1970s—probably beginning in 1969 with MSP-BASF—was the decade of a virtual deluge of imported jazz albums; it occurred too fast to keep up with. I was in Syracuse in the early 1970s writing about some of this music, and my buddy Joe Bova was broadcasting it on his weekly show on the NPR affiliate. You had those musically fascinating yet financially controversial recordings by Americans touring with

Archie Shepp and others for Byg-Actuel and the America label; ECM brought numerous central and northern European musicians to the American consciousness; you had Frie Musik Production; jazz avant-garde from England; Gunter Hampel and Jeanne Lee; Enja; Jappo; Underwear. Then around 1973 or so albums by Miles and others on Nippon Columbia showed up—Miles's was the Sam Rivers edition of his '60s quintet; the Three Blind Mice label also came from Japan and several musicians from there, like Chin Suzuki, Hondo, and others, Ryo Kawasaki, toured and settled here. The Italians issued Red Records, and then Black Saint and Soul Note, albeit featuring Americans. Then Jason Hwang and other musicians from the Chinatowns of New York and San Francisco played Studio Rivbea. There was so much activity, so much music in these little out-of-the-way venues.

I think the greatest irony in the arrival of these internationally made jazz recordings is that they and the domestic independents like HatHut and Strata-East created a phenomenon, largely involving free-bop and outright new jazz or avant-garde, that sustained the health of jazz during the severe period of imposed decline of jazz's mainstreams. American expatriates like Steve Lacy, Mal Waldron, and Frank Wright visited. But we have to give credit to Dexter Gordon's return, and to Johnny Griffin's visits. Then, I began noticing that Jo Berendt's discourses on the Globe Unity Orchestra extolled it as superior to Sun Ra's Arkestra based on elements like precision of execution. The merry-go-round continued, but personally I could see it better for what it was.

CG: So the notion you expressed in the essay—that you have to keep this music in the black community and protect it from outside influences—has become a non-issue.

RW: I think there are two things here which may seem like hair-splitting. Commercialization: Obviously, there is a certain degree of commercialization, which is going to produce a commodity such as a recording and produce the machinery to take a band or an orchestra to Prague or Moscow or Melbourne. So that kind of commercialization has always been there. What the essay is dealing with is the sort of take-over of those who may have generated the commodity to take it in some other direction.

OK. Put it back in time a little bit. There used to be ten-year cycles of major stylistic change in jazz. If we start with the Original Dixieland Jazz Band as the "first" jazz recordings, then you have swing that comes in, then you have a movement known as bebop, and then you have a movement known as West Coast. These movements have always been racial in character. It really wasn't necessarily a cultural tug of war, but there were things that were happening with . . . you had the Paul Whiteman Orchestra on the one hand, and then you had Fletcher Henderson, Duke Ellington, and Jelly Roll Morton on the other. And the press attention was going more to Paul Whiteman. In the '30s the press went to Glenn Miller and Benny Goodman. When you look at the jazz polls in *Downbeat* and *Metronome*, Duke Ellington was on the list sometimes behind twenty white bands.

I'd like to amend what I said about "the no-talent guys" in bebop. I wrote this at a time when I made the presumption that they were talking about white musicians. I was trying to read into it [something] that wasn't there. And it was really shortly after [writing] this that I began to realize that's not what happened. It was essentially a cultural movement where the black musicians may have been in the foreground. You could call it black-led, but it wasn't a black musician's thing in an exclusive sense. And neither was the '60s avant-garde because it just wasn't so. But since I didn't come through the '40s, I had to go by what the musicians were saying in print. And musicians coming out of the '30s and '40s are notoriously vague about a number of political happenings. It's easy to read into it, and I fell for it.

To reiterate: That sound that Jimi Hendrix helped create, that wall of metal, I found irritating, and I still do. And my son [Elliot] likes to listen to it! It's more the sound than the musicians [that disturbed me]. I felt that the regrouping that needed to take place in black musical communities was to stay away from that sound, because I thought that sound was dangerous. It seemed to me that the people who were singing [rock] were fighting the music. It was something that I simply could not get into. I couldn't do it. I could see certain musical groups and musical sounds coming into jazz and just ruining it.

CG: So you saw it as insidious.

RW: Yes! Attendant with it was the fact that young people my age or younger would talk about how they liked jazz and then it would be Blood, Sweat and Tears. There were things by Blood, Sweat and Tears that I liked but I didn't really consider them to be a jazz group.

It's more the aesthetic that I've tried to look at over the years. What I'm calling the aesthetic are those components and principles that constitute the identity and character of the culture. It's been that which I was mostly bothered by. You come to the realization that it ain't Stan Getz that you should go after just because he came to the fore and Cannonball Adderley or some of the others may have had a drop in record sales. It's not

Stan Getz. It's the machinery that created the situation. It exploits and dis-figures the person put out there as well as the person who was, let's say, replaced. And it confuses the audience and the public.

[Toward the end of the interview, I read Ron Welburn comments on the black aesthetic I had elicited from John Loehrke and Alva Nelson, and juxtaposed them with a quotation from "The Black Aesthetic Im-perative."] From Alva Nelson: "We *do* do things in *our* rhythm. We walk a certain way. It's not better or worse—it's just *how* . . . *we* . . . *walk*. Because we're walking to our music. Now, to say that a white musician, or white performer, or white person does not have rhythm, it's an individual thing. You cannot say that white people don't have rhythm the way they dance. If they're dancing to [black] music and they're not seeped in the culture, why would they be able to? At least they're sharing, though. I never learned to dance. So when we got to a party I'd probably dance like a white guy. I'd do the 'mashed potatoes' like James Brown and just embar-rass everybody."

From John Loehrke: "What they mean by 'too white' is not being idio-matic to the jazz style. I myself think in those terms. Usually what I mean is that it sounds *tight*. There is a looseness in the black aesthetic. The beat is wider and deeper in a black band like Duke Ellington's than, say, in Buddy Rich's band, where the beat is in a razor-sharp place. In a white blues band it's—*bn-ti chk-i bn-ti chk-i*. In a black blues band it's got more of a rolling sound—*zoo-ka za-ka zoo-ka za-ka*. That's why a lot of this rap music sounds very white too me. It's very sharp, there's no depth to the beat and a lot of the aesthetic seems to be artificial. It's not natural, flowing-out-of-the-dance rhythms the way jazz music is. The way Elvin Jones plays the drums, for example. A lot of what makes it sound so good is that even though he's doing a lot of complex things, they physically flow in a natural way from his body."

From Ron Welburn, "The Black Aesthetic Imperative": "In *The Negro and His Music* (1936), Alain Locke advocated we 'become musical by nurture and not rest content with being musical by nature.' We should all, then, re-establish ourselves as musicians: every black American can at least become a drummer or learn to play on a simple reed flute, just as every black person can dance."

RW: That's what I said, yeah. Uh . . . bullshit!

I think that what they each said was right on the money. I think that their perceptions are accurate. I find beauty in the kind of tolerance that musicians have. There's something especially in jazz musicians that re-veals an openness that is remarkable in that you don't find it in other people. The jazz experience engenders a knowledge of a wider scale of music appreciation. Jazz is kind of like in the middle, in that you need to appreciate the classical and also the very popular as well as folk.

I think everybody should have some kind of musical experience which is ongoing because it tells us who we are as people and what culture or nation we come from.

Racial Identity Embedded in Performance

YOU ARE MY SUNSHINE BY ARETHA FRANKLIN

You Are My Sunshine was composed in 1939 by Charles Mitchell and Jimmy Davis. Davis, the better-known member of this songwriting team, was a country and gospel singer who occasionally sang risqué songs like *Pistol Packin' Papa* and *Pussy Blues*. In addition to writing classic country favorites like *It Makes No Difference Now, Nobody's Darling but Mine*, and *Sunshine,* he acted in a few B-movies and served as Louisiana's governor from 1944 to 1948. Davis was elected to the Country Music Hall of Fame at the age of seventy in 1972.

What did Aretha Franklin—and Ray Charles before her—have in mind when they recorded a song that seems on the surface to be "too white" for a soul singer? Although the differences between a country musician's version of the song and Aretha Franklin's *Sunshine* with its striking divergences from the original's text and melody are obvious, there are a few important similarities. Both soul music and country music come out of and are directed to groups of people reared in the South. Soul singer Jerry Butler remarked that soul music and country both deal with mundane concerns:

[They] stay around because they talk about everyday situations; they talk about true-to-life things. They don't get hung
up in fantasyville and they don't get hung up on Broadway.
They talk to people about things that happen to people.[1]

This 1967 performance, along with others recorded at around the
same time, established Aretha Franklin as the "queen of soul." Although
the Atlantic recording sessions are considered to be some of the finest
black music of the period, most of the session musicians were white
southerners and the musical director was Arif Mardin, a Turkish-born
Berklee School of Music graduate. Despite the cross-racial and cultural
amalgam that produced this version of *Sunshine*, Franklin's performance
is clearly African-American.

To uncover the meanings of Franklin's performance I will begin with a
description of the features that mark it as different from the original. This
will be followed by an interpretation of the ways that the marked linguistic and musical features bring meaning to the song.

Franklin's version begins with an out-of-tempo, rambling, testimonial-
like introduction not present in any form in the original version. Accompanied by tremolo figures played by keyboard, guitar, and bass guitar,
Franklin tells us that she understands how everyone has felt the deep
emotions she is feeling: "Into each life some rain has sure 'nough fallen."
A chorus made up of her sisters Erma and Carolyn repeats or responds to
Franklin whenever she pauses.

The melody of the original has been completely supplanted by one
based entirely on the blues mode. Even the melodic contour of the original is absent in this new version. The simple, four-square rhythm has been
replaced by one that uses much off-beat phrasing. A brief comparison of
the first line of the refrain in the original text and Franklin's text will suffice
to make these points and the scope of the changes in the text obvious:

Original: "You are my sunshine, my only sunshine."

Franklin: "Baby, baby, baby, baby, baby, you are my sunshine."

Franklin omits the second verse of the original, with its threat: "But if you leave me to love another, you'll regret it all some day." Where the original concludes with a repeat of the refrain Franklin goes on, "Baby, don't you take my" (she leaves out the expected "my sunshine away"), and adds a new phrase: "You promised me . . . that you'd never, never, never leave me." (Both lyrics—the Charles Mitchell-Jimmy Davis original and Aretha Franklin's—are at the end of the chapter.)

Franklin's structural additions to the original text (the introduction and coda) are rich in incomplete sentences and pronouns with unclear antecedents. In the introduction Franklin begins a conditional statement, "If some rain has got to fall," but doesn't complete it. The lines that follow are three parenthetical confessions beginning: "And I've had enough rain . . . And I'm so glad . . . And I believe it . . . " The coda begins with the following sentence sung in call-and-response form. Left out of each statement, of course, is the word "sunshine:"

> *Franklin*: I don't want you to take my
>
> *Chorus*: O baby don't you take my
>
> *Franklin*: Baby don't you take my
>
> *Chorus*: O baby don't you take my

By shaping *You Are My Sunshine*'s melody and text to her own creative purposes, Franklin conveys the story about the lover gone astray in a far more powerful delivery than anyone singing the song as it was originally written could achieve. The chorus lends emphasis to Franklin's statements by repeating words she has just sung:

> *Franklin*: You know that I hung back
>
> *Chorus*: You know that I hung back

Franklin uses more words than the grammarians of standard English would consider to make her case to her departing lover: "You told me once you did." She favors chain repetitions of key words: "You'll never, never, never, never know," and "Baby, baby, baby, baby, baby." There are passages of a kind of additive repetition in which words are repeated and then followed by words that complete or add to the meaning:

> *Franklin*: If some rain
>
> *Chorus*: If some rain

Franklin: If some rain has got to fall

There are anaphoric constructions:

They tell me that into each life some rain has sure 'nough fallen

They tell me that everybody has sho has sho 'nough cried

The text gains rhetorical power from the manner in which Franklin sets her text to music, executing it in small groups of words separated by pauses. One group of words is often succeeded by another one of equal length, a rhetorical device called isocolon. Attention is brought to particular words when their stresses go against the drummer's strongly accented 4/4 beat:

and you'll ne - ver, ne - ver, ne   -   ver know

All the linguistic devices I have mentioned are common elements of black lyrics or black expression in general. Dozens of examples could be brought forth. I will mention only a few. Muddy Waters' recording of *Rolling Stone* is awash with elliptical phrases the singer leaves to the listener to make sense of. He sings, "O well he's a . . . , O well he's a . . . ," leaving the listener to understand the unsung words are "rolling stone." Anaphora is found in the Rev. Martin Luther King Jr.'s famous "I have a dream" speech. Additive repetition is just one of several devices—including stuttering—black singers and preachers use to delay the completion of a phrase.[2] The use of a responding chorus is a ubiquitous element of soul music. African-American discourse is full of phrases in which the pronoun "it" occurs with an unclear reference, for example, "get it on" and "getting it together." Finally, the text uses the phrase "sho 'nough," which in the 1960s was used primarily by black speakers addressing other black speakers.

The relationship in both texts begins on an unequal footing: The lover chooses his actions while the protagonist hopes she will benefit from them. But from the first refrain on, the protagonist in Franklin's text uses less sentimental terms of endearment than the protagonist of the original text. Franklin appears to go out of her way to avoid old-fashioned sentimentality. In her version she stays clear of "dear" and "I love you." For the latter she substitutes "I need you." She consistently omits the phrase "My only sunshine." The protagonist in the original text will do anything to keep her lover from leaving, including making threats: "But if you leave me to love another, you'll regret it all some day." In Franklin's text the protagonist becomes increasingly assertive from the second refrain on. By its end the message has become "Treat me right," a common sentiment of black lyrics. The message of the original is "Give me love," a common sentiment in white American popular music.[3]

Franklin's performance took place when African Americans were involved in a struggle to affirm their solidarity as a people and take pride in their culture. Franklin and many other black artists were devoted to the struggle. The lyrics and the ways they were sung stressed pride, sincerity, endurance, shared experience, and confidence. This is indicated by such song titles as *Tell It Like It Is* (Aaron Neville), *Just Keep Holding On* (Sam and Dave), *Keep Pushing* (the Impressions), and *Say It Loud, I'm Black and I'm Proud* (James Brown).

Franklin doesn't need lyrics to prove her sincerity. She more than proves it by the way she seems as if she's struggling against the words, so full of emotion that she can hardly get them out. As far as confidence is concerned, Franklin's musicality is a model of appropriate action. She and her sisters know just when to hold a phrase or break it off, maintain a texture or vary it, accent a note or leave it alone, and fall on the beat or go against it.

Franklin's text is all about shared experience: "Into each life some rain has sure 'nough fallen." The solidarity of the black community is suggested by the way the chorus supports and lends emphasis to Franklin's statements. This paradigm of communal involvement promotes a sense of community: "The sight and sound of a common problem being acted out, talked out, and worked out on stage promotes catharsis, and the fact that all present are participants in the solution creates solidarity."[4]

Everything about Franklin's performance supports a sacred interpretation. Since "rain has got to fall on everybody" and sunshine clears up the rain, "sunshine" could be a spiritual force, not just a straying lover. The text is conveyed as an act of testifying taking place within a community symbolically represented by the chorus. With her wide vibrato and melismatic treatment of words (sometimes referred to as "worrying the line"[5]) Franklin puts her listeners in church.

FRANKLIN   **ORIGINAL**

Introduction

They tell me that into each
life some rain has sure
'nough fallen. They tell me

FRANKLIN   **ORIGINAL**

that everybody has sho, has
sho 'nough cried some-
times. If some rain [Chorus:
Some rain]; if some rain has
got to fall [Chorus: Some
rain] on everybody . . . And
I've had enough rain in my
life . . . And I'm so glad right
now I've got a little love
around me to keep the rain
off my head. Yeah, yeah.
And I believe it . . . I believe
it . . . I believe it because
[One member of the chorus:
Tell me why do you believe]
I believe it because . . .

Verse

On the other night   The other night dear
As I lay sleepin'   As I lay sleeping
And I lay my head on you   I dreamed
I held you in my arms, yeah   I held you in my arms
But when I woke up   When I awoke dear
And found out I was mis-   I was mistaken
taken, yeah

You know that I hung back   And I
[Chorus: You know that I
hung back]

Hung my head and I cried   Hung my head and cried.
[Chorus: Head and I cried].

Refrain

Baby, baby, baby, baby, baby
You are my sunshine [Cho-   You are my sunshine
rus: Babe!]

                                                 My only sunshine
Ya shore make me happy,   You make me happy
baby
For when the skies are gray   When skies are gray

FRANKLIN	ORIGINAL
And you'll never, never, never know	You'll never know dear
'Bout how much I need you	How much I love you
I don't want you to take my [Chorus: O baby don't you take my]	Please don't
Take my sunshine away [Chorus: Sunshine away].	Take my sunshine away.

Verse

I'll always love you
And make you happy
If you will only say the same
But if you leave me
To love another
You'll regret it all some day.
[*Refrain* repeated in the original]

Verse

You told me once you did	You told me once dear
That you really loved me	You really loved me
And no one else could ever	And no one else
Could ever come between, yeah.	Could come between
And now you're thinkin' about a leavin' me [Chorus: Leavin']	But now you've left me
For another, yeah [Chorus: Leave]	And love another
If you do	
You know you're gonna shatter	You have shattered
Shatter every one of my dreams [Chorus: One of my dreams].	All of my dreams.

FRANKLIN   **ORIGINAL**

Refrain

Because baby, baby, baby,
baby, baby

You are my sunshine [Cho-   You are my sunshine
rus: Babe!]

                                 My only sunshine

Ya shore make me happy   You make me happy

For when the skies are gray,   When skies are gray
yeah.

And you'll never, never,   You'll never know dear
never, never, never know

'Bout how much I need you   How much I love you
[Chorus: How much I really
need you]

I don't want you to take my   Please don't take my
[Chorus: O baby don't you   sunshine away.
take my]

Baby don't you take my
[Chorus: O baby don't you
take my]

You promised me [Chorus:
O baby don't you take my]

That you'd never, never,
never, never leave me

You promised me [Chorus:
Sunshine sho 'nough]

That you'd never, never,
never leave, baby [Chorus:
Sunshine sho 'nough]

You're gonna find that I
[Chorus: Sure 'enough]

Don't ever take it away
[Chorus: O baby don't you
take my].

BLUE MONK BY THE JIMMY GIUFFRE 3

In the late 1950s, The Jimmy Giuffre 3 consisted of the leader on clarinet, tenor or baritone sax; valve trombonist Bob Brookmeyer; and guitar-

ist Jim Hall. Before a live audience in December 1958, they recorded Thelonious Monk's *Blue Monk* for Atlantic Records. Giuffre admired Monk's music and stated that he "liked the way he makes a statement, the conviction with which he plays and writes." Hearing Monk and Sonny Rollins over a period of time persuaded Giuffre that his music-making was overly cautious: "It was as if half the music I had inside me wasn't coming out. I was holding it until I got the sound straight."[6]

Monk's famous blues composition is a carefully wrought melody with unexpected dissonances that serve as a sardonic commentary on old-timey music. In other words, it is high camp. Giuffre's version is Monk's music without Monk's spirit. While Monk's performance of his composition is taut and angular, Giuffre's is languid and dreamy. Giuffre removes all the sarcasm from *Blue Monk* and transforms it into the old-timey country blues it was never intended to be. But does it really matter? This is jazz after all, a music in which the composer's intentions are typically subsumed by the expressive needs of the individual, in which substituting new chord progressions for "square" ones and changing the original tempos are common practices.

On the other hand, jazz musicians like Barry Harris consider Monk's music to be a special case, a music in which jazz musicians must respect the composer's intentions. At the Thelonious Monk Competition, for example, he criticized pianist Alva Nelson's slow tempo on Monk's *'Round Midnight*. In most respects I am sympathetic to Harris's reverence for Monk's music, and with few exceptions (Giuffre's version of *Blue Monk* being one) I dislike performances of Monk in which his melodies are played incorrectly and his subsidiary lines and inner voicings are omitted.

If one listens to Giuffre's version of *Blue Monk* while setting aside the question of whether Giuffre is guilty of desecration, it is easy to appreciate its originality and quietly intense beauty. Held aloft by Jim Hall's simple four-square accompaniment, Giuffre and Brookmeyer create long, flowing melodies. A sophisticated harmonic sensibility is harnessed to the creation of pure song. Although the music definitely swings, rhythmic vitality is a secondary consideration. Like much of Giuffre's music of the period, it is more Basie than bebop.

Giuffre's music was an anti-hip statement. Turning away from hard bop riffs and harmonies, loud drummers, and pyrotechnics, Giuffre moved toward melodies with (in his words) "a folk-songy, bluesy, down-homey, old-timey, natural, funky air."[7] Giuffre exhibited a decidedly analytical approach to his music that was at odds in a jive-talking jazz community. Here, for example, is Giuffre describing one of his compositions,

Crawdad Suite: "It has two themes. One is pure blues, the other a folkish tune in a distant minor key. The contrast is interesting. The minor key is quite free of tempo. In the coda, both themes are played together combining the two moods." It is difficult to imagine Monk or Horace Silver describing one of their own pieces in such a way. At a time when advances in jazz were tied to a harder rhythmic feel, Giuffre was going in the other direction:

> I've come to feel increasingly inhibited and frustrated by the insistent pounding of the rhythm section. With it, it's impossible for the listener or the soloist to hear the horn's true sound, I've come to believe, or fully concentrate on the solo line. An imbalance of advantages has moved the rhythm section from a supporting to a competitive role.[8]

On the occasions when Giuffre uses drums, he uses them primarily for coloristic effects rather than to drive the band in the manner of, say, Art Blakey. On the 1955 recording *Tangents in Jazz* with trumpeter Jack Sheldon, bassist Ralph Pena, and drummer Artie Anton, he notated the areas in the improvised sections where the bass player and drummer could and could not play.[9] Although it works well in Giuffre's music, few drummers and bassists enjoy playing within such circumscribed roles on a full-time basis. In fact, Giuffre admitted to me (I studied with him off and on from 1967 to 1974) that most of his sidemen really wanted to play bebop.

Giuffre can in some respects be accused of subscribing to the Paul Whiteman school of thought: being satisfied with jazz only when it sacrifices something of its basic nature—when it acts like a lady, not a whore. Giuffre's music is deeply influenced by the blues, but it is a blues reinterpreted by someone dedicated to classical standards of aesthetic beauty—balance, symmetry, and clarity. Some jazz critics would have us believe that only Jimmy Giuffre and other white musicians adhere to these standards, neglecting the fact that black jazz musicians like John Lewis of the Modern Jazz Quartet and classical composers like William Grant Still have also fallen under classicism's spell.

A comparison of Giuffre's version with the recording of *Blue Monk* by the Monk Quartet of the 1950s featuring tenor saxophonist Johnny Griffin demonstrates how Giuffre's music ran counter to the mainstream jazz ethos of the time. Griffin's solo in particular hews close to this ethos. While Griffin's playing is full of bebop phrases, hard bop blues riffs, and change-running arpeggios, Giuffre plays slow melodies within a small range of notes. While Griffin's sound is tough and dynamic, Giuffre's is persistently quiet, unencumbered by a prodding rhythm section at a time when jazz groups were getting louder because of increasingly assertive rhythm sections and better amplification equipment. When one hears Johnny Griffin, one can imagine him playing with a rhythm-and-blues group and fitting right in because of his sound and fervor. But Giuffre's quiet, well-rounded, pearl-like tones would fail to make the mark. A constant flow of blues phrases mixed into bebop lines marks Griffin as African American, just as their scarcity in Giuffre's music marks him as *not* African American.

The Right of Swing

[T]he blues is black man's music, and whites diminish it at best or steal it at worst. In any case they have no moral right to use it.
—Jazz critic Ralph J. Gleason[1]

Joel Rudinow, a philosophy professor at Sonoma State University, has written an essay titled "Race, Ethnicity, Expressive Authenticity: Can White People Sing the Blues?" that grew out of a course in the philosophy of art and contemporary rock and soul music. His students quickly dismissed the question: Can white people sing the blues? For them, the white blues guitarist Stevie Ray Vaughn had made it a non-issue. They had little respect for jazz and rock critic Ralph Gleason's opinion that white people can't play the blues and have no right to perform a musical idiom closely tied to African-American culture.

In the face of large numbers of white blues artists—a long list including Mike Bloomfield, Paul Butterfield, Nick Gravenites, Rory Block, and Charlie Musselwhite—and white sidemen closely affiliated with black artists—Jesse Edwin Davis with Taj Mahal and Albert Gianquinto with James Cotton—the blues appears to Rudinow to be an idiom that knows no racial boundaries. The question is thus one of credibility. What does it take to be recognized as an authentic blues musician? Rudinow describes authenticity as "a value—a species of the genus credibility. It's the kind of credibility that comes from having the appropriate relationship to an original source."[2] Since the "original source" of blues is African-American culture, black nationalists argue that without being black you cannot be a blues person. Rudinow disagrees. While whites can never be authentic in the sense of being flesh-and-blood descendants of African-American history, he argues, those who make the effort to uncover the blues idiom's textual and textural secrets have just as much a right to membership in the blues community as any African American does.

PAYING DUES

The ultimate test of authenticity in both the blues and jazz worlds is peer acceptance, and there is more to peer acceptance than the ability to play music. A musician is judged partly on the quality of his or her experiences, scoring highest by accumulating time spent working for recognized musical stylists, but also for enduring drug addiction, racial prejudice, and other travails.

Paying dues is also giving due respect. The jazz community of the 1950s and 1960s expected its younger members to gain experience as sidemen before attempting a solo career. "Paying dues" was the "official" way of being authenticated as a jazz musician. Few jazz musicians received any widespread critical success who had not first played as sidemen with prominent bandleaders like Miles Davis, Cannonball Adderley, Art Blakey, and Horace Silver. Ornette Coleman and Cecil Taylor are among the few successful musicians from the 1950s who didn't gain their initial fame as sidemen. The absence of a mentor may not have stopped their careers but it certainly created grave difficulties during their formative years. Despite receiving a good reception from the audience at a Brooklyn club in the black neighborhood of Bedford-Stuyvesant, Taylor was fired by the manager, who told him, "We don't want this music in here." According to A. B. Spellman, who wrote about the incident in his chapter on Taylor in *Four Lives in the Bebop Business,* influential musicians in the audience were angered that Taylor was already working as leader of his own group without having come up through the ranks.[3]

Taylor and Coleman are exceptions. Most musicians who never paid their dues as sidemen are unable to achieve anything like Taylor's and Coleman's ascendancy even if they achieve financial success. Forever the jazz community outsider, Brubeck got on the cover of *Time* magazine but has consistently received little or no respect from each generation of jazz musicians and fans (with a few prominent exceptions like Anthony Braxton).

Paying sidemen dues is important for becoming a success in the jazz world, but life dues—enduring hardships stemming from racial prejudice, drug addiction, alcoholism, and poverty—are valued in a different way. An old adage of the blues community is that in order to play the blues, you must *live* the blues. This concept of experience as enlightening is frequently alluded to by jazz musicians. Charlie Parker once said: "If you don't live it, it won't come out of your horn."

The blues and jazz communities adhere to the principle that "the more directly one's knowledge claims are grounded in first-hand experience, the more unassailable one's authority."[4] Musicians are judged by the quality and extent of the dues they've had to pay. Black nationalists put experiencing racial prejudice ahead of all other forms of dues paying. Being black is their prima facie requirement for induction into the blues. Whites need not apply. For everyone besides black nationalists, race may still be important, but the primary basis for acceptance is work experience. The closer a musician has been to style-setters like Miles Davis, the more esteem he or she can expect. "Who has he (or she) played with?" becomes the essential question, rather than "Is she (or he) black?"

AUTHENTIC SPEAKERS AND REBELS

Stylistic authenticity is a matter of performing in accordance with the practices of style-setting musicians. In many respects stylistic authenticity is surprisingly similar to speaking a language. The linguists Alan M. Perlman and Daniel Greenblatt have correctly noted that jazz improvisation has a specific syntax: "The implicit goal of the jazz improviser is to create an impromptu melody that sounds like jazz."[5] Jazz improvisers choose phrases and melodic devices recognized as "jazz" by other jazz musicians and play them with "jazz-appropriate" articulation and timbre.

Although the jazz community is noted for its tolerance—looking with amusement and even admiration at aberrant behavior; forgiving what music pedagogues consider improper ways of playing instruments (Dizzy Gillespie's puffed cheeks, Thelonious Monk's uncurled fingers) and serious failings in musicianship (poor reading skills, "bad" intonation)—it can be as rigid about the jazz idiom's vocabulary as the Académie Française, is about the French language. As the iconoclastic clarinetist Don Byron points out, "Everybody wants to be jazz and then say that something they don't like isn't jazz."6

During the iconoclastic heydays of avant-garde jazz in the mid-1960s and continuing into the years when fusion took the jazz world by storm, musicians questioned the value of authenticity. If they were beholden to anything, it was to rejecting the orthodox jazz practices of hard bop. But even then the leading musicians demonstrated a mastery of most, if not all, of the jazz vernacular. Bassists and drummers were still judged on their mastery of playing time; horn players still played with jazz phrasing.

But what avant-garde jazz musicians didn't do was play chord changes. In order to judge whether they deserved a jazz pedigree, many in the jazz community felt it was less important to judge the music these musicians played than to know if they had the ability to play *All the Things You Are* and other core jazz repertoire items. John Coltrane had a better reputation than Ornette Coleman because the latter never really learned how to play over chord changes.

The end of the 1970s marked a turn away from the free-wheeling approaches of the avant-garde and fusion. Musicians began to dedicate themselves to defining and promoting the vocabulary and syntax of the jazz language. Wynton Marsalis rode to fame on this new wave of conservatism and became its symbol. He got help in spreading his vision by the jazz education movement, which had begun to make impressive strides in establishing programs in universities and arts high schools and inspiring a cottage publishing industry of jazz theory and instrumental method books. In tandem with jazz educators, Marsalis has strived to institutionalize a vision of the music that with the exception of the music of the Miles Davis Quintet of the 1960s (a strong influence on Marsalis), includes only those developments that hit the jazz world before Ornette Coleman came to New York in 1959 and changed the face of jazz.

Marsalis has always been motivated to protect jazz from disappearing into pop music on the one hand, and from poor standards of musicianship on the other. His preservationist zeal and unembarrassed elitism have succeeded in raising public awareness of jazz as an artistic pursuit and securing institutional support. At the same time Marsalis's conservatism has been divisive. Bassist John Loehrke insists that

> it's leading to an increasingly closed-minded concept of the music. This kind of rigid idea: "In a *real* jazz band the bass plays down low and plays mostly quarter-notes and walks"—not running over the bass and playing counter-

rhythms the way Gary Peacock did with Albert Ayler. This retro hard bop attitude: "Jazz is *this*. In a jazz band the drummer does mainly *boom chucka doom chucka doom chucka doom*."

Bassist Anthony Jackson has even harsher words:

I maintain that this latest crop of "redeemers" is more artistically bankrupt, morally hypocritical, and historically irrelevant than any that has come before. We are, in my opinion, witnessing no less than a modern cultural parallel to Germany in the 1930s, with a megalomaniacal "arbiter of good taste" undertaking a redefinition and reclassification of a country's expressive potential, ostensibly to weed out contaminating influences. The underlying purpose is simply the muzzling and suppression of people whose expressive power, originality, and vitality are likely stronger than that of the leaders.[7]

"I've gotten to the point where I can't care what other jazz cats think," says Don Byron, one of the leading members of New York's downtown new-music scene. Byron has gotten mixed messages from the jazz community. While *Down Beat* has lauded him, giving him a "Jazz Artist of the Year" award and voting him "Favorite Clarinet Player" of 1993, the Lincoln Center crowd does not consider him a jazz musician. Stanley Crouch, artistic consultant for *Jazz at Lincoln Center*, respects Byron's musicianship but doesn't "hear the elements that make jazz sound like it sounds."[8]

Byron, who gained fame as clarinetist with the Klezmer Conservatory Band, takes a postmodernist approach to authenticity. When he performs the music of Jewish comedian Mickey Katz, he makes an exact copy of the original and transforms it, as Stephen Sherrill pointed out in a *New York Times* feature on Byron:

If Byron doesn't look the part of a klezmer musician, well, that's the point. Authenticity for him involves not fulfilling expectations but upending them—presenting the music so out of context, and mastering the music to such a degree, that listeners will be forced to disconnect what they're hearing from any preconceived notions of what someone playing such music looks like. "I don't want to be the mainstream guy. I just want to be the weird guy," Byron later explains. "I want to be the guy who's got the weird thing of his own, and then I want to be that in several different contexts."9

Some in the audience at a Brooklyn performance of "Don Byron Plays the Music of Mickey Katz" just didn't get it. Or if they did, they weren't interested in Byron's twisted authenticity. Those looking for a Mickey Katz revival were disappointed. Yes, he was faithfully executing Katz's music from exact transcriptions. But the singers weren't singing the Yiddish properly and Katz's humor was nowhere to be found.

The klezmer scholars were aghast that Byron's championing of Mickey Katz was making a klezmer legend out of someone they considered a comedian with incidental ties to true klezmer. Byron defended his authenticity as well as Katz's against their criticism:

> None of these klezmer cats are doing what they're doing any more authentically than I am. . . . Some of the same types of cats said this stuff about Mickey, too: "No, this isn't really klezmer." As if klezmer is only one thing. Well, this is really Mickey Katz, and if they want to make a value judgment about that, that's their business. But to say it's not real—it's really what it is.10

Byron wearily accepts that he will always be "the black guy who plays klezmer." Like white jazz musicians, he is the subject of psychological characterizations and cultural slander. In the back of his mind he realizes that someone is always judging whether he has the right to play Yiddish swing.

Notes

INTRODUCTION

1. LeRoi Jones, *Blues People:The Negro Experience in White America and the Music That Developed from It* (New York: Morrow Quill Paperbacks, 1963), p. 153.

2. Michael Bane, *White Boy Singin' the Blues: The Black Roots of White Rock* (Middlesex, England: Penguin Books, 1982), p. 155.

3. I am not alone in recognizing that racial relations were strained in New York City's jazz community of the late 1960s. Pianist Richie Beirach has stated that whites often encountered hostility from black musicians: "I can tell you many, many personal experiences of extremely strained relationships with blacks. This was especially true in clubs in the Lower East Side like Slugs." Ronald Radamo, *New Musical Figurations: Anthony Braxton's Cultural Critique* (Chicago: University of Chicago Press, 1993), p. 156, n. 57.

4. Radamo, *New Musical Figurations*, p. 46.

5. Ruth M. Stone, *Let the Inside Be Sweet: The Interpretation of Music Event Among the Kpelle of Liberia* (Bloomington, Ind.: Indiana University Press, 1982), p. 8.

6. Kwame Anthony Appiah, *In My Father's House: Africa in the Philosophy of Culture* (New York: Oxford University Press, 1992), p. 194.

7. Stone, *Let the Inside Be Sweet,* p. 8.

CHAPTER ONE

1. J. A. Rogers, "Jazz At Home." In Addison Gayle Jr., ed., *The Black Aesthetic* (Garden City, N.Y.: Doubleday, 1971), p. 107.

2. Ibid., p. 72.

3. Bob Wilber, *Music Was Not Enough* (New York: Oxford University Press, 1988), p. 43.

4. Cited in Gene Lees, *Cats of Any Color: Jazz, Black and White* (New York: Oxford University Press, 1994) p. 241.

5. Michael L. Hecht, Mary Jane Collier, and Sidney Ribeau, *African American Communication: Ethnic Identity and Cultural Interpretation* (Newbury Park, Calif.: Sage Publications, 1993), p. 2.

6. Robert Wright, "The Perversion of Darwinism" (Review of Pat Shipman, *The Evolution of Racism), New York Times Book Review* (July 31, 1994), p. 7.

7. Lawrence Wright, "One Drop of Blood," *New Yorker* (July 25, 1994), p. 55.

8. bell hooks, *Yearning: Race, Gender, and Cultural Politics* (Boston: South End Press, 1990), p. 37.

9. Charles Keil, *Urban Blues* (Chicago: University of Chicago Press, 1966), p. 174, n. 10.

10. Ibid., p. 97

11. Ray Charles and David Ritz, *Brother Ray* (New York: Warner, 1978), pp. 167–68.

12. LeRoi Jones, *Blues People: The Negro Experience in White America and the Music that Developed from It* (New York: Morrow Quill Paperbacks, 1963), p. 153.

13. In Gayle, Jr., ed., *The Black Aesthetic.*

14. Cited in Frank Kofsky, *Black Nationalism and the Revolution in Music* (New York: Pathfinder, 1970) p. 120.

15. Ibid., p. 11.

16. Miles Davis with Quincy Troupe, *Miles: The Autobiography* (New York: Simon & Schuster, 1989), p. 380.

17. Ibid., p. 405.

18. Ibid., p. 119.

19. Ben Sidran, *Black Talk: How the Music of Black America Created a Radical Alternative to the Values of Western Literary Tradition* (New York: Holt, Rinehart and Winston, 1971), p. 122.

20. Ian Carr in *Miles Davis* (New York: William Morrow, 1982) offers a completely different view of the *Birth of the Cool* rhythm section in another set of recordings—live recordings from broadcasts: "The rhythm section, fired by Max Roach, and with very muscular chord work from John Lewis, really drives along in the polyrhythmic bebop manner" (p. 36).

21. Jones, *Blues People*, p. 213.

22. Lees, *Cats of Any Color,* p. 197.

23. Art Pepper and Laurie Pepper, *Straight Life: The Story of Art Pepper* (New York: Da Capo, 1994. Reprint of New York: Schirmer Books, 1979), pp. 113–14.

24. Cited in Lees, *Cats of Any Color,* p. 235.

25. hooks, *Yearning,* p. 37.

26. LeRoi Jones, "The Changing Same" (R&B and New Black Music). In Gayle, Jr., ed., *The Black Aesthetic,* p. 125.

27. Rafi Zabor and Vic Garbarini, "Wynton vs. Herbie: The Purist and the Crossbreeder Duke It Out." In Mark Rowland and Tony Scherman, eds., *The Jazz Musician* (New York: St. Martin's Press, 1994), pp. 97–128.

28. James Lincoln Collier, *Jazz: The American Theme Song* (New York: Oxford University Press, 1993), Chap. 8.

29. Gary Giddins, *Celebrating Bird: The Triumph of Charlie Parker* (New York: Beech Tree Books William Morrow, 1987), p. 112.

30. Collier, *Jazz,* p. 214.

31. Stanley Crouch, "Sketches of Pain," *New Republic* (Feb. 12, 1990), pp. 30–37.

32. Ibid.

33. Ibid.

34. Ibid.

35. Jimmy Stewart. "Introduction to Black Aesthetics in Music." In Gayle Jr., ed., *The Black Aesthetic,* p. 84.

36. Dizzy Gillespie with Al Fraser, *To Be, or Not to Bop: Memoirs—Dizzy Gillespie* (Garden City, N.Y.: Doubleday, 1979), p. 287.

37. Ibid., p. 371.

38. Musicologist James Patrick calculated that blues constitute 20.6 percent of Parker's repertory. The rest of his repertory was composed of popular songs and original compositions. "Charlie Parker and Harmonic Sources of Bebop Composition: Thoughts on the Repertory of New Jazz in the 1940s," *Journal of Jazz Studies* 2, No. 2, p. 3.

39. Jones, *Blues People,* p. 182.

40. Ibid., p. 118.

41. Ibid., pp. 217–18.

42. John Storm Roberts. *Black Music of Two Worlds* (New York: Praeger, 1972), p. 28.

43. Jones, *Blues People,* p. 153.

44. Cited in Carol Cooper, "New Pop Gospel by the Winans." *Newsday* (Nov. 17, 1994), p. B11.

45. William Howland Kenney, *Chicago Jazz: A Cultural History, 1904–1930* (New York: Oxford University Press, 1993), p. 119.

46. Mezz Mezzrow and Bernard Wolfe, *Really the Blues* (New York: Random House, 1946; reprint, Garden City, N.Y.: Doubleday, 1972), p. 130.

47. Burton Peretti, *The Creation of Jazz: Music, Race, and Culture in Urban America* (Urbana, Ill.: University of Illinois Press, 1992), p. 81.

48. Dan Morgenstern, Introduction to Louis Armstrong, *Swing That Music* (New York: Da Capo Press, 1993. Reprint of London: Longmans, Green, 1936), p. ix.

49. Armstrong, *Swing That Music,* p. 9–10.

50. Gillespie, *To Be, or Not to Bop,* p. 393.

51. Ibid., p. 157.

52. Bob Wilber assisted by Derek Webster, *Music Was Not Enough* (New York: Oxford University Press, 1988), p. 48.

53. Lees, *Cats of Any Color,* p. 200.

54. Jones, *Blues People,* p. 163. In Alan Pomerance's, *Repeal of the Blues: How Black Entertainers Influenced Civil Rights* (New York: Citadel Press, 1988), p. 39, Alan Pomerance also discusses how much Goodman paid arrangers. If Pomerance is referring to the same period in Goodman's career, the amount paid to Henderson should be doubled: "A weekly allowance for eight new arrangements at 75 dollars each enabled John and Goodman to hire people of the caliber of Fletcher Henderson, Jimmy Mundy and Edgar Sampson to do them."

55. André Hodeir, *Jazz: Its Evolution and Essence* (New York: Grove Press, 1956. Revised edition, 1979), p. 31.

56. Stanley Dance, *The World of Duke Ellington* (New York: Charles Scribner's Sons, 1970), p. 108.

57. Davis, *Autobiography,* p. 119.

58. Collier, *Jazz: The American Theme Song,* p. 207.

59. Cited in Nat Hentoff, "The Murderous Mode of Jazz," *Esquire* (Sept. 15, 1960), p. 90.

60. Mary Lou Williams' comments were cited in Nat Shapiro and Nat Hentoff, eds., *Hear Me Talkin' to Ya: The Story of Jazz as Told by the Men Who Made It* (New York: Rinehart, 1955; reprint, New York: Dover Publications, 1966), pp. 340–41.

61. Leslie R. Rout, "Reflections on Post-War Jazz." In Gayle Jr., ed., *The Black Aesthetic,* p. 147.

62. Gillespie, *To Be or Not to Bop,* p. 139.

63. Ibid., p. 143.

64. Ron Welburn, "The Black Aesthetic Imperative." In Gayle Jr., ed., *The Black Aesthetic,* p. 133. The Gillespie quotation appears in Nat Shapiro and Hentoff, *Hear Me Talkin' to Ya,* p. 337.

65. Davis, *Autobiography,* p. 117.

66. Gillespie, *To Be or Not to Bop,* p. 411.

67. Davis, *Autobiography,* p. 156.

68. Robert Gordon, *West Coast Jazz: The Los Angeles Jazz Scene of the 1950s* (London: Quartet Books, 1986), p. 72.

69. Cecil Taylor cited A. B. Spellman, *Four Lives in the Bebop Business* (New York: Pantheon Books, 1966), p. 62. Note that Taylor says that the egg-throwing "reputedly" took place. Gillespie does not mention it in his autobiography, nor does he express any ill feelings toward Dave Brubeck.

70. Ibid., p. 33.

71. Frank Kofsky, *Black Nationalism and the Revolution in Music* (New York: Pathfinder, 1970), p. 34.

72. Ibid., p. 32.

73. Ronald Sukenick. *Down and In: Life in the Underground* (New York: Collier Books, 1987).

74. Hodeir, *Jazz: Its Evolution and Essence*, p. 120.

75. Jones, *Blues People*, p. 30.

76. Kofsky, *Black Nationalism and the Revolution in Music*, p. 36n.

77. Spellman, *Four Lives in the Bebop Business*, pp.142–43.

78. Cited in Kofsky, *Black Nationalism and the Revolution in Music*, pp. 65–66.

79. Cited in Arthur Taylor, *Notes and Tones: Musician to Musician Interviews* (New York: Perigee Books, 1977), pp. 249, 250–51.

80. Cited in Spellman, *Four Lives in the Bebop Business*, pp. 141–42.

81. Jones, *Blues People*, p. 154.

82. Ibid., p. 30.

83. Ibid., p. 29.

84. Cited in Spellman, *Four Lives in the Bebop Business*, p. 62.

85. Wayne Enstice and Paul Rubin, *Jazz Spoken Here: Conversations with Twenty-Two Musicians* (Baton Rouge: Louisiana State University, 1992. Reprint of New York: Da Capo, 1984), p. 206.

86. Ibid., p. 177.

87. Ibid., p. 246.

88. Cited in Helen Myers, "African-American Music." In Helen Myers, ed., *Ethnomusicology: Historical and Regional Studies* (New York: W. W. Norton, 1993), pp. 427–28.

89. Cited in Whitney Balliett, *American Musicians: Fifty-Six Portraits in Jazz* (New York: Oxford University Press, 1986), p. 342–43.

90. Len Lyons, *The Great Jazz Pianists: Speaking of Their Lives and Their Music* (New York: Quill, 1983), pp. 227–28.

91. Enstice and Rubin, *Jazz Spoken Here*, p. 39.

92. Cited in Collier, *Jazz: The American Theme Song*, p. 90.

93. Nat Hentoff, "Race Prejudice in Jazz: It Works, Both Ways," *Harper's Magazine* (June 1959), pp. 74–76.

94. Ibid.

95. Gary Giddins, *Riding on a Blue Note* (Oxford, England: Oxford University Press, 1981), p. 256.

96. Billy Taylor, *Jazz Piano: A Jazz History* (Dubuque, Iowa: Wm. C. Brown, 1983), pp. 3, 8.

97. Irving Louis Horowitz and Charles Nanry, "Ideologies and Theories About American Jazz," *Journal of Jazz Studies* 2, No. 2 (June 1975), p. 33.

98. Bob Wilber, a protégé of the famous Creole musician Sidney Bechet, remembers that Bechet "never thought of himself as a black man," and sometimes made anti-black statements. *Music Was Not Enough,* p. 48.

99. Collier, *Jazz: The American Theme Song,* p. 201.

100. Kwame Anthony Appiah, *In My Father's House: Africa in the Philosophy of Culture* (New York: Oxford University Press, 1992), p. 74.

101. Cited in Lees, *Cats of Any Color,* p. 241.

102. Taylor, *Jazz Piano,* p. 62.

103. Bert Primack, "Critical Analysis: Jazz Critics Under the Microscrope," *Jazz Times* 24, No. 7 (September 1994), p. 39.

CHAPTER TWO

1. Cited in Clifford J. Levy, "Study to Examine Bones From Blacks' Burial Site," *New York Times* (Aug. 13, 1991), p. B1.

2. Michael W. Harris, *The Rise of Gospel Blues: The Music of Thomas Andrew Dorsey in the Urban Church* (New York: Oxford University Press, 1992), discusses how black churches such as the African Methodist Episcopal Church (AME) attempted to diminish the influence of indigenous black culture on African Americans.

3. Cited in Kwame Anthony Appiah, *In My Father's House: Africa in the Philosophy of Culture* (New York: Oxford University Press, 1992), pp. 22–23.

4. Claude McKay, "Garvey as a Negro Moses." In Herbert Aptheker, ed., *A Documentary History of the Negro People in the United States,* vol. 3 (Secaucus, N.J.: Citadel Press, 1951–74), p. 370.

5. Melville Herskovits, *The Myth of the Negro Past* (New York: Harper & Bros., 1941).

6. Ibid., p. 141.

7. Ibid., p. 133.

8. Greg Tate, "Above and Beyond Rap's Decibels," *New York Times* (March 6, 1994), Sec. 2, p. 36.

9. Ibid., p. 56.

10. Appiah, *In My Father's House,* p. 25.

11. Paul Oliver, *Savannah Syncopators* (New York: Stein & Day, 1970), p. 23.

12. D. J. Epstein, *Sinful Tunes and Spirituals: Black Folk Music to the Civil War* (Urbana, Ill.: University of Illinois Press, 1977), p. 14.

13. Ibid., pp. 53–54.

14. Michael Theodore Coolen, "The Fodet: A Senegambian Origin for the Blues?" In *Black Perspective in Music* 10, no. 1 (Spring 1982), p. 75.

15. The use of a high drone string on the banjo has been erroneously attributed to Joel (also called Joe) Walker Sweeney, a white musician and the first nationally known banjoist. A watercolor titled "The Old Plantation" done in the late eighteenth century clearly shows a banjo with three full-length strings and a characteristically short thumb string, Jay Scott Odell, "Banjo." In *New Grove Dictionary of Music and Musicians,* ed. Stanley Sadie (Washington, D.C.: Grove's Dictionary of Music, 1980).

16. Coolen, "The Fodet," p. 75.

17. Samuel Charters, *The Roots of the Blues: An African Search* (New York: Perigee, 1981), p. 60. Ethnomusicologist Philip Schuyler is surprised that Charters didn't recognize that the sound of an early American fretless banjo with gut strings is "very much like that of the African prototype" (personal correspondence, July 1994).

18. The fodet is also the name given to the tuning used to play a song. There is a body of songs that can be played with each tuning.

19. Coolen, "The Fodet," p. 77.

20. Philip D. Curtin. *The Atlantic Slave Trade: A Census* (Madison, Wis.: University of Wisconsin Press, 1966). Winifred Vass, *The Bantu Speaking Heritage of the United States* (Los Angeles: UCLA, Center for Afro-American Studies, 1979). Peter H. Wood, *Black Majority: Negroes in Colonial South Carolina From 1670 Through the Stono Rebellion* (New York: Knopf, 1974). Joseph E. Holloway, "The Origins of African-American Culture." In Joseph Holloway, ed., *Africanisms in American Culture* (Bloomington, Ind.: Indiana University Press, 1991).

21. John Storm Roberts, *Black Music of Two Worlds* (New York: Praeger, 1972), remains the definitive study of African musical elements in jazz and other American idioms.

22. Jones's *Blues People* must be credited for predating much of the published studies on African aesthetics. In it he considered the use of the word "cool" in the literal translation of a Twi dialect phrase—"cool he heart give him," meaning "to calm a person." Jones suggested that it might tell us something about the roots of African-American sensibility.

23. Richard Majors and Janet Mancini Billson, *Cool Pose: The Dilemmas of Black Manhood in America* (New York: Touchstone, 1993), p. 4.

24. Roy Carr, Brian Case, and Fred Dellar, *The Hip: Hipsters, Jazz and the Beat Generation* (London: Faber and Faber), p. 11.

25. Cited in Lewis Porter, *Lester Young* (Boston: Twayne Publishers, 1985), p. 2.

26. Robert Farris Thompson, *African Art in Motion: Icon and Act in the Collection of Katherine Coryton White* (Los Angeles: University of California Press, 1974), p. 43.

27. Robert Farris Thompson, "An Aesthetic of the Cool," *Africa Arts* 7, No. 1 (Fall 1973), pp. 43, 89–90n. 23.

28. Ibid., p. 90.

29. Ibid., p. 41.

30. Warren D'Azevedo, cited in Thompson, "An Aesthetic of the Cool," p. 41.

31. Cited in Porter, *Lester Young,* p. 16.

32. Ibid., pp. 2–3.

33. Ibid., p. 21.

34. Robert Farris Thompson, *Flash of the Spirit: African and Afro-American Art and Philosophy* (New York: Vintage Books, 1984), p. 63.

35. Cited in John Miller Chernoff, *African Rhythm and African Sensibility: Aesthetics and Social Action in African Musical Idioms* (Chicago: University of Chicago, 1971), p. 108.

36. Richard Alan Waterman, " 'Hot' Rhythm in Negro Music," *Journal of the American Musicological Society* 1 (Spring 1948), p. 37.

37. Richard Alan Waterman, "African Influence on the Music of the Americas." In Sol Tax, ed., *Selected Papers of the 29th International Congress of Americanists, Vol. 2: Acculturation in the Americas* (Chicago: University of Chicago Press, 1952), p. 211.

38. David Locke, *Drum Gahu: A Systematic Method for an African Percussion Piece* (Crown Point, Ind.: White Cliffs Media, 1987), p. 125.

39. Hewitt Pantaleoni, "Three Principles of Timing in AN LO Dance Drumming," *African Music Society Journal* 2 (1972), p. 62.

40. Olly Wilson, "The Significance of the Relationship Between Afro-American Music and West African Music," *Black Perspectives in Music* (Spring 1974), p. 6.

41. Waterman, "African Influence on the Music of the Americas," p. 217.

42. Locke, *Drum Gahu,* p. 10.

43. Waterman, " 'Hot' Rhythm in Negro Music," pp. 24–37.

44. Charles Keil, *Urban Blues* (Chicago: University of Chicago Press, 1966), pp. 45–46.

45. LeRoi Jones, *Blues People* (New York: Morrow Quill Paperbacks, 1963), p. 172.

46. Keil, *Urban Blues,* p. 45

47. Gunther Schuller, *Early Jazz: Its Roots and Musical Development* (Oxford, England: Oxford University Press, 1968), pp. 5, 10–32, 40–62, 184n.

48. Appiah, *In My Father's House,* p. 26.

49. Cited in Christopher Waterman, "Africa." In Helen Myers, ed., *Ethnomusicology: Historical and Regional Studies,* (New York: W. W. Norton, 1993), p. 240.

50. Ibid.

51. Frank J. Gillis and Pekka Gronow, Review of Gunther Schuller, *Early Jazz: Its Roots and Musical Development, Ethnomusicology* 13, No. 3 (1969), p. 564.

52. Jones, *Blues People,* p. 27.

53. Joachim E. Berendt, *The Jazz Book: From Ragtime to Fusion and Beyond* (Westport, Conn.: Lawrence Hill, 1981), p. 154.

54. Ernest Borneman, *A Critic Looks at Jazz* (London: Jazz Music Books, 1946), p. 9.

55. Norman C. Weinstein, *A Night in Tunisia: Imaginings of Africa in Jazz* (Metuchen, N.J.: Scarecrow Press, 1992), p. viii.

56. Ibid., p. 11.

57. Ibid., p. 137.

58. Ibid., p. 73.

59. John Miller Chernoff, *African Rhythm and African Sensibility* (Chicago: University of Chicago Press, 1971).

60. Weinstein, *A Night in Tunisia,* p. 53.

61. Ibid., p. 35.

62. Ibid., p. 108.

63. Cited in Weinstein, *A Night in Tunisia,* pp. 51–52.

64. Asadata Dafora, Papers. Schomburg Center for Research in Black Culture of the New York Public Library.

65. Ibid.

66. Mickey Hart with Jay Stevens, *Drumming at the Edge of Magic: A Journey Into the Spirit of Percussion* (San Francisco: Harper SanFrancisco, 1990), pp. 214–15.

67. Berendt, *The Jazz Book,* p. 285.

68. C. O. Simpkins, *Coltrane: A Biography* (Baltimore: Black Classic Press, 1989), p. 232.

69. Donald Clarke, ed., *The Penguin Encyclopedia of Popular Music* (London: Penguin, 1990), p. 1213.

70. Roberts, *Black Music of Two Worlds,* p. 258.

71. My brother Phillip Gerard, a former Peace Corps volunteer in neighboring Lesotho, recalls that in South Africa the term *gangster* is used to describe a person—not necessarily a member of a gang—who behaves in a gangster style.

72. Don Palmer, "Abdullah Ibrahim: Capetown Crusader," *Down Beat* 52 (January 1985), pp. 20–22.

73. Brian Case and Stan Britt, *The Harmony Illustrated Encyclopaedia of Jazz,* 3rd ed. Revised and edited by Chrissey Murray (New York: Harmony Books, 1986), "Hugh Masakela."

74. Duke Ellington, *Music Is My Mistress* (New York: Doubleday, 1973), p. 109.

75. Ibid., p. 337.

76. Dizzy Gillespie with Al Fraser, *To Be or Not to Bop: Memoirs—Dizzy Gillespie* (Garden City, N.Y.: Doubleday, 1979), pp. 317–25.

77. Ibid. p. 490.

78. Frank Malabe and Bob Weiner, *Afro-Cuban Rhythms for Drumset* (New York: Manhattan Music, Drummers Collective Series, 1990), p. 9.

79. Gillespie, *To Be or Not to Bop*, p. 290.

80. Ibid., pp. 290–91.

81. Jessie Gaston Mulira, "The Case of Voodoo in New Orleans." In Joseph Holloway, ed., *Africanisms in American Culture* (Bloomington, Ind.: Indiana University Press, 1991), p. 35.

82. Ibid., p. 290.

83. Cited in Berendt, *The Jazz Book*, p. 285.

84. Cited in Arthur Taylor, *Notes and Tones: Musician to Musician Interviews* (New York: Perigee, 1982), p. 242–43.

85. Cited in Herb Nolan, "New Message From Art Blakey," *Down Beat* 16 (November 1979), p. 20.

86. Ibid., p. 242.

87. Weinstein, *A Night in Tunisia*, p. 109.

88. Taylor, *Notes and Tones*, pp. 19, 30.

89. Ibid., p. 30.

90. Cited in Jacob Drachler, ed., *Black Homeland/Black Diaspora: Cross-Currents of the African Relationship* (Port Washington, N.Y.: Kennikat Press, 1975), p. 253.

91. Ibid., p. 23.

92. Ibid., p. 26.

93. Simpkins, *Coltrane*, p. 128.

94. Ibid., p. 17.

95. Ibid., pp. 128, 232, 240.

96. See, for example, Frank Kofsky, *Black Nationalism and the Revolution in Music* (New York: Pathfinder, 1970).

97. Taylor, *Notes and Tones,* p. 43.

98. Kofsky, *Black Nationalism and the Revolution in Music.*

99. Ibid., p. 101.

100. Ronald M. Radamo, *New Musical Figurations: Anthony Braxton's Cultural Critique* (Chicago: University of Chicago Press, 1993), p. 99.

101. I am indebted to Brandon's chapter "Continuity and Change" in *Santeria from Africa to the New World* for his use of many of the same ideas in his discussion of the dichotomy between Catholic and African in Cuban society.

CHAPTER THREE

1. Albert J. Raboteau, "Afro-American Religions: Muslim Movements." In Mircea Eliade, ed., *The Encyclopedia of Religion* (New York: Macmillian, 1987), pp. 100–103.

2. Ibid.

3. Wilfred Cantwell Smith, "Ahmadiyya." In H.A.R. Gibb, J. H. Kramers, W. Lévi-Provençal, and J. Schacht, eds, *Encyclopaedia of Islam*, new edition (Leiden: E. J. Brill, 1979).

4. Hazrat Mirza Ghulam Ahmad of Quadian, *Jesus in India* (Islamabad: Islam International Publications, 1989), pp. 22–23.

5. Tony Poon-Chiang, "Case Study of the Missionary Stance of the Ahmadiyya Movement in Islam in North America" (Ph.D. diss., Northwestern University, 1973).

6. Nazir Ali Jairazbhoy, "Pakistan." In Helen Myers, ed., *Ethnomusicology: Historical and Regional Studies* (New York: W. W. Norton, 1993), p. 294. See also Abu Bilal Mustafa Al-Kanadi, *The Islamic Ruling on Music and Singing: In Light of the Quraan* (Jedda, Saudi Arabia: Abdul-Qasim Bookstore, 1991).

7. C. O. Simpkins, *Coltrane: A Biography* (Baltimore: Black Classic Press, 1975), p. 39.

8. Herb Nolan, "New Message From Art Blakey." *Down Beat* (November 1979), p. 20.

9. Bob Rusch, "Yusef Lateef Interview," *Cadence* (January 1989), p. 9.

10. J. Gordon Melton, ed., *The Encyclopedia of American Religions: Religious Creeds* (Detroit: Gale Research, 1988), p. 785.

11. Dizzy Gillespie with Al Fraser, *To Be, or Not to Bop: Memoirs—Dizzy Gillespie* (Garden City, N.Y.: Doubleday, 1979), pp. 291–92.

12. Joe Goldberg, *Jazz Masters of the Fifties* (New York: Macmillian, 1965), p. 56.

13. Nat Hentoff, liner notes to the Larry Young album *Heaven on Earth*, 1969.

14. Miles Davis with Quincy Troupe, *Miles: The Autobiography* (New York: Simon & Schuster, 1989), p. 411.

15. *Muhammed Speaks*, Dec. 15, 1962, pp. 20–21; Dec. 30, pp. 20–22.

16. Arthur Taylor, *Notes and Tones: Musician to Musician Interviews* (New York: Perigee, 1977), p. 106.

17. Gillespie, *To Be, Or Not to Bop*, p. 292.

18. Ibid., 473–74.

19. Ibid., p. 488.

20. Murano Senchu, "Nichirenshu." In Eliade, ed., *The Encyclopedia of Religion*, Vol. 10, pp. 427–30.

21. Robert S. Ellwood, *Religious and Spiritual Groups in Modern America* (Englewood Cliffs, N.J.: Prentice-Hall, 1973), pp. 267–75.

22. Lyons, *The Great Jazz Pianists: Speaking of Their Lives and Music* (New York: Quill, 1983), p. 276.

23. Ellwood, *Religious and Spiritual Groups*, pp. xii–xiii.

24. Simpkins, *Coltrane: A Biography*, pp. 57–58, 60.

25. Ibid., p. 200.

26. Ronald M. Radamo, *New Musical Figurations: Anthony Braxton's Cultural Critique* (Chicago: University of Chicago Press, 1993), p. 100.

27. Simpkins, *Coltrane: A Biography*, p. 233.

28. "Our Times: African Orthodox Church Dedicated to John Coltrane," *Life* (December 1992), p. 92. The church is on Divisadero Street.

CHAPTER FOUR

1. Robert A. Stebbins, "A Theory of the Jazz Community." *Sociological Quarterly* 9, No. 3 (Summer 1968), pp. 318–31.

2. Steven P. Piazzale, " 'Deviant' Subcultural Formation and Art World Change: The Case of Jazz" (Ph.D. diss., Stanford University, 1979).

3. James Lincoln Collier, *Jazz: The American Theme Song* (New York: Oxford University Press, 1993), p. 186.

4. Ira Gitler, *Swing to Bop: An Oral History of the Transition in Jazz in the 1940s* (New York: Oxford University Press, 1985), p. 282.

5. Miles Davis with Quincy Troupe, *The Autobiography of Miles Davis* (New York: Simon & Schuster, 1989), pp. 129, 247.

6. Claude Brown, *Manchild in the Promised Land* (New York: Macmillan, 1965), pp. 187–88.

7. Ibid., p. 80.

8. Gitler, *Swing to Bop*, p. 282n.

9. Davis, *Autobiography*, p. 130.

10. A. B. Spellman, *Four Lives in the Bebop Business* (New York: Pantheon Books, 1966), p. 158.

11. Gitler, *Swing to Bop,* p. 277.

12. Ibid., pp. 277–78.

13. Charles Winick, "The Use of Drugs by Jazz Musicians," *Social Problems* 7 (Winter 1959–60), p. 241.

14. Ibid., p. 366.

15. Ibid., pp. 366–67.

16. Davis, *Autobiography,* p. 96.

17. Gitler, *Swing to Bop*, p. 283.

18. Winick, "The Use of Drugs by Jazz Musicians," p. 245.

19. Cited by Spellman, *Four Lives in the Bebop Business*, p. 138.

20. Spellman, *Four Lives in the Bebop Business,* p. 195.

21. Winick, "The Use of Drugs by Jazz Musicians," p. 240.

22. Dizzy Gillespie with Al Fraser, *To Be or Not to Bop: Memoirs–Dizzy Gillespie* (Garden City, N.Y: Doubleday, 1979), p. 400.

23. Ronald Sukenick, *Down and In: Life in the Underground* (New York: Collier Books, Macmillan, 1987), pp. 167–68.

24. Robert Levin, "The Jazz Composers Guild: An Assertion of Dignity" *Down Beat* (May 6, 1965), pp. 17–18.

25. Ibid., pp. 17–18.

26. Valerie Wilmer, *As Serious as Your Life: The Story of the New Jazz* (Westport, Conn.: Lawrence Hill, 1980), pp. 214–15. Spellman, *Four Lives in the Bebop Business,* pp. 25–27.

27. Leslie B. Rout Jr., "AACM: New Music (!) New Ideas (?)," *Journal of Popular Culture* 1, No. 2 (1968), p. 130.

28. Wilmer, *As Serious as Your Life,* p. 116.

29. Ronald M. Radamo, *New Musical Figurations,: Anthony Braxton's Cultural Critique* (Chicago: University of Chicago Press, 1993), p. 131–32.

30. Rout, "AACM," p. 139.

31. Radamo, *New Musical Figurations,* p. 91.

32. Wilmer, *As Serious as Your Life,* p. 118–19.

33. John Litweiler, *The Freedom Principle: Jazz After 1958* (New York: William Morrow, 1984), p. 187.

34. Wilmer, *As Serious as Your Life,* p. 216.

CHAPTER FIVE

1. In David Levering Lewis, ed., *The Portable Harlem Renaissance Reader* (New York: Penguin Books, 1994), pp. 110–17.

2. Norman Weinstein, *A Night in Tunisia: Imaginings of Africa in Jazz* (Metuchen, N.J.: Scarecrow Press, 1992), p. 19.

3. James Lincoln Collier, *Jazz: the American Theme Song* (New York: Oxford University Press, 1993), pp. 7–8. The notion of the black experience as a curative to repressive sexual mores has been in vogue for most of the century, and was at times given expression in Freudian terms. For instance, Frank Zappa wrote that "any parent who tried to keep his child from listening to or participating in this musical ritual was, in the eyes of the child, trying to castrate him."

4. Norman Mailer, *The White Negro* (San Francisco: City Lights Books, 1969. Reprinted from *Dissent,* 1957), p. 6.

5. Michael Bane in his *White Boy Singin' the Blues: The Black Roots of White Rock* (Middlesex, England: Penguin Books, 1982), mentions the pamphlet. Norman Mailer also wrote an article by the same name, so it is likely that Bane is referring to Mailer's article.

6. Bane, *White Boy Singin' the Blues,* p. 210.

7. Noel Ignatiev, "Treason to Whiteness Is Loyalty to Humanity," *Utne Reader* (November/December 1994), pp. 84–85.

8. Mezz Mezzrow and Bernard Wolfe. "Ecstatic in Blackface: The Negro as a Song-and-Dance Man (1947–8)." In *Really the Blues,* (Garden City, N.Y.: Doubleday, 1972), p. 301.

9. Bane, *White Boy Singin' the Blues,* p. 195.

10. Mezzrow, "Ecstatic in Blackface," p. 301.

11. Zora Neale Hurston called the white writers whose black characters were the embodiment of primitivism "Negrotarians." Chip Rhodes, "Writing Up the New Negro: The Construction of Consumer Desire in the Twenties," *Journal of American Studies* 28, No. 2 (1994), p. 192.

12. Mezzrow, "Ecstatic in Blackface," p. 295.

13. Ibid., pp. 303–4.

14. Loften Mitchell, "I Work Here to Please You." In Addison Gayle, Jr., ed., *The Black Aesthetic* (Garden City, N.Y.: Doubleday, 1972), pp. 282, 286.

15. This phrase was coined by the cultural theorist Stuart Hall. See George Lipsitz, *Time Passages: Collective Memory and American Popular Culture* (Minneapolis: University of Minneapolis Press, 1990), pp. 120ff, p. 283 n.33.

16. Constance Rourke, *American Humor: A Study of the National Character* (New York: Harcourt, Brace, 1931), p. 86.

17. Lipsitz, *Time Passages,* pp. 122–23.

18. Ibid., p. 22.

19. Willie "The Lion" Smith, *Music on My Mind* (London: MacGibbon & Kee, 1964). See the copy of Smith's business card on the back cover.

20. Mezzrow, *Really the Blues,* p. 290.

21. Ibid., p. 42.

22. Bane, *White Boy Singin' the Blues,* p. 195.

23. Michael Rogin, "Blackface, White Noise: The Jewish Jazz Singer Finds His Voice," *Critical Inquiry* 18, No. 3 (Spring 1992), p. 434.

24. Liner notes to Ben Sidran's *Life Is a Lesson,* Go Jazz Records, 1993.

25. William Howland Kenney, *Chicago Jazz: A Cultural History, 1904–1930* (New York: Oxford University Press, 1993), p. 99.

26. Johnny Otis, *Listen to the Lambs* (New York: W.W. Norton, 1968), pp. 98, 163.

27. Frank Zappa, "The Oracle Has It All Psyched Out," *Life Magazine* (June 28, 1968), pp. 82–91.

28. Lipsitz, *Time Passages,* p. 122.

29. Mezzrow, *Really the Blues,* p. 315.

30. Ibid., p. 41.

31. Mark Rowland and Tony Scherman, eds., *The Jazz Musician* (New York: St. Martin's Press, 1994), p. 144.

32. Burton W. Peretti, *The Creation of Jazz: Music, Race, and Culture in Urban America* (Urbana, Ill.: University of Illinois Press, 1992), p. 206.

33. John Howard Griffin, *Black Like Me* (Boston: Houghton Mifflin, 1977).

34. Otis, *Listen to the Lambs,* p. 12.

35. Ibid., pp. 162–63.

36. Mezzrow, *Really the Blues,* p. 15.

37. Musicologist Thomas Owens believes that despite Mezzrow's dedication to jazz he remained a third-rate talent (personal correspondence, June 1995).

38. Mezzrow, *Really the Blues,* p. 51.

39. Amy Linden. "A Career Made of Being Where He Doesn't Belong," *New York Times* Arts and Entertainment section, (July 31, 1994), p. 25.

40. William J. Schafer and Johannes Riedel, *The Art of Ragtime: Form and Meaning of an Original Black American Art* (New York: Da Capo Press, 1977. Reprint edition of Baton Rouge: Louisiana State University, 1973), p. 80.

41. The convention probably took place in 1968, not 1969. Most likely Penn is referring to the 1968 convention in Atlanta of the National Association of Radio and Television Announcers (NARTA) in which Wexler was hanged in effigy. There is a description of it in the entry on soul music in Donald Clarke, ed., *The Penguin Encyclopedia of Popular Music.* (London: Penguin Books, 1990), p. 1098.

42. Linden, "A Career," p. 25.

43. Lipsitz, *Time Passages,* p. 265.

44. James O. Young, "Should White Men Play the Blues?" *Journal of Value Inquiry* 28 (September 1994), pp. 415–24.

45. Bane, *White Boy Singin' the Blues,* p. 155.

46. Ibid., p. 161.

47. Neil Strauss, "Scottology," *The Village Voice* (Nov. 3, 1992), p. 69.

48. Described in Joe Goldberg, *Jazz Masters of the Fifties* (New York: Macmilian, 1965. Reprinted New York: Da Capo Press, 1983), p. 138.

49. Joel Lewis, "Raymond Scott, Maestro of Tunes for Toons: The Polymorphic Musical Career of an 'Absurdist' Tone Poet," *Forward* (March 5, 1993), p. 9.

50. Ibid.

51. Billy Taylor, *Jazz Piano: A Jazz History* (Dubuque, Iowa: Wm. C. Brown, 1982), p. 9. I have changed Taylor's line of thought slightly. Taylor's exact words were: "The evolution of jazz styles does not progress only from one great individual artist to another, as many writers would have us believe, but rather from generation to generation." I stress the impact of the generation-to-generation evolution a bit more than Taylor does.

52. Michelle Wood, "The Men Who Made the Music: Raymond Scott." *The Swing Era: Vintage Years of Humor,* Time-Life Records, 1991.

53. Raymond Scott, "Swing Is 'stagnant' Syncopation," *Billboard* (Nov. 27, 1937), p. 22.

54. Strauss, "Scottology," p. 69.

55. Len Lyons, *The Great Jazz Pianists: Speaking of Their Lives and Music* (New York: Quill, 1983), p. 265.

CHAPTER SIX

1. Statement made to a *New York Magazine* reporter. Cited in Nelson George, *The Death of Rhythm & Blues* (New York: E. P. Dutton, 1989), p. 173.

2. George, *The Death of Rhythm & Blues*, pp. 3–4.

3. Ibid., p. 10.

4. Ibid., pp. 108–9.

5. Liner notes to Jimi Hendrix's *Electric Ladyland.* MCA Records, 1993.

6. Ian Carr, *Miles Davis A Biography* (New York: William Morrow, 1982), p. 172.

7. Ibid., p. 201.

8. Miles Davis with Quincy Troupe, *Miles: The Autobiography* (New York: Simon & Schuster, 1989), p. 324.

9. Carr, *Miles Davis,* p. 217.

10. Ibid., p. 328.

11. Ibid., p. 214.

12. Ibid., p. 329.

13. Mark Rowland and Tony Scherman, eds., *The Jazz Musician* (New York: St. Martin's Press, 1994), p. 118.

14. Ibid., p. 121.

15. Ibid.

16. George, *The Death of Rhythm & Blues,* p. 174.

17. James T. Jones IV, "Racism in Jazz: Same as it Was . . . Or Worse?" *Jazz Times* (March 1995), p. 55.

18. Ibid., p. 56.

CHAPTER SEVEN

1. A. B. Spellman, *Four Lives in the Bebop Business* (New York: Pantheon Books, 1966), pp. 142–43.

2. Michael Bane, *White Boy Singin' the Blues: The Black Roots of White Rock* (Middlesex, England: Penguin Books, 1982), p. 155.

3. Arthur Taylor, *Notes and Tones: Musician to Musician Interviews* (New York: Perigee Books, 1977), p. 249.

4. Ibid., pp. 242–43.

5. Herb Nolan, "New Message From Art Blakey," *Down Beat* 16 (November 1979), p. 20.

6. Letter printed in *Jazz Times,* July/August 1995.

7. W. F. Lucas is the author of *Bottom Fishing: A Novella & Other Stories* (Knoxville, Tenn.: Carpetbag Press, 1974).

8. Posted by Matthew C. Weiner (mcwst5+pitt.edu), University of Pittsburgh.

9. Ronald G. Welburn, "American Jazz Criticism, 1914–1940." (Ph.D. diss., New York University, 1983).

CHAPTER EIGHT

1. Simon Frith, *Sound Effects: Youth, Leisure, and the Politics of Rock 'n' Roll* (New York: Pantheon Books, 1983), p. 24.

2. Charles Keil, *Urban Blues* (Chicago: University of Chicago Press, 1966), p. 125.

3. Jeff Todd Titon, *Early Downhome Blues* (Urbana, Ill.: University of Illinois Press, 1977), p. 189.

4. Keil, *Urban Blues,* p. 137.

5. Pearl Williams-Jones, "A Crystallization of the Black Aesthetic," *Ethnomusicology* 19, No. 3 (1975), pp. 373–85.

6. Liner notes to Jimmy Guiffre's *Western Suite.* Atlantic Records, 1959.

7. Liner notes *The Jimmy Giuffre 3.* Atlantic Records 1254, n.d.

8. Ålun Morgan, liner notes to *Tangents in Jazz.* Pausa Jazz Origin series, 1986.

9. Ibid.

CHAPTER NINE

1. Joel Rudinow, "Race, Ethnicity, Expressive Authenticity: Can White People Sing the Blues?" *Journal of Aesthetics and Art Criticism* 52, No.1 (Winter 1994), p. 127.

2. Ibid., p. 129.

3. A. B. Spellman, *Four Lives in the Bebop Business* (New York: Pantheon Books, 1966), pp. 20–21.

4. Rudinow, "Race, Ethnicity, Expressive Authenticity," p. 132.

5. Alan M. Perlman and Daniel Greenblatt, "Miles Davis Meets Noam Chomsky: Some Observations on Jazz Improvisation and Language Structure." In Wendy Steiner, ed., *The Sign in Music and Literature* (Austin: University of Texas Press, 1981), pp. 169–83.

6. Stephen Sherrill, "Don Byron," *New York Times Magazine* (Jan. 16, 1996), p. 21.

7. Gene Lees, *Cats of Any Color: Jazz, Black and White* (New York: Oxford University Press, 1994), p. 230.

8. Sherill, "Don Byron," p. 21.

9. Ibid., p. 30.

10. Ibid., p. 20.

Selected Bibliography

RACE & JAZZ

Carter, Sandy. "Jazz Race." *Z Magazine* (February 1995).

Collier, James Lincoln. *Jazz: The American Theme Song.* New York: Oxford University Press, 1993.

Hentoff, Nat. "Race Prejudice in Jazz: It Works Both Ways." *Harper's Magazine* (June 1959).

_____. "The Murderous Modes of Jazz." *Esquire* (September 15, 1960).

Horowitz, Irving Louis, and Charles Nanry. "Ideologies and Theories About American Jazz." *Journal of Jazz Studies* 2, No. 2 (June 1975).

Jones, James T, IV. "Racism and Jazz: Same as It Ever Was . . . or Worse?" *Jazz Times* (March 1995).

Kinnon, Joy Bennett. "Are Whites Taking or Are Blacks Giving Away the Blues?" *Ebony* (September 1997).

Lees, Gene. *Cats of Any Color: Jazz, Black and White.* New York: Oxford University Press, 1994.

Olsher, Dean, moderator. *Jazz Musicians Discuss Racism in the Jazz World.* National Public Radio two-part series (January, 1996)

Peretti, Burton W. *The Creation of Jazz: Music, Race, and Culture in Urban America.* Urbana, Ill.: University of Illinois Press, 1992.

Radamo, Ronald M. *New Musical Figurations: Anthony Braxton's Cultural Critique.* Chicago: University of Chicago Press, 1993.

Spellman, A. B. *Four Lives in the Bebop Business*. New York: Pantheon Books, 1966.

Szwed, John F. "Musical Style and Racial Conflict." *Phylon* 27, No. 4 (Winter 1966).

Teachout, Terry. "The Color of Jazz." *Commentary* 100, No. 3 (September 1995).

AFRICAN-AMERICAN IDENTITY

Baraka, Amiri. *See* Jones, LeRoi.

Brown, Claude. *Manchild in the Promised Land*. New York: Macmillan, 1965.

Childs, John Brown. *Leadership, Conflict, and Cooperation in Afro-American Social Thought*. Philadelphia: Temple University Press, 1989.

Cleaver, Eldridge. *Soul on Ice*. New York: Dell, 1968.

Crouch, Stanley. *Notes of a Hanging Judge: Essays and Reviews 1979–1989*. New York: Oxford University Press, 1990.

_____ . "Sketches of Pain." *New Republic* (February 12, 1990).

Ellison, Ralph. *Shadow and Act*. 1964. Reprint, New York: Vintage International, 1995.

Harris, Eddy. *Native Stranger: A Black American's Journey into the Heart of Africa*. New York: Vintage Departures, 1992.

Hecht, Michael L., Mary Jane Collier, and Sidney A. Ribeau. *African-American Communication: Ethnic Identity and Cultural Interpretation*. Newbury Park, Calif.: Sage Publications, 1993.

hooks, bell. *Yearning: Race, Gender, and Cultural Politics*. Boston: South End Press, 1990.

Jones, LeRoi. *Blues People: The Negro Experience in White America and the Music That Developed From It*. New York: Morrow Quill Paperbacks, 1963.

_____ . "The Changing Same (R & B and New Black Music)." In *The Black Aesthetic*, edited by Addison Gayle, Jr. Garden City, N.Y.: Doubleday, 1971.

Keil, Charles. *Urban Blues*. Chicago: University of Chicago Press, 1966.

Kofsky, Frank. *Black Nationalism and the Revolution in Music*. New York: Pathfinder, 1970.

Levy, Clifford J. "Study to Examine Bones from Black's Burial Site." *New York Times* (August 13, 1991).

Liyong, Taban lo. "Negroes Are Not Africans." In *Black Homeland/Black Diaspora: Cross Currents of the African Relationship*, edited by Jacob Drachler. Port Washington, N.Y.: National University Publications/ Kennikat Press, 1975.

Majors, Richard, and Janet Mancini Billson. *Cool Pose: The Dilemmas of Black Manhood in America*. New York: Touchstone, 1993.

Manning, Kenneth R. "Race, Science and Identity." In *Lure and Loathing: Essays on Race, Identity and the Ambivalence of Assimilation*, edited by Gerald Early. New York: Penguin Books, 1993.

Mboya, Tom. "Africa and Afro-America." In *Black Homeland/Black Diaspora: Cross Currents of the African Relationship*, edited by Jacob Drachler. Port Washington, N.Y.: National University Publications/Kennikat Press, 1975.

Mitchell, Luften. "I Work Here to Please You." In *The Black Aesthetic*, edited by Addison Gayle, Jr. Garden City, N.Y.: Anchor Books, 1972.

Neal, Larry. "Some Reflections on the Black Aesthetic." In *The Black Aesthetic*, edited by Addison Gayle, Jr. Garden City, N.Y.: Doubleday, 1971.

Sidran, Ben. *Black Talk: How the Music of Black America Created a Radical Alternative to the Values of Western Literary Tradition*: New York: Holt, Rinehart and Winston, 1971.

Stewart, Jimmy. "Introduction to Black Aesthetics in Music." In *The Black Aesthetic*, edited by Addison Gayle, Jr. Garden City, N.Y.: Anchor Books, 1972.

Walton, Ortiz. "Comparative Analysis of the African and the Western Aesthetics." In *The Black Aesthetic*, edited by Addison Gayle, Jr. Garden City, N.Y.: Doubleday, 1971.

Weinstein, Norman C. *A Night in Tunisia: Imaginings of Africa in Jazz*. Metuchen, N.J.: Scarecrow Press, 1992.

Welburn, Ron. "The Black Aesthetic Imperative." In *The Black Aesthetic*, edited by Addison Gayle, Jr. Garden City, N.Y.: Doubleday, 1971.

Yvonne. "Black Catholics: Cultural Exiles, Literary Exiles." In *Daily Fare: Essays from the Multicultural Experience*, edited by Kathleen Aguero. Athens, Ga.: University of Georgia Press, 1993.

WHITES AND AFRICAN-AMERICAN CULTURE

Bane, Michael. *White Boy Singin' the Blues: The Black Roots of White Rock*. Middlesex, England: Penguin Books, 1982.

Hooper, Joseph. "A Saxophonist Who Doesn't Wear Armani." *New York Times* (January 15, 1995).

Ignatiev, Noel. "Treason to Whiteness Is Loyalty to Humanity." *Utne Reader* (November/December 1994).

Kenney, William Howland. *Chicago Jazz: A Cultural History, 1904–1930*. New York: Oxford University Press, 1993.

Linden, Amy. "A Career Made of Being Where He Doesn't Belong." *New York Times* (July 31, 1994).

Mailer, Norman. *The White Negro*. San Francisco: City Lights Books, 1969.

Mezzrow, Mezz, and Bernard Wolfe. *Really the Blues*. New York: Random House, 1946. Reprint, Garden City, N.Y.: Doubleday, 1972.

Otis, Johnny. *Listen to the Lambs*. New York: W. W. Norton, 1968.

Rogin, Michael. "Blackface, White Noise: The Jewish Jazz Singer Finds His Voice." *Critical Inquiry* 18, No. 3 (Spring 1992).

Rudinow, Joel. "Race, Ethnicity, Expressive Authenticity: Can White People Sing the Blues?" *Journal of Aesthetics and Art Criticism* 52, No. 1 (Winter 1994).

Young, James O. "Should White Men Play the Blues?" *Journal of Value Inquiry* 28 (September 1994).

RELIGIOUS INFLUENCES
Islam

Ahmad, Harzart Mirza Ghulam, of Quadian. *Jesus in India*. Islamabad: Islam International Publications, 1989.

Ahmad, Rashid, as told to Les Brownlee. "True Islam." *Sepia* (July 1960).

Lincoln, C. Eric. *The Black Muslims in America*. Queens, N.Y.: Kayode Publications, 1971. Reprint, 1991.

Poon-Chiang, Tony. "Case Study of the Missionary Stance of the Ahmadiyya Movement in Islam in North America." Ph.D. diss., Northwestern University, 1973.

Raboteau, Albert J. "Afro-American Religions: Muslim Movements." In *The Encyclopedia of Religion*, edited by Mircea Eliade. New York: Macmillian, 1987.

Smith, Wilfred Cantwell. "Ahmadiyya." In *Encyclopedia of Islam*, edited by H.A.R. Gibb, J. H. Kramers, W. Lévi-Provençal, J. Schacht. Leiden: E. J. Brill, 1979.

Santería

Brandon, George. *Santeria from Africa to the New World: The Dead Sell Memories*. Bloomington, Ind.: Indiana University Press, 1993.

Canizares, Raul. *Walking with the Night: The Afro-Cuban World of Santeria*. Rochester, Vt.: Destiny Books, 1993.

Murphy, Joseph M. *Santeria: African Spirits in America*. Boston: Beacon Books, 1988.

JAZZ COMMUNITIES

Becker, Howard S. *Outsiders: Studies in the Sociology of Deviance*. New York: The Free Press, 1963.

Levin, Robert. "The Jazz Composers Guild: An Assertion of Dignity." *Down Beat* (May 6, 1965).

Piazzale, Stephen P. " 'Deviant' Subcultural Formation and Art World Change: The Case of Jazz." Ph.D. diss., Stanford University, 1979.

Radamo, Ronald M. *New Musical Figurations: Anthony Braxton's Cultural Critique.* Chicago: University of Chicago Press, 1993.

Rout, Leslie R. "AACM: New Music (!) New Ideas (?)." *Journal of Popular Culture* 1, No. 2 (1968).

Stebbins, Robert A. "A Theory of the Jazz Community." *Sociological Quarterly* 9, No. 3 (Summer 1968).

Werner, Craig. "Leon Forrest, the AACM and the Legacy of the Chicago Renaissance." *The Black Scholar* 23, Nos. 3/4 (Summer 1993).

Wilmer, Valerie. *As Serious as Your Life: The Story of the New Jazz.* Westport, Conn.: Lawrence Hill, 1980.

Index

About the Author

CHARLEY. GERARD is a jazz musician and the author of several books on jazz subjects, including *Salsa: The Rhythm of Latin Music* (1989) and *Hard Bop Piano: Jazz Compositions of the 50s and 60s* (1993).